A green basilisk lizard races across the surface of water in Santa Rica, Costa Rica.

NATIONAL
GEOGRAPHIC
KiDS

ALMANAC 2019

NATIONAL GEOGRAPHIC
WASHINGTON, D.C.

National Geographic Kids Books
gratefully acknowledges the following people for their help with the
National Geographic Kids Almanac 2019.

Anastasia Cronin of the
National Geographic Explorers program

Amazing Animals

Suzanne Braden, Director, Pandas International

Dr. Rodolfo Coria, Paleontologist, Plaza Huincul, Argentina

Dr. Sylvia Earle, National Geographic Explorer-in-Residence

Dr. Thomas R. Holtz, Jr., Senior Lecturer, Vertebrate Paleontology,
Department of Geology, University of Maryland

Dr. Luke Hunter, Executive Director, Panthera

Dereck and Beverly Joubert,
National Geographic Explorers-in-Residence

Nizar Ibrahim, National Geographic Emerging Explorer

"Dino" Don Lessem, President, Exhibits Rex

Kathy B. Maher, Research Editor, *National Geographic* magazine

Kathleen Martin, Canadian Sea Turtle Network

Barbara Nielsen, Polar Bears International

Andy Prince, Austin Zoo

Christopher Sloan

Julia Thorson, translator, Zurich, Switzerland

Dennis vanEngelsdorp, Senior Extension Associate,
Pennsylvania Department of Agriculture

Science and Technology
Space and Earth

Tim Appenzeller, Chief Magazine Editor, *Nature*

Dr. Rick Fienberg, American Astronomical Society,
Press Officer and Director of Communications

Dr. José de Ondarza, Associate Professor,
Department of Biological Sciences, State University
of New York, College at Plattsburgh

Lesley B. Rogers, Managing Editor (former),
National Geographic magazine

Dr. Enric Sala, National Geographic Visiting Fellow

Abigail A. Tipton, Director of Research (former),
National Geographic magazine

Erin Vintinner, Biodiversity Specialist,
Center for Biodiversity and Conservation at the
American Museum of Natural History

Barbara L. Wyckoff, Research Editor (former),
National Geographic magazine

Going Green

Eric J. Bohn, Math Teacher, Santa Rosa High School

Stephen David Harris,
Professional Engineer, Industry Consulting

Catherine C. Milbourn, Senior Press Officer, EPA

Brad Scriber, Senior Researcher, *National Geographic* magazine

Paola Segura and Cid Simões,
National Geographic Emerging Explorers

Dr. Wes Tunnell, Harte Research Institute for
Gulf of Mexico Studies, Texas A&M University—Corpus Christi

Natasha Vizcarra, Science Writer and Media Liaison,
National Snow and Ice Data Center

Culture Connection

Dr. Wade Davis, National Geographic Explorer-in-Residence

Deirdre Mullervy, Managing Editor,
Gallaudet University Press

Wonders of Nature

Anatta, NOAA Public Affairs Officer

Dr. Robert Ballard,
National Geographic Explorer-in-Residence

Douglas H. Chadwick, wildlife biologist and contributor to
National Geographic magazine

Susan K. Pell, Ph.D., Science and Public Programs Manager,
United States Botanic Garden

History Happens

Dr. Sylvie Beaudreau, Associate Professor,
Department of History, State University of New York

Elspeth Deir, Assistant Professor, Faculty of Education,
Queens University, Kingston, Ontario, Canada

Dr. Gregory Geddes, Professor, Global Studies,
State University of New York–Orange,
Middletown-Newburgh, New York

Dr. Fredrik Hiebert, National Geographic Visiting Fellow

Micheline Joanisse, Media Relations Officer,
Natural Resources Canada

Dr. Robert D. Johnston,
Associate Professor and Director of the
Teaching of History Program, University of Illinois at Chicago

Dickson Mansfield, Geography Instructor (retired),
Faculty of Education, Queens University,
Kingston, Ontario, Canada

Tina Norris, U.S. Census Bureau

Parliamentary Information and Research Service,
Library of Parliament, Ottawa, Canada

Karyn Pugliese, Acting Director, Communications,
Assembly of First Nations

Geography Rocks

Glynnis Breen, National Geographic Special Projects

Carl Haub, Senior Demographer,
Conrad Taeuber Chair of Public Information,
Population Reference Bureau

Dr. Toshiko Kaneda, Senior Research Associate,
Population Reference Bureau

Dr. Kristin Bietsch, Research Associate,
Population Reference Bureau

Dr. Walt Meier, National Snow and Ice Data Center

Dr. Richard W. Reynolds,
NOAA's National Climatic Data Center

United States Census Bureau, Public Help Desk

Contents

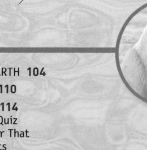

Wonders of Nature

200

History Happens

220

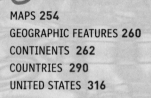

Geography Rocks

252

NATIONAL GEOGRAPHIC KIDS
ALMANAC CHALLENGE 2019

The results are in!
Which shark was the favorite in our 2018 online pole? See page 193.

Want to become part of the 2019 Almanac Challenge? Go to page 192 to find out more.

Butterflies are projected onto St. Peter's Basilica in Vatican City in an effort to raise awareness about climate change.

New Recruits

MARTIN THE CAT WITH A DEPUTY INSPECTOR

These four-legged animals are as clever as they are cute, and they are ready to help enforce the law.

Around the world, some cute cats and darling dogs are on paw patrol! Specifically, in Brooklyn, New York, U.S.A., and in Taipei, the capital city of Taiwan, adorable animals have honorary spots on the local police squad. And while they may not be solving cases or catching bad guys, these cuties spread plenty of cheer to their entire stations.

FELINE DETECTIVE

At the Coney Island police precinct in Brooklyn, New York, U.S.A., Martin the tabby is definitely the cat's meow. The cute kitty was abandoned when he was just months old before being discovered by police, who took him in and made Martin an unofficial member of the local squad. While Martin doesn't do much to fight crime, he does hunt down mice. As for his other daily "duties"? Martin typically eats leftovers (he especially loves turkey sandwiches), lounges around, and cuddles with police officers during their downtime.

PUPPY POLICE

At the New Taipei Police Department, these itty-bitty Labradors are the real V.I.P.s (that's very important *puppies*,

of course!). When they were just one month old, the crop of canines started training to become police dogs. After about a year of training, the dogs will be accompanying officers to crime scenes to sniff out clues. Cute and clever—what's not to love about these precious pups?

ONE-MONTH-OLD LABRADOR PUPPY POLICE RECRUIT IN TAIWAN

MR. TRASH WHEEL

IT'S SOLAR POWERED!

THIS INNOVATIVE TRASH SKIMMER IS CREDITED WITH REMOVING MORE THAN 500,000 GROCERY BAGS AND SOME 600,000 PLASTIC BOTTLES FROM THE WATER.

With its big, googly eyes and rounded shape, "Mr. Trash Wheel" doesn't look so intimidating. But this trash skimmer has a serious job to do: It pulls debris from the water surrounding Baltimore, Maryland, U.S.A. And plenty of it. To date, Mr. Trash Wheel has removed some 1.4 million pounds (635,029 kg) of garbage from the Jones Falls watershed, which empties into Baltimore's Inner Harbor. The floating filth-remover harnesses power from the water's current, as well as from the sun, to turn a waterwheel and a conveyor belt. As Mr. Trash sits at the end of the watershed, its wheel sucks garbage—from bottles and bags to cigarette butts and sports balls—up onto the conveyor belt and into a Dumpster barge. And that's no trash talk!

Baby Boom

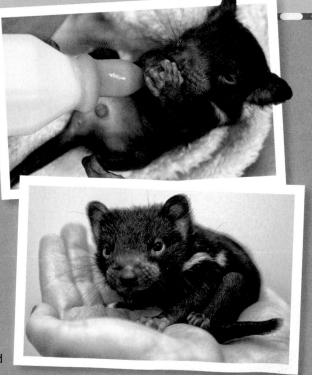

Sad fact: More than 80 percent of the wild Tasmanian Devil population has been affected by a highly contagious cancer that was first identified in 1996. But some conservationists are hoping to boost the animal's numbers by breeding them, and possibly protecting them from the deadly disease that they're exposed to in the wild. The plan just may work: A record 51 Tasmanian Devil joeys were born at a free-range breeding facility in Australia in 2017. That's a welcome baby boom that could save these marsupials from extinction.

ROBOT HOTEL

Where can a dino be the face of the future? A robot hotel, of course!

GUESTS ARE GREETED BY A ROBOTIC DINOSAUR.

A HUMANOID ROBOT INTERACTS WITH GUESTS.

The Henn-na Hotel in Japan gives guests a glimpse of a futuristic world where robots rule, literally. Head to the front desk and you'll be greeted by an automated velociraptor wearing a hat and bow tie that will direct you to enter your info on a touchscreen tablet. You might also interact with a humanoid host. You'll then be escorted to your room by a bright-red self-propelled trolley that will carry your luggage, too.

ROBOTIC FISH SWIM IN A LOBBY TANK.

When you need to enter your room, just place your face in front of a screen. Facial recognition technology will allow you to open a locked door without even having to swipe your key. Feeling a bit warm? No need to turn up the AC: Controlled by a sensor, the room's air will adjust based on your own body temperature. There are also robots that'll wash the windows, vacuum, take out your trash, and turn the lights off for you. Aside from the actual guests and a few human staff members, nearly everything that moves in the hotel—including the fish in the lobby's tank—are robots.

Why robots? The Henn-na Hotel owners say they can save money by having a staff of machines that work for free. So the next time you're daydreaming about leaping to the future? No need to find a time machine. Just check into this high-tech hotel instead!

"OWL" ALWAYS LOVE THESE GUYS.

Nest Best Thing

Snowy the owl may be a stuffed animal, but her "adopted" babies sure give a hoot about her! After five tawny owl chicks were found orphaned, rescuers at the New Forest Otter, Owl, and Wildlife Park in Southampton, England, placed them with the cuddly toy to help the babies feel more comfortable. At first the chicks were afraid of the large white bird. But when animal manager John Crooks warmed Snowy on the radiator, the chicks crawled under her wings to take advantage of her "body heat." After several months, the chicks were ready to leave the nest. What happened to dear old stuffed mom? "She was a bit messy from all the babies," Crooks says. So Snowy took her own trip—to the washing machine!

To feed her chick, a female owl brushes food against the whiskers above the chick's beak, and the baby opens its mouth.

Eat Your Lawn

FARMING A LAWN IN ORLANDO, FLORIDA, U.S.A.

Grow food. Not lawns!

FLEET FARMING

FLEETFARMING.COM ⓕ ⓨ @FLEETFARMING

PICTURE THIS: It's lunchtime and you're craving a salad. But instead of heading to the store, you walk outside. There, you pluck a variety of veggies—from carrots to cucumbers—right from your front lawn. That's just what some homeowners in Orlando, Florida, U.S.A., are doing these days, thanks to FleetFarming. This program turns lawns into neat rows of blooming gardens, filled with fruits and veggies ripe for the taking.

Microfarming—farming a small area—is convenient, and it's good for the environment, too. Instead of traveling thousands of miles to get from a farm to the store, which increases the amount of greenhouse gas emissions in our environment, your veggies go straight to your plate. Which means that by farming your lawn, you can protect the planet—and stay super healthy while you're at it.

#CuteAnimalTweetOff

How do you determine the cutest animal on Earth? You take to Twitter! At least that's what several zoos and aquariums from around the country recently did in a lighthearted Twitter battle, one-upping each other by posting pics of their most adorable residents. The Twitter chain included snaps of a baby sifaka lemur, the world's smallest deer, a tiny gorilla clinging to its mom's leg, and a sea otter waving hello. Hashtag *swoon*.

 National Zoo
@NationalZoo

We welcomed a gray seal pup Jan. 21.The pup appears to be nursing, moving & bonding well w/ mom. #Squee
10:06 AM-Jan 25, 2017

 Zoo Atlanta
@ZooATL

We're always down for a #cuteanimaltweetoff!
11:53 AM-Jan 25, 2017

 Virginia Aquarium
@VAAquarium

#challengeaccepted We see @NationalZoo's seal pup, and raise an otter/osprey combo.
11:03 AM-Jan 25, 2017

 Tennessee Aquarium
@TNAquarium

Challenge accepted! #CuteAnimalTweetOff @NatlAquarium
12:51 PM-Jan 25, 2017

 National Zoo
@NationalZoo

@VAAquarium This is Redd, our endangered Bornean orangutan infant. And he is the cutest. Do you fold yet?
#challengeaccepted 11:42 AM-Jan 25, 2017

 **Los Angeles Zoo and Botanical Gardens**
@LAZoo

I got here as fast as I could... #cuteanimaltweetoff
3:24 PM-Jan 25, 2017

HOT MOVIES in 2019*

- *Frozen 2*
- *Wonder Woman 2*
- *Star Wars Episode IX*
- *Minecraft*
- *Spongebob Squarepants 3*
- *The Lion King (live action)*
- *Captain Marvel*

*Release dates and titles are subject to change.

IRISH ISLAND FEELS THE FORCE

SKELLIG MICHAEL

VISITORS CAN CLIMB MORE THAN 600 STEPS.

RUINS

A MONASTERY WAS FOUNDED ON THE ISLAND BETWEEN THE SIXTH AND EIGHTH CENTURIES.

"SKELLIG" MEANS "STEEP ROCK."

The Star Wars movies are set in a galaxy far, far away, but some scenes are filmed in real-life places right here on Earth. Take Skellig Michael, for example. This island off the coast of Ireland serves as a backdrop in *The Force Awakens*, specifically as a hideout for Luke Skywalker. With its rocky terrain and jagged peaks (the island is actually the top of a 400-million-year-old sandstone mountain), Skellig Michael definitely looks the part of an otherworldly land. And now, fans are flocking to the island to get an up-close-and-personal view of this mystical mountain—and have their very own Star Wars moment.

15

Cool Events in 2019

International Whale Shark Day

Show big love for these gentle giants, which can grow to be the size of a bus!

August 30

International Kite Day

GO FLY A KITE!
In Gujarat, India, locals celebrate winter beginning to turn to summer by **launching kites and fireworks** into the air.

January 14

Scooby-Doo Turns 50!

The first episode featuring this mystery-solving pooch and pals aired on this day in 1969!

September 13

Super Bowl LIII

America's top two professional teams go head-to-head in Atlanta, Georgia, U.S.A., to determine the champion of the 2018 season.

February 3

Rugby World Cup

Rugby fans from around the world will **cheer their team to a trophy** in matches throughout Japan.

September 20–November 2

World Emoji Day

TEXT your favorite winky face or emoticon.

July 17

International Black Cat Awareness Month

Who are you calling unlucky?
Black Cats are PURRFECT, too.

October

Moon Landing Anniversary

The first successful mission to the moon is marked today— 50 years after Apollo 11's historic trip.

July 20

Pushkar Camel Festival

Some 50,000 camels participate in parades, beauty contests, and races at this **festival** in India.

November 4–12

SNOW COOL

FINNEGAN THE FISH

CREATING GIANT SNOW SCULPTURES FOR A CAUSE

Austin, Trevor, and Connor Bartz don't just create colossal snow sculptures for the fun of it. The brothers use their impressive handiwork to raise money for causes close to their hearts, like providing clean water for communities in Malawi, Africa. After collecting snow from their neighborhood in New Brighton, Minnesota, U.S.A., it takes the brothers some two weeks working in 12-hour blocks to complete their impressive icy artwork. Now *that*'s one way to spend a snow day!

OCTAVIUS THE OCTOPUS

SNOW SEA TURTLE

Floating Home

Talk about getting away from it all: One couple lives on their own man-made island off the coast of British Columbia's Vancouver Island. Built on top of a dozen interlocking steel docks, the compound floats in Clayoquot Sound, some 10 miles (16 km) from the nearest town. The island has several structures, including a home, a greenhouse, a dance studio, gardens, and even a waterfall for freshwater. Completely self-sufficient, the couple generates electricity from solar and water power, grows their own fruits and veggies, and catches fish for most meals. Sure brings new meaning to living off the land—and the water!

Blacktip sharks swim in a lagoon near Caroline Island in the central Pacific.

Amazing Animals

19 Cutest Animals of 2019

Fuzzy, fluffy, soft, and sweet: These critters are as cute as they come! Read on to find out why there's more to these animals than just their lovable looks.

1

HEADSTAND

A baby white-fronted capuchin monkey flips his view on the world by turning on its head. The playful primates, found in South America, communicate using vocalizations that include squeals, whistles, and purrs.

2

WHALE OF A TIME

A beluga whale pops out of the water to say hello. Mostly found in the Arctic Ocean's coastal waters, baby belugas are born dark gray. It can take up to eight years for a whale to turn completely white.

3

HANGING ON

Cold weather? *Snow* problem! Thanks to a coat of thick, shiny fur, the American marten stays active all winter long. The small mammal also uses its sharp, curved claws to climb trees and hang on branches with ease.

4

CLOWNING AROUND

A trio of clownfish swim around the anemone they call home. Clownfish and anemones are actually dependent on one another for survival: The fish clean and protect the plant while receiving food and shelter in return.

5

TASTE THE RAINBOW

A pair of rainbow lorikeets playfully peck at each other as a third bird looks on. These colorful creatures—found in Australia and Indonesia—are known for their dramatic display during mating season, including swinging upside down.

6 CURVE APPEAL

A giant peacock moth caterpillar makes its way up the curve of a small branch. The colorful insect will eventually turn into one of the most massive moths in the world, with a five-inch (13-cm) wingspan.

7 BRACE YOURSELF

Wesley the golden retriever has a smile just a bit different than other dogs. That's because he wore braces on his teeth to correct a severe underbite that made eating difficult. The metal mouth was just temporary—and now Wesley has a pearly white smile.

8 REST TIME

A white-handed gibbon finds the perfect nook to relax high in the tree canopy. This endangered species of monkey found in Southeast Asia certainly earns its rest: It spends most of its days swinging in the trees and can "fly" up 40 feet (12 m) through the air before landing.

9

TONGUE'S OUT

This giraffe's not being rude: It simply spends a lot of time with its tongue hanging out to reach leaves on the top of trees. As for the tongue's dark color? Scientists say that may be built-in protection from the sun's harmful UV rays.

10

FURRY FRIEND

Sloths are known for clinging to trees, not toys. But Edward the baby two-toed sloth—who lives at the London Zoo—enjoys clutching to his stuffed animal. Neglected by his mom, Edward hangs on to the toy to build up the same muscles he'd use to hold onto a parent.

11

GO FISH

The mandarinfish may look pretty, but watch out! The tropical fish—native to lagoons and reefs in the Pacific Ocean—is actually covered by a slimy, smelly substance that's poisonous to predators.

12

ONE SERIOUS SWIMMER

Why, hello there. A hippo emerges from the water for a quick breath, but it won't stay there for long: The giant animals can spend up to five minutes underwater without coming up for air.

23

13

SWEET DREAMS

A ring-tailed lemur gets cozy by curling up and wrapping its long tail around its body—a sleep position displayed by the entire species. One more thing to love about lemurs? They purr while they snooze, too!

14

PIGGING OUT

Pigs may not fly, but they can swim! On Pig Beach on Big Major Cay in the Bahamas, a colony of wild swine roam along the sand and swim in the crystal-blue waters. Visitors to the island can splash alongside the popular pigs.

15

HELLO, UP THERE!

A tree frog's head makes an unlikely landing spot for a butterfly. The tiny amphibians, found on all continents except Antarctica, are known to eat insects. Watch out, butterfly!

16

SPOT ON

Now that's some fierce focus! This margay—a small cat species native to Central and South America—is likely eyeing its prey while licking its chops. These felines typically feast on small mammals like rats, squirrels, and porcupines.

17

LITTLE LAMB

Just days old, this adorable lamb is already able to run and jump. Extremely active and social, young sheep are often spotted playing games like "follow the leader" while roaming around a farm.

18

BEAR IT

In Australia, the koala is known as a native bear, although it's actually not a bear at all. A marsupial mammal, the iconic animal earned its nickname because of its bearlike appearance.

19

RIDE ALONG

Birds of a feather ... ride together? This pair of parrots display impressive talent while rolling on tiny bikes for a fun photo op.

SPYING ON SLOTHS

RESEARCHERS USE TECHNOLOGY TO LEARN ABOUT LIFE IN THE SLOW LANE.

A BROWN-THROATED THREE-TOED SLOTH IN COSTA RICA

A HOFFMANN'S TWO-TOED SLOTH HANGS OUT WITH HER BABY.

Tucked in a tree canopy in Panama's rain forest, a three-toed sloth and the newborn baby clinging to her belly are all but invisible to the naked eye. This is the sloths' defense strategy: hiding from predators by camouflaging themselves. But their stealth behavior also makes it tricky for researchers to study them. Spying on the sloths has been hard to do, but now, cool technology allows sloth scientists to "see" what this animal does all day long.

COOL TOOLS

"Spying" tools include using a harmless, sticky substance to glue a tiny cap on a sloth's head. Inside is a monitor that records brain activity, so researchers can tell when the sloth is awake and asleep. Radio collars track sloths' travel—they typically move just 80 feet (24 m) a day—to understand how much space they need to thrive. And outfitting the animals with custom backpacks helps researchers record body temperature and geographic location. After four weeks, an automatic latch opens, and the backpack falls to the forest floor. The data inside give clues about the best spots to set sloths free in the wild.

SAVING THE SLOTHS

Learning about the daily habits and routines of sloths is helpful in developing protected areas for these animals. And thanks to these high-tech tools, researchers have behind-the-scenes information that can help ensure that sloths hang around for a long time to come.

How many toes? Sloths come in two models: two-toed and three-toed. They resemble each other, but they're two completely different families. Two-toed sloths are feistier and faster than three-toed sloths. Two-toed sloths can move quickly in the trees, while sloths with three toes usually move more slowly.

TWO-TOED

THREE-TOED

Undercover Polar Bears

Scientists use cool technology to spy on these animals.

In northern Alaska, a female polar bear curls up in her den. She's warm despite the frigid temperatures outside. Right now it's just her in the shelter, but in a couple of weeks she'll give birth to cubs. The family will then ride out the rest of the winter in their den.

Suddenly, a small plane flies overhead recording video of the frozen ground. Even though the soon-to-be mom is tucked under a few feet of snow, the images taken by the plane's cameras reveal her presence.

Because polar bears are hard to spot throughout the winter, experts have come up with surprising ways to gather information on these elusive—and vulnerable—animals. Using new technology, like this plane, scientists can learn more about polar bears and figure out how to protect them.

Heat Wave

How do the plane's video cameras spot this undercover animal? The gadgets are designed with special technology that allows them to pick up ground temperatures. "A polar bear in a den emits heat that is transferred to the surface of the snow," biologist Craig Perham says. "When a plane flies overhead, its cameras sense that the spot has a slightly warmer temperature than its surroundings."

Scientists like Perham rely on these gadgets to help them track down dens. Once they know the location of a den, researchers can prevent people from accidentally disturbing the shelter by building in or driving through the area.

Drone On

Flying drones with cameras are also being used on these den-finding missions. Todd Brinkman, a researcher with the University of Alaska in Fairbanks, is testing a drone called the Ptarmigan (named after the Arctic bird) to see if it can find polar bear dens. Once the drone is ready, it may help scientists protect the dens' furry inhabitants more quickly.

Using Tech to Protect

The long-term goal for using these gadgets? To gather as much information as possible about polar bears. Says Elisabeth Kruger, a program officer for the World Wildlife Fund, "New technology is helping us protect these animals as much as possible without getting in their way."

A male polar bear can weigh as much as six men.

Polar bear cubs stay with their mothers for about two years.

A newborn polar bear cub is about the size of a guinea pig.

A MOTHER HANGS OUT WITH HER CUB.

A polar bear's paw can measure as much as 12 inches across.
(30 cm)

Frog VERSUS Fungus

Scientists race to save amphibians from a deadly threat.

You can call a group of frogs an army or colony.

FRINGED LEAF FROGS LIVE IN THE SOUTH AMERICAN COUNTRIES OF BRAZIL, COLOMBIA, ECUADOR, PERU, AND PROBABLY BOLIVIA.

FRINGED LEAF FROG

More than 6,500 known species of frogs and toads exist.

A dark-green fringed leaf frog croaks softly as it sits on a tree branch in a wooded area of Brazil. Suddenly, it jumps to another branch. As the frog soars, it flaunts its brilliant orange-yellow tummy. Other fringed leaf frogs hop around and show off their stomachs too, adding streaks of color to the green habitat.

The bright bellies of these small animals aren't their only attention-grabbing feature. The species, which lives in tropical forests of South America, has somehow been able to survive a threat endangering amphibians worldwide. The menace—a deadly fungus called chytrid (KIH-trid) that attacks amphibians' skin—has wiped out certain frog species in some forests. But the fringed leaf frog still remains healthy. Scientists are examining these frogs and others that seem less affected by chytrid to learn how other animals can beat the threat.

CROAKER SOAKER

Chytrid began spreading rapidly in the 1990s, according to some scientists. It thrives in rivers and streams, where amphibians typically hang out. By attacking the animals' delicate skin, the fatal fungus suffocates its victims.

CUBAN TREE FROG

Scientists estimate that when chytrid invades an area, 80 percent of the amphibian species can become infected. It's hit many countries, from Brazil to Japan to Australia. "Chytrid has had a devastating impact," conservation biologist and amphibian specialist Danté Fenolio says. The good news is that chytrid is easily cured. An infected frog can take a soak in an antifungal bath a few minutes a day for about 10 days to clear it up.

But first scientists have to find infected frogs, so they trek into forests. They scoop up as many animals with chytrid as possible and bring them to zoos and sanctuaries for treatment.

Once introduced to their new pads, relocated amphibians are treated like VIPs. Keepers give them healing baths and place them in superclean aquariums to prevent the fungus from spreading. They also provide their "guests" with tasty snacks of live crickets, grasshoppers, ants, and katydids—the same things that they'd eat in the wild.

Though a lot of the rescued animals have recovered completely, keepers haven't been able to return them to their natural habitat. Unfortunately, the antifungal baths don't provide immunity to chytrid. And scientists haven't figured out a way to remove the fungus from the animals' homes. So if they're brought back to the forests, they could be exposed to chytrid again and reinfected. Now

RED-EYED TREE FROG

scientists are turning to the frogs' cousins—amphibians that seem to be unaffected by chytrid—to lend a webbed hand.

REASONS FOR HOPE

The populations of certain amphibians such as the fringed leaf frog, marine toad, and red-eyed tree frog haven't declined because of chytrid. What's happening? For certain species such as the fringed leaf frog, the answer remains unclear. But scientists think that some of these animals may naturally host types of bacteria on their skin that prevent the fungus from growing. Other amphibians with poison glands might produce special chemicals along with their toxins that help the animals resist chytrid. And certain animals may simply have inherited a natural immunity to the fungus.

PANAMANIAN GOLDEN FROG

Frogs were the first land animals to have vocal cords.

To help animals that might get infected, researchers are trying to reproduce the fungus-fighting bacteria that naturally grow on some captive Panamanian golden frogs. They may then be able to transfer the bacteria to vulnerable amphibians. Researchers from the University of South Florida have also found that Cuban tree frogs can build more and more of a resistance to chytrid if they are repeatedly infected and treated. It's too early to know if these treatments will work on a large scale and allow relocated frogs to return to their homes. But they offer hope.

"We look forward to the day when we can return rescued frogs and other amphibians to the wild where they belong," Fenolio says. Forests that host a chorus of croaks? That's definitely a reason to jump up and down!

WHAT IS Taxonomy?

Since there are billions and billions of living things, called organisms, on the planet, people need a way of classifying them. Scientists created a system called **taxonomy,** which helps to classify all living things into ordered groups. By putting organisms into categories we are better able to understand how they are the same and how they are different. There are seven levels of taxonomic classification, beginning with the broadest group, called a domain, followed by kingdom, down to the most specific group, called a species.

Biologists divide life based on evolutionary history, and they place organisms into three domains depending on their genetic structure: Archaea, Bacteria, and Eukarya. (See p. 87 for "The Three Domains of Life.")

Where do animals come in?

Animals are a part of the Eukarya domain, which means they are organisms made of cells with nuclei. More than one million species of animals have

Chinese stripe-necked turtle

been named, including humans. Like all living things, animals can be divided into smaller groups, called phyla. Most scientists believe there are more than 30 phyla into which animals can be grouped based on certain scientific criteria, such as body type or whether or not the animal has a backbone. It can be pretty complicated, so there is another, less complicated system that groups animals into two categories: vertebrates and invertebrates.

SAMPLE CLASSIFICATION
JAPANESE MACAQUE

Kingdom:	Animalia
Phylum:	Chordata
Class:	Mammalia
Order:	Primates
Family:	Cercopithecidae
Genus:	*Macaca*
Species:	*fuscata*

TIP:
Here's a sentence to help you remember the classification order:
King Phillip Came Over For Good Soup.

BY THE NUMBERS

There are 13,267 vulnerable or endangered animal species in the world. The list includes:

- **1,204 mammals,** such as the snow leopard, the polar bear, and the fishing cat.

- **1,469 birds,** including the Steller's sea eagle and the black-banded plover.

- **2,386 fish,** such as the Mekong giant catfish.

- **1,215 reptiles,** including the American crocodile.

- **1,414 insects,** including the Macedonian grayling.

- **2,100 amphibians,** such as the Round Island day gecko.

- **And more,** including 170 arachnids, 732 crustaceans, 239 sea anemones and corals, 190 bivalves, and 1,992 snails and slugs.

Vertebrates Animals WITH Backbones

Fish are cold-blooded and live in water. They breathe with gills, lay eggs, and usually have scales.

Amphibians are cold-blooded. Their young live in water and breathe with gills. Adults live on land and breathe with lungs.

Reptiles are cold-blooded and breathe with lungs. They live both on land and in water.

Birds are warm-blooded and have feathers and wings. They lay eggs, breathe with lungs, and usually are able to fly. Some birds live on land, some in water, and some on both.

Mammals are warm-blooded and feed on their mothers' milk. They also have skin that is usually covered with hair. Mammals live both on land and in water.

Bird: Bald eagle

Fish: Clown anemonefish

Invertebrates Animals WITHOUT Backbones

Sponges are a very basic form of animal life. They live in water and do not move on their own.

Echinoderms have external skeletons and live in seawater.

Mollusks have soft bodies and can live either in or out of shells, on land or in water.

Arthropods are the largest group of animals. They have external skeletons, called exoskeletons, and segmented bodies with appendages. Arthropods live in water and on land.

Worms are soft-bodied animals with no true legs. Worms live in soil.

Cnidaria live in water and have mouths surrounded by tentacles.

Worm: Earthworms

Cnidaria: West Coast sea nettle

Cold-blooded versus Warm-blooded

Cold-blooded animals, also called ectotherms, get their heat from outside their bodies.

Warm-blooded animals, also called endotherms, keep their body temperature level regardless of the temperature of their environment.

BIG CATS

A young male jaguar

The National Geographic Big Cats Initiative's goal is to stop the decline of lions and other big cats in the wild through research, conservation, education, and global awareness. Visit natgeo.org/big-cats to learn more.

Not all wild cats are big cats, so what are big cats? To wildlife experts, they are the four living members of the genus *Panthera*: tigers, lions, leopards, and jaguars. They can all unleash a mighty roar and, as carnivores, they survive solely on the flesh of other animals. Thanks to powerful jaws; long, sharp claws; and daggerlike teeth, big cats are excellent hunters.

WHO'S WHO?

BIG CATS MAY HAVE a lot of features in common, but if you know what to look for, you'll be able to tell who's who in no time.

FUR

Most tigers are orange-colored with vertical black stripes on their bodies. This coloring helps the cats blend in with tall grasses as they sneak up on prey. These markings are like fingerprints: No two stripe patterns are alike.

TIGERS

JAGUARS

A jaguar's coat pattern looks similar to that of a leopard, as both have dark spots called rosettes. The difference? The rosettes on a jaguar's torso have irregularly shaped borders and at least one black dot in the center.

LEOPARDS

A leopard's yellowy coat has dark spots called rosettes on its back and sides. In leopards, the rosettes' edges are smooth and circular. This color combo helps leopards blend into their surroundings.

LIONS

Lions have a light brown, or tawny, coat and a tuft of black hair at the end of their tails. When they reach their prime, most male lions have shaggy manes that help them look larger and more intimidating.

JAGUAR
100 to 250 pounds
(45 TO 113 KG)

5 to 6 feet long
(1.5 TO 1.8 M)

LEOPARD
66 to 176 pounds
(30 TO 80 KG)

4.25 to 6.25 feet long
(1.3 TO 1.9 M)

BENGAL TIGER
240 to 500 pounds
(109 TO 227 KG)

5 to 6 feet long
(1.5 TO 1.8 M)

AFRICAN LION
265 to 420 pounds
(120 TO 191 KG)

4.5 to 6.5 feet long
(1.4 TO 2 M)

1 Jaguar jaws are strong enough to crush turtle shells.

2 Researchers have sprayed pricey perfume around camera traps to lure jaguars to them.

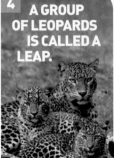

4 A GROUP OF LEOPARDS IS CALLED A LEAP.

5 THE DARKER A LION'S MANE, THE OLDER THE FELINE IS.

3 A snow leopard's **big paws act like snowshoes,** allowing it to **walk on snow without sinking.**

19 Cool THINGS ABOUT

6 UNLIKE MOST BIG CATS, WHICH USUALLY HAVE YELLOWISH EYES, A SNOW LEOPARD'S EYES ARE GRAY OR LIGHT GREEN.

7 Using its strong hind paws and claws, a clouded leopard can hang upside down from a tree branch.

9 Cheetah cubs have a long silver stripe of fur that may help keep them camouflaged in tall grass.

8 LIONS SURVIVE DROUGHTS IN AFRICA'S KALAHARI DESERT BY EATING JUICY MELONS.

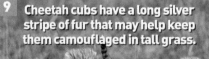

10 A leopard with a strawberry-blond coat was spotted in Africa.

11 During India's **ONAM FESTIVAL,** people disguised as tigers perform a dance to honor the big cat.

12 SNOW LEOPARDS HAVE BEEN SPOTTED AT ELEVATIONS OF OVER 18,000 FEET (5,486 M).

13 Stone carvings of **jaguars** that date back **500 or more years** have been discovered in **Mexico.**

BIG CATS

14 A cheetah can accelerate to 70 miles (112 km) an hour in three seconds—that's faster than most sports cars.

15 A lion can eat 40 pounds (18 kg) of meat—the same as 160 hamburgers—in one sitting.

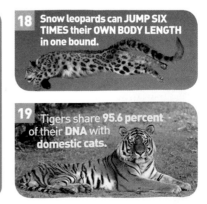

16 The lines that run from a cheetah's eyes to its mouth may protect it from sun glare.

17 THE CHEETAH SOMETIMES **PURRS** WHEN IT FEELS RELAXED, JUST AS DOMESTIC CATS DO.

18 Snow leopards can JUMP SIX TIMES their OWN BODY LENGTH in one bound.

19 Tigers share **95.6 percent** of their **DNA** with domestic cats.

top spOt

How the jaguar's one-of-a-kind features make it stand out from other wild cats

The word "jaguar" comes from a Native American word meaning "he who kills with one leap."

A jaguar's spots are called rosettes.

A STEALTHY PREDATOR glides along a river in South America. Noticing a group of alligator-like animals called caimans floating by the shore, the hunter silently cruises toward the reptiles. It swims between plants to mask its movements and pauses beside an unsuspecting caiman. Then the animal shoots through the water at its target, sinking its teeth into the reptile's scaly skin.

With its prey clamped between its jaws, the creature climbs from the water and onto the riverbank. In doing so, it reveals its true identity. The dripping-wet hunter is a jaguar.

"We knew jaguars were good swimmers," says wildlife ecologist Alan Rabinowitz, who runs a big cat conservation organization called Panthera and witnessed the splashy smackdown while on an expedition. "But we were astonished to learn that they can hunt as they swim."

Snagging prey while swimming is something no other feline does. Then again, the jaguar stands out from the rest of the cat crowd in many ways.

ON THE ON HUNT

One thing that makes a jaguar unique from other cats is its hunting techniques. This cat hunts for food on the ground, in trees, and while swimming in water. No other cat does this. "Even lions and tigers—the closest relatives of the jaguar—don't go after prey in all three spots," Rabinowitz says. "They usually just nab prey on the ground."

What's more, jaguars use a different hunting strategy from most other felines. A lot of cats chase targets over long distances. A jaguar silently sneaks up to prey such as tapirs before ambushing its meal. The animal creeps closer to its mark than even the tiger. When jaguars finally strike, they do so in their own special way. Most felines struggle with prey before overpowering it. But a jaguar has the largest jaws of any big cat, so its bite is so strong it's often able to take down its target with just one chomp.

But just because jaguars slay it with their hunting skills doesn't mean they like to fight. They only scuffle when necessary.

ADAPTATION NATION

So why is the jaguar so different from other felines? Over their four-million-year existence, jaguars have developed adaptations to help deal with unique challenges in their habitats. For instance, it's hard to chase prey through the forests where the cats live. That's why they creep right up to their target.

Deadly parasites thrive in the cat's habitat. If the jaguar is wounded, it could become exposed to infection. Um, no thank you! "Avoiding face-offs means that the jaguar is less likely to get a cut that could become infected," Rabinowitz says. That also may be why the cat developed its jumbo-size jaws, which allow it to quickly knock out prey. A swift takedown means less opportunity for infection-causing cuts. The jaguar's adaptations help it survive. "We're still figuring out everything. And we can't wait to uncover more jaguar secrets." Rabinowitz says.

The jaguar's roar sounds like a deep cough.

Jaguar Genetics

Scientists once thought that the jaguar species—like all other big cat species—was divided into smaller groups called subspecies. These form when groups of one type of animal become isolated from each other. The members within each group breed with one another. Over time, the groups develop slightly different genetics (codes passed from parents to offspring that determine traits).

In 2001 experts examined the DNA (or sets of genetics) in the fur and droppings of jaguars from Mexico to Argentina. Results revealed that no subspecies exist— all jaguars belong to one genetic group. "Every other big cat has subspecies," says wildlife ecologist Alan Rabinowitz. "This really makes the jaguar unique."

Scientists believe that jaguars move around so much that they don't have a chance to form isolated groups that can turn into subspecies. "That's good," Rabinowitz says. "Isolated animal groups are more vulnerable to extinction." Meaning that a jaguar's travel habits might actually take the species far in life.

Jaguars are near threatened. About 15,000 exist in the wild.

NORTH AMERICA

ATLANTIC OCEAN

SOUTH AMERICA

PACIFIC OCEAN

Where jaguars live

PENGUIN CITY

Chinstraps rule the roost in these loud, crowded colonies.

Chinstraps usually dive to depths of around 150 feet (46 m).

a sprawling city bustling with the loud racket of morning rush hour, crowds of commuters hurry past each other. Suddenly, one traveler bumps into another and sets off a shouting match. Others in the vicinity join in with loud honks and screeching noises. Eventually the gridlock eases and the commuters continue, ready to get on with their day.

This may seem like a typical morning in, say, New York City. But the scene is set in Antarctica, and these commuters are really chinstrap penguins on their way to their foraging ground. Chinstraps are flightless, two-foot (0.6-m)-tall birds that live in and around Antarctica and nest in crowded communities called colonies, home to hundreds of thousands of individuals.

BIRD CITIES

Every November, near the start of summer in Antarctica, members of different colonies arrive at their breeding grounds

Chinstrap penguins are named for facial markings that resemble helmet chinstraps.

on Antarctica's shores, squawking practically nonstop.

After building a nest out of pebbles for their chicks, chinstrap moms and dads take turns squatting right on top of them to keep them warm. When a parent isn't babysitting, it heads off to find food, commuting from its home to the ocean along well-worn footpaths. Like city streets, the paths bustle with individuals—and traffic.

After traveling a mile (1.6 km) or more from their nesting site, the penguins finally reach the colony's "food district" at the edge of the sea. From here they dive into the water and use their speedy swimming skills to catch krill. Then they emerge from the water and get back on the penguin expressway toward home.

Back at the nest, the returning parent feeds its hungry offspring by regurgitating some of the krill it devoured. With regular meals, the youngest members of the penguin city begin to grow.

SUMMER BREAK

In late January, about a month after chinstrap penguin chicks hatch, offspring are left in groups so that both moms and dads can search for food. The groups—which are sort of like day-care centers—huddle together for warmth and protection. Eventually the chicks begin to roam the colony together. By late March (the start of the fall), the colonies disperse. Members spend the next several months at sea. Next November, the birds will return to re-create their metropolis. New residents will hatch, and parents will once again prepare their chicks for life in the big city.

TWO CHINSTRAPS IN A COLONY COURT EACH OTHER WITH LOUD VOCALIZATIONS.

These penguins eat snow to cool down when they feel too warm.

UNICORNS
OF THE SEA

SCIENTISTS TRY TO **SOLVE THE MYSTERY** OF THE NARWHAL'S **GIANT TUSK.**

Chilly water laps against an iceberg in the Arctic Ocean. Suddenly, a pod of narwhals—a species of whale that sports a unicorn-like horn on its head—emerges from the sea near the iceberg's edge.

Narwhals live in the Arctic Ocean. Like most whales, they're jumbo-size—up to 3,500 pounds (1,588 kg)—and surface to breathe. And like some whale species such as orcas, they live in pods. (Narwhals usually have 15 to 20 in their group.) But there's one thing a narwhal has that no other whale does: a giant tusk growing out of its noggin.

For centuries people have been trying to figure out what this tusk—actually an enlarged tooth—is used for. Luckily, scientists have come up with some theories that may help solve this gnawing puzzle.

TUSK, TUSK

A narwhal's swordlike tusk first pokes from its jaw through the animal's upper lip when it's about three months old. This is the only tooth the whale develops. Over time, the tusk can grow to be the half the length of the whale's body. New research shows that narwhals may use these long appendages to snag prey like arctic cod using quick jabs to stun the fish before they eat them.

TOOTH SLEUTHS

Another theory is that male narwhals likely use the tooth to attract females. Similar to a peacock's flashy feathers, the tusk makes them stand out to potential mates. The animals have been observed scraping their tusks together, as though they are in a fencing match. This may be a way for male members of the pod to identify one another.

While there's still plenty scientists don't know about narwhals, they will continue to look for answers. In the meantime, it appears that these mysterious whales still have a few secrets up their tusks.

SURFACING ABOVE WATER, A GROUP OF NARWHALS TAKES A BREATH OF AIR.

THIS POD OF MALES SWIMS THROUGH ARCTIC WATERS.

A NARWHAL MOM TRAVELS WITH HER BABY.

BRAINWAVES

Inside the Amazing Minds of Dolphins

SCIENTISTS STUDY THE BEHAVIOR OF THESE AND OTHER BOTTLENOSE DOLPHINS AT THE ROATÁN INSTITUTE FOR MARINE SCIENCES IN HONDURAS, CENTRAL AMERICA.

ALFONZ AND KIMBIT EACH TAKE HOLD OF A ROPE TO PULL APART THE PIPE WITH A TREAT INSIDE.

In an experiment at a research center in Florida, U.S.A., two dolphins try to solve a puzzle. Named Alfonz and Kimbit, the dolphins examine a pipe that scientists have stuffed with tasty fish and dropped into the water. To get to the snack, each dolphin must tug on a rope connected to a cap on each end of the pipe. Neither dolphin can open the pipe alone, so to solve this puzzle, Alfonz and Kimbit must work together.

They don't waste any time. Gripping the ropes with their teeth, the dolphins yank off the caps. Success! They split the treat inside. Their feat reveals a lot about the amazing minds of these marine mammals. Alfonz and Kimbit demonstrate that they can communicate, cooperate, and plan—three behaviors scientists consider signs of intelligence in animals. But intelligence is tricky to measure in animals, and researchers are figuring out new ways to answer an old question. "We shouldn't be asking, 'How smart are dolphins?'" says Stan Kuczaj, an expert on dolphin intelligence. "We should be asking, 'How are dolphins smart?'"

STRANGE BRAINS

Scientists see signs of intelligent life throughout the animal kingdom. Octopuses can solve puzzles. Wolves communicate. Crows use tools. But dolphins possess *all* of these brainy abilities. Some people think that the only animals smarter than dolphins are humans.

But dolphin brains are very different from our own. Dolphins have adapted for life in the ocean. They sleep with half their brains awake to stay alert for sharks and other dangers. "These animals live in a very different world," underwater photographer Brian Skerry says. "They're best described as an alien intelligence."

They even have an otherworldly ability: echolocation, a way to "see" by bouncing sound waves of high-speed clicks off objects hundreds of yards away. Dolphins use this sixth sense in intelligent ways. They listen to each other's signals to cooperate while hunting. "I suspect they also use echolocation to read the emotions of other animals," Kuczaj says. Ever notice how your muscles grow tense when you're anxious or your heart races when you get scared? Using echolocation, dolphins can sense these characteristics in other animals. They can even tell if another dolphin is sick. "Knowing the mood of other animals in the group is an important ability when you're such a social animal," Kuczaj says.

PROBLEM SOLVERS

In the shallow waters off Florida, a group of dolphins goes fishing. One darts into action, swimming in speedy circles around a school of fish to kick up a netlike wall of mud. Trapped, the fish leap over the mud—and right into the open mouths of the other dolphins. In other places, dolphins have devised their own brainy means of landing lunch. Orcas in Argentina trap sea lions on the beach. Dolphins off another coast of South America cooperate to scare fish into easier-to-chomp schools. Like Alfonz and Kimbit, these wild dolphins are cooperating to solve problems.

SOCIAL SWIMMER

Dolphins form decades-long friendships and team up to hunt for food, find mates, and protect the group. Partnerships fall apart and re-form according to complex social rules that scientists are still figuring out. If a dolphin gets sick or hurt, the entire group will follow and look after it. "Social behavior is a key to their survival," Skerry says.

A PIECE OF SEAWEED BECOMES A TOY AS THESE BOTTLENOSE DOLPHINS PLAY TOGETHER.

AFTER FORCING FISH TO CLUMP TOGETHER, DUSKY DOLPHINS GRAB AN EASY MOUTHFUL. A PENGUIN (BOTTOM) EVEN SNEAKS IN FOR THE FEAST.

Signs of Dolphin Smarts

THEY COMMUNICATE. Scientists suspect dolphins "talk" about everything from basic facts like their age and gender to whether they're happy or sad. When faced with a shark or other threats, they'll even call group members for backup.

THEY COOPERATE. Intensely social animals, dolphins establish complex relationships that scientists still don't understand. They team up to hunt, protect each other, find mates, and just play.

THEY INVENT. Dolphins demonstrate a humanlike ability to adapt to different situations. Some even use tools. Dolphins in Australia wear sponges to protect their noses when they dig in the seafloor for food.

Name That TIDE POOL ANIMAL

When the tide goes out in rocky, coastal areas, some water gets left behind in pools and crevices. These spots are called tide pools, and many different creatures like to hang out in them. See if you can name these tide pool animals.

A

This creature is always on the lookout for a new home. Snail shells are usually its preference, but with five pairs of legs, you can't call it a slowpoke!

A tide pool is one tough neighborhood! When the tide is in, waves come crashing; when the tide is out, animals are exposed to sun, cold weather, and even freshwater from rain. When you look closely at tide pool creatures, you'll find they all have adaptations to survive these harsh conditions.

C The webbing between this animal's short, triangular arms is a clue to its name. Sensors on the end of each of its arms can sense light and detect prey.

B These drifters don't have much say about where they end up, but often they show up in tide pools. They may be soft and squishy, but their tentacles are stunning.

D Nemo and his father lived inside one of these. When their tentacles are open, they are ready for food; when they're folded in, they're likely munching.

E After grazing on algae, this tide pool creature finds the perfect parking spot on a rock and hunkers down, sealing water underneath itself to keep its body moist during low tide.

F Call it a tide pool salad. This leafy green creature can get dry and stiff at low tide, but it bounces right back once the water comes in.

A. Hermit crab. B. Jellyfish. C. Bat star. D. Sea anemone. E. Limpet. F. Sea lettuce

SEA TURTLE

A lost and freezing loggerhead gets help from warmhearted volunteers.

The freezing sea turtle can barely manage another stroke as she struggles to keep herself warm in the frigid waters of Cape Cod Bay off Massachusetts, U.S.A. The reptile is suffering from the turtle version of human hypothermia—when body temperature falls below normal levels. Her strength is fading fast.

She bobs lifelessly on the surface of the water before a gust of wind propels her toward land. Washed up on the shore of Crosby Landing Beach, she lies motionless in the sand, bitterly cold. If she doesn't get help soon, she won't have a chance.

LIFEGUARDS ARRIVE

Taking a morning stroll along the beach,

Brian Long spots the large turtle. He can't tell if she's alive, so he immediately phones the Massachusetts Audubon Society, a conservation organization. The call reaches director Bob Prescott, who rushes to the beach in a pickup truck and identifies the 2.5-foot (.76-m)-long creature as a loggerhead sea turtle. An endangered species, they spend their summers in the north and their winters in warmer southern waters, but this turtle likely got lost while navigating down the coast and missed the chance to migrate before cold weather set in. The animal's eyes are closed, and she's not visibly breathing. But when

Some Pacific loggerheads migrate over 7,500 miles (12,000 km) between nesting beaches.

A cooler loggerhead nest will produce more male hatchlings, while a warmer one will produce more females.

THE WEAK TURTLE ARRIVES AT THE REHAB CENTER.

Prescott gently touches her neck, the big-beaked reptile slowly raises her head. She's hanging on but urgently needs medical care. The two men hoist the huge animal onto the bed of the truck, and she's taken to New England Aquarium in Boston, Massachusetts. Here, she can begin her recovery.

These turtles may live for 50 years or more in the wild.

SHELL-SHOCKED

At the aquarium's marine animal rehabilitation center, staff name the turtle Biscuits and give her an exam. She weighs in at 165 pounds (75 kg)—slightly underweight for a loggerhead of Biscuits's age. She has developed open wounds, she's dehydrated, and she has pneumonia. She is also cold-stunned, a condition that affects reptiles if their temperature drops too low. As their bodies cool, the animals' blood circulation slows, causing the animals to enter a coma-like state, practically unable to move.

Now her caretakers' goal is to raise her body temperature from an extremely low 48°F (9°C) to between 70°F and 80°F (21°C and 25°C). But it won't be easy—warming her too quickly could be deadly. She's moved into a

GEORGIA SEA TURTLE CENTER STAFF UNLOAD BISCUITS FROM THE PLANE.

TURTLE TAKEOFF

Soon, Biscuits is ready for to be moved to the Georgia Sea Turtle Center on Jekyll Island, which is located closer to her release site. Here the staff will continue to prepare her for reentry into the wild. Along with three other recovering turtles, she's flown to Georgia, U.S.A., on a private jet. Once there, Biscuits is placed in a tank where she can continue practicing her swimming strokes. Caretakers also put live blue crabs and horseshoe crabs in her tank so she can get used to catching prey again. These critters are some of a loggerhead's favorite foods in the wild, and Biscuits quickly remembers how to snatch up the tasty treats in her beak.

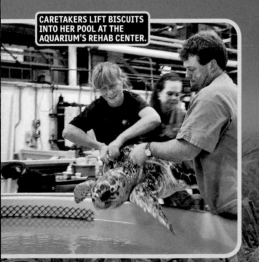

CARETAKERS LIFT BISCUITS INTO HER POOL AT THE AQUARIUM'S REHAB CENTER.

BISCUITS RETURNS TO THE SEA.

temperature-controlled pool set to 55°F (13°C). Each day the rehabbers raise the thermostat a little higher. As the temperature rises, Biscuits begins to move normally again.

To help her regain energy, the staff offer healthy meals of fish and squid, and they rehydrate her with daily injections of nutrient-filled fluids. Biscuits also receives antibiotics for her pneumonia and soothing ointment for her skin.

BACK TO THE SEA

A month later Biscuits is ready to return to the ocean. She's heavier, now weighing 180 pounds (82 kg), and has proven she can catch live prey. She's driven by her rehabilitation team to a release site in Florida, U.S.A. When the team lowers her onto the sand at the water's edge, she immediately crawls into the crashing waves and swims off, healthy and happy at last.

Tips for Being a
COATI

There comes a time, if you're a coati, that you'll join a band of other coatis. Here are five pointers for fitting in.

BE A TEAM PLAYER.

Your coati band has as many as 30 members, and you'll have to get along with everyone—that means females of all ages and immature males. (When males are two to three years old they leave the band.) So don't dawdle as you travel together searching for food. Have your pals' backs as you keep each other safe.

KEEP YOUR NAILS SHARP.

Shh. Hear the insect larvae squirming inside that log but have no idea how to get at them? Just use your long, sharp claws to gouge and rip into the wood. Mounds of grubs are now yours anytime you want.

BE COOL—DON'T BEG.

There's no sharing in coati bands; you'll have to find your own meals. Don't just stand there drooling if you see an adult eating something interesting. It's totally OK to put your nose right up to her mouth and take a big whiff. You can even follow her around to see how she finds more.

GO BACK FOR SECONDS— AND THIRDS, AND FOURTHS.

You can eat practically everything in the forest—as long as it's small enough. Meals include fruits, beetles, centipedes, scorpions, termites, insect larvae, and spiders. And it's not gross to crave something chewy on the outside and crunchy on the inside, such as a frog, lizard, rodent, or bird.

CROCODILE HATCHLING

CHILL OUT.

After a hard day of eating bugs and dodging predators, you deserve a little fun. So leap from branch to branch with your bandmates. Scale to the treetop, use your mighty tail to balance way up high, and scramble straight down. You might be having a blast, but playing also helps build muscle and speed. You'll need both to track down tasty frogs and escape hungry predators—and that's what being a full-fledged coati is all about.

NINJA GIRAFFES

These animals have some seriously stealthy moves.

You might not think giraffes would have much in common with ninja, skilled combatants who prowled through 15th-century Japan on spy missions. After all, giraffes move awkwardly, and their superlong necks hardly seem stealthy. But these hoofed creatures are surprisingly sleek and agile. Discover how giraffes kick it up a notch, ninja style.

HIDE-AND-SEEK

Often hired by rulers who were competing for power, ninja would dress up as farmers or merchants to spy on their leader's opponent. Giraffes may have a distinctive appearance, but they sport the perfect camouflage for blending into their surroundings. Their brown spots look like the shadows created by sunlight shining through the trees, keeping them protected from predators.

THE NEED FOR SPEED

Ninja trained to become swift runners so they could easily slip away from foes during a chase. Giraffes are also excellent sprinters, using their long, muscular legs. At full gallop, these animals can reach 35 miles an hour (56 km/h), which helps them evade predators, like lions.

SPECTACULAR SENSES

People once believed that ninja could see in the dark and hear tiny movements. This likely wasn't true for ninja, but giraffes really do have superb vision and hearing. Using their keen eyesight, they can spot a moving animal more than a half mile (0.8 km) away. They also hear noises that humans can't detect. Could giraffes be even better warriors than ninja?

WEAPON MASTERS

When ninja came face-to-face with their rivals, they used swords and daggers to defeat the enemy. Giraffes have their own built-in weapons: hooves with sharp edges. In fact, a giraffe can be deadly when it uses its feet to kick other giraffes and predators. Two male giraffes might also fight for dominance by clubbing each other with their heavy heads and necks.

GOOFBALLS

THE WAY ARMADILLOS BEHAVE WILL CRACK YOU UP.

If you held a contest for the funniest animal on the planet, the prize would have to go to an armadillo. Get ready to LOL as NG shows off the silly side of armadillos.

Armadillos live mostly in Central and South America. Only the nine-banded armadillo lives in the United States.

An armadillo looks hilarious.

Armadillos look like a mixture of a huge roly-poly bug, a pig, and a medieval knight—with a bit of giant insect mixed in. But they're actually mammals, closely related to anteaters and sloths. They have long snouts and piglike ears, and their bodies are covered with protective bony plates that look like a knight's armor.

They turn into balls.

Armadillos usually aren't fighters. When threatened, the three-banded armadillo protects itself by rolling into a ball. The result looks so much like a soccer ball that a three-banded armadillo named Fuleco was the mascot of the 2014 World Cup in Brazil.

Armadillos are mostly nocturnal. They stay inside their burrows when it's hot and come out at dawn or dusk or at night to look for food.

They leap straight up when startled.

If something startles a nine-banded armadillo by touching it on the back, it responds by jumping straight up into the air, sometimes as high as four feet (1.2 m). It's a reflex that probably helps them get away from predators. (Or maybe it just makes the predators laugh so hard they forget to chase the armadillo.)

They're likely to get into traffic jams.

If you frighten an armadillo, it might run away to hide in the nearest burrow. But sometimes when one armadillo is trying to get into the burrow, another armadillo (or two!) is trying to get out. They get stuck!

Armadillos have been around for at least 65 million years.

They stick out their tongues to eat.

Armadillos use their long, sticky tongues to feel around in ant nests, slurping up lots of ants at a time. A nine-banded armadillo can eat thousands of ants at one meal. Ants may not be *your* favorite food, but don't make fun of an armadillo's snack—it might stick out that extra-long tongue at you!

TONGUE

ROOM

A nine-banded armadillo uses its huge front claws to dig its burrow. It might have several burrows but uses only one for its babies. That burrow is up to 25 feet (7.6 m) long and can have several rooms and connecting tunnels.

TUNNEL

49

WOLVERINE!

How to track a wild, mysterious super-predator

Wolverines are small but ferocious bearlike animals. They're so mysterious that scientists don't even know how many there are in the wild. But researchers like Gregg Treinish are working to help this wild species continue to survive.

"It's February and I'm on the top of a mountain in Montana, U.S.A., all alone. The snow-caked forest is silent. All of a sudden, I spot a wolverine track. I start following his trail.

"Tracking a wolverine is like following a ghost through the forest. They're so fast—covering 20 miles (32 km) in a day—and stealthy that I've never seen one in the wild. But if I pay close attention to the trail this one left, I can learn a lot about him.

"The tracks are grouped side by side instead of one after the other, showing that the wolverine was bounding fast, hunting something. I see another set of wolverine tracks. Then two more, crossing each other. Something was going on here. Ahead, I spot a four-foot (1.2-m) hole in the snow. Dirt and blood are scattered around the edge. I peer in to see an elk leg—a tasty meal for the wolverine.

A WOLVERINE CHOWS DOWN ON A LARGE ANIMAL'S LEG BONE.

Wolverines are highly intelligent. People have reported seeing them climb trees, wait, and then pounce on deer that walk by.

"I search the hole and find two wolverine hairs, which I place in a bag. Later, scientists will extract DNA from the hairs, and that will help them discover how many wolverines live in this area, what they're eating, and how far they're traveling.

"As climate change warms the planet, wolverines' snowy habitat is disappearing. The clues I find will help scientists track the population to learn whether we need to take action to prevent these phantoms of the forest from disappearing forever."

Mistaken IDENTITY

Sugar gliders seem to think that they're birds and soccer players. Find out why.

The sugar glider appears to be one mixed-up mammal. Mostly found in the forests of Australia and on the nearby island of New Guinea, this tree-dweller exhibits a mishmash of traits seen in other animals and humans. Is it confused, or does it just have bizarre behaviors? Read on and decide for yourself.

A SUGAR GLIDER'S TAIL IS LONGER THAN ITS BODY.

THEY HAVE BIRDLIKE MOVES.

When the sugar glider wants to travel long distances, it leaps from its treetop home into the air and spreads its limbs as if they're wings. Luckily, skin flaps on either side of its body connect the front and back legs. With the flaps extended, the critter can sail on air. Sugar gliders aren't birds, but they definitely have soaring skills.

MALE SUGAR GLIDERS HAVE A BALD PATCH ON THEIR HEADS.

THEY ACT LIKE BALL PLAYERS.

Sugar glider families sleep inside tree hollows. At naptime they heap together like soccer stars who have just scored a big win. Huddling like this keeps the animals warm. But not just any glider is welcome on the "victory pile." If an unrelated sugar glider sneaks onto a family's turf, the clan will chase it away. Now that's good defense.

THEY BEHAVE LIKE KIDS.

You probably have a serious sweet tooth. And sugar gliders act like, well, a kid in a candy store when they're around sweet stuff. This animal devours foods that are high in sugar, such as flower nectar and tree sap.

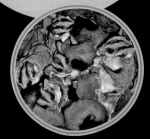

Wild Hamsters

FARMERS TRY TO MAKE PEACE WITH THESE PESKY CRITTERS.

In a sun-dappled wheat field in France, a prowling barn cat meets a black-bellied hamster. Too far from her burrow to run for shelter, the wild hamster rises on her hind legs to face her enemy. She puffs out her cheeks, flashes her black underbelly, growls, and bares her teeth. The cat backs away. That black-bellied hamster is one tough rodent.

"They're afraid of nothing," says Alexandre Lehmann, a biologist who has worked with these wild hamsters for the past 12 years. "They fight against cats and dogs and even farmers. They try to fight against tractors. The Germans call them small bears."

Good thing the black-bellied hamster won't go down without a fight. Because in France, where only 500 to 1,000 remain in the wild, these cranky critters are in a fight for their lives.

During hibernation a hamster's heart beats only about six times a minute.

There are around 25 different species of wild hamsters.

TWO-DAY-OLD HAMSTERS

The earliest hamsters lived more than 2.5 million years ago.

ENTRANCE TO A HAMSTER BURROW

CAPTIVE-BRED HAMSTERS ARE READY FOR RELEASE INTO THE WILD.

A NEST INSIDE A BURROW

FEISTY RODENTS

Don't confuse the black-bellied hamster with its puny tame relative, the golden hamster. At about 12 inches (30 cm) long, the black-bellied hamster is twice as big. And it's way more feisty.

In fact, black-bellied hamsters historically have been considered public enemy number one—rodents on the wrong side of the law. Ranging from the eastern steppes of Russia to the plains of Alsace in France, black-bellied hamsters have long been seen as pests because of their appetite for farmers' grains, beets, and cabbage. And since mother hamsters can give birth to as many as 14 babies a year, sometimes the population has exploded. The hamsters earned a bad rap, and humans tried everything to get rid of them. Some older farmers remember a time when, as kids, they were paid as bounty hunters to kill hamsters and bring their tails to city hall.

The war on hamsters continued until just a few decades ago, when naturalists noticed the rodents were in trouble. Although plenty of hamsters were in Russia and Ukraine, their numbers had been dwindling in western Europe. A movement began to save the hamsters. In 1993 France passed a law protecting them as an endangered species.

FRANCE — EUROPE
ATLANTIC OCEAN

HELPING HANDS

At the Stork and Otter Reintroduction Centre in Alsace, Lehmann and his colleagues breed captive hamsters and release their pups into the wild. But breeding black-bellied hamsters isn't easy. Remember, these critters have attitude. Forget humans—they don't even like each other.

If all goes well, the mother hamster will give birth to a litter of about seven pups in three weeks' time. One year later the pups will be ready for release into the wild.

GROWING HABITAT

Black-bellied hamsters might think of themselves as tough guys. But to a fox or an eagle, they're just a four-legged snack. To survive, hamsters need to be released into a field with lots of leafy hiding places. That's a problem in Alsace, where most farmers plant corn. The corn hasn't sprouted in early spring, when hamsters come out from winter hibernation. In the bare fields the hamsters are easy targets for predators.

Some older farmers don't want hamsters on their property because of their reputation as pests. But most are willing to help, especially since the French government will pay farmers to grow early-sprouting crops, such as alfalfa and winter wheat, and allow hamsters to be released on their lands. It's a way to protect not just the hamsters, but also other small animals that thrive in a landscape of leafy fields.

Sounds like the bad beast on the block is up to some good after all.

Awesome
INSECT AWARDS

We're buggin' out! The Earth is crawling with over 800,000 species of insects. And whether they're teeny-tiny or superstrong, some of those six-legged species certainly stand out. Here are seven of the biggest, baddest, ickiest bugs out there!

Heavy Lifter

Loud Mouth

The *rhinoceros beetle,* which gets its name from the hornlike structure on the male's head, is capable of carrying up to 850 times its own body weight.

The distinctive call of a male *African cicada* is about as loud as a rock concert or an ambulance siren. The call comes from special structures on the bug's belly, which vibrate to deter predators or attract another cicada's attention.

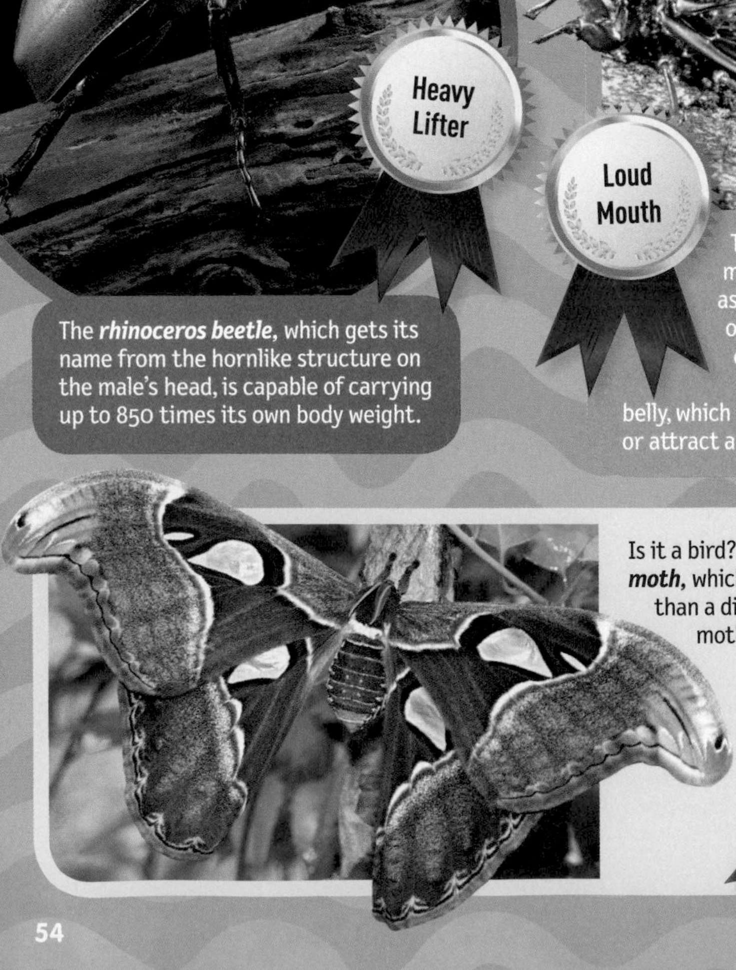

Is it a bird? A bat? No, it's the *Atlas moth,* which has a wingspan wider than a dinner plate—the largest moth wings on the planet.

Biggest Wings

The **monarch butterfly** has a king-size appetite! A large monarch caterpillar can chomp an entire milkweed leaf in less than four minutes.

Big Eater

Sharpest Defense

It's common to mistake the **walking leaf** for an actual leaf, thanks to its large, feathery wings. This clever camouflage provides protection from potential predators.

Coolest Camo

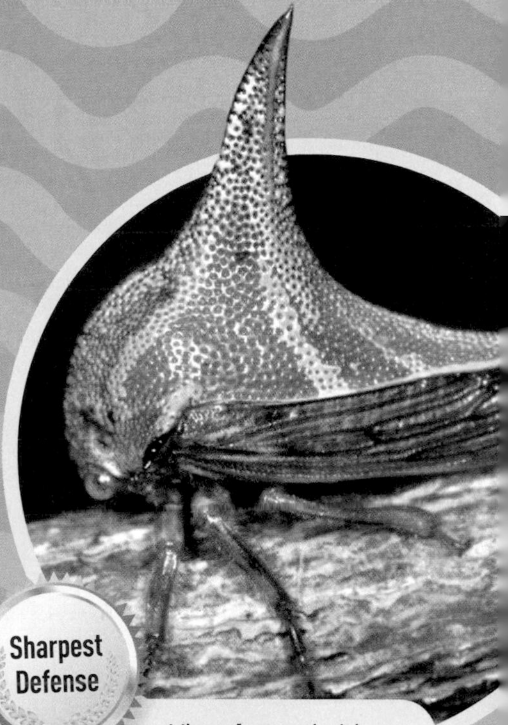

When clustered with others on a branch, a tiny **thorn bug** becomes part of a prickly pack no bird wants a bite of!

Colossal Crawler

The **Goliath beetle** weighs about as much as a quarter-pound hamburger, making it one of the heaviest bugs on Earth.

55

EXTRAORDINARY Animals

HOW DO YOU LIKE MY DOG-GLES?

DOG DRIVES BOAT

NEXT TIME I GO ON A VACATION, I'LL GO ON A CRUISE.

Chicago, Illinois, U.S.A.
Forget dog-paddling—Duma the Jack Russell terrier prefers driving speedboats. The pooch is a star performer in boat shows across the United States.

Duma first hit the water when she was a puppy, going for rides on Lake Michigan with owner Cliff Bode. At first she just sat on Bode's lap while he drove, but one day she put her paws on the wheel. "After a couple of times in the driver's seat, she thought that was her place," Bode says.

Duma, who always wears a life jacket when she's on the water, steers the boat with her paws. Bode controls the speed throttle and points Duma where to go with his free hand. Next up for Duma? Waterskiing!

LOST PARROT GIVES ADDRESS

Nagareyama, Japan
When Yosuke (YOH-su-kay) the parrot's owner took him outside for some fresh air, Yosuke flapped away. "We looked for Yosuke for three days, but we couldn't find him," Yoshio Nakamura says.

What Nakamura didn't know was that police had found the African gray parrot and took him to a veterinarian. At first Yosuke was shy. Then he started singing. Suddenly, after about 10 days, he squawked, "I'm Mr. Yosuke Nakamura" and recited his address. African grays are known for their intelligence and vocabulary. Yosuke knows about 50 phrases and took about a month to learn his address. Good thing he did—getting lost is strictly for the birds.

CHIMP
OUTSMARTS HUMANS

YES, I AM SMARTER THAN A FIFTH GRADER.

Kyoto, Japan

Think you're brainier than a chimpanzee? Most people do—unless they've met Ayumu the chimp. According to researchers, he has a better memory than most humans.

Ayumu and three other chimps took the same memory test that college students did. Numbers in random order flashed on a screen, and then turned into white squares. Participants had to touch the squares in numerical order to demonstrate memory skills. Ayumu was so accurate he outscored other chimps *and* students.

Scientist Tetsuro Matsuzawa, who led the study, says many people think humans are better than animals in every way. He says this test proves that isn't always true and hopes his research will motivate people to treat animals with more respect.

AYUMU PUTS HIS MEMORY SKILLS TO THE TEST.

YOU COULD SAY I RECEIVED KOALA-TY CARE.

KOALA
SURVIVES
WILD
RIDE

STAFF AT THE AUSTRALIA ZOO WILDLIFE HOSPITAL TREAT TIMBERWOLF.

Gympie, Australia

Spotting a koala in Australia isn't unusual—but discovering one clinging to the front of your car is. That's just what a family of five found when they stopped for gas after a long night of driving.

The koala was likely crossing a freeway when the family's car struck him, and no one realized the vehicle had hit the animal. Instead of falling onto the road, the little marsupial survived the journey by gripping the front bumper of the car.

"Koalas live in trees and are able to hold on to branches in very strong winds," says Amber Gillett, a veterinarian at the Australia Zoo Wildlife Hospital where the koala, later named Timberwolf, was taken after the family called rescuers.

In fact, the only injury Timberwolf suffered was a broken nail. After just a few weeks of rest, he was ready to return to the wild.

Incredible Animal Friends

OUTFOXED AGAIN!

FOX PLAYS WITH TERRIER

PATTERLAND TERRIER

ORIGIN
Most likely England

WEIGHT
Between 10 and 17 pounds (4.5 and 7.7 kg)

DIG IT
Terriers love to dig. In fact, the word "terrier" comes from *terra*, a Latin word for earth.

ONE OF MANY
There are more than 25 different terrier breeds.

Corwen, Wales, U.K.
Rosie the orphan fox pup loves playtime with her adopted sister, Maddy the Patterland terrier. They even frolic in the family's living room. "The fox likes to run along the top of the sofa and jump over the coffee table to meet Maddy. The room is usually a wreck," says owner Richard Bowler, who took in the fox after she was abandoned.

It's an odd friendship, since Maddy's parents were actually bred to hunt foxes. Nobody told *this* dog, though. She spends most of her time rolling around with Rosie in an outdoor vegetable garden.

The furry friends do settle down for nap time, though—but not before Maddy gives Rosie a sloppy good-night kiss.

RED FOX

RANGE
North America, Europe, Asia, and northern Africa

WEIGHT
Between 8 and 15 pounds (3.6 and 6.8 kg)

SOLO ACT
As solitary animals, red foxes don't typically form packs like wolves.

HERE I AM!
Red foxes often use their tails as signal flags for fox-to-fox communication.

NEXT TIME, I GET TO SPLASH THE TOURISTS.

DOLPHIN SWIMS WITH SEA LION

INDO-PACIFIC BOTTLENOSE DOLPHIN

RANGE
Waters off of Asia, Africa, and Australia

LENGTH
6 to 10 feet (1.8 to 3 m)

HIGH JUMP
They have been seen leaping as high as 16 feet (4.9 m) from the water's surface.

SCALING SEALS
This mammal sheds its outermost layer of skin every two hours.

Coffs Harbour, Australia

Miri the sea lion loves giving Jet the bottlenose dolphin smooches. "Miri has been known to stop whatever she's doing, glide over to Jet, and plant a big kiss on him," says Angela Van Den Bosch of Dolphin Marine Magic water park, where the friends live.

Jet and Miri became best buds during the marine center's playtime, when the park's sea lions hang out with the dolphins. Although some sea lions like to sun themselves outside the dolphin pool, Miri slides into the water to chill with her friend. The two enjoy chasing each other and munching on snacks. The pair even "talk" to one another. Jet makes clicking noises at his sea lion buddy, while Miri barks in response. Sounds like these two speak fluent BFF.

AUSTRALIAN SEA LION

RANGE
Waters off of western and southern Australia

LENGTH
4.5 to 8 feet (1.4 to 2.4 m)

SPECIES ALERT
Only 10,000 to 15,000 Australian sea lions remain in the wild.

SCALING SEALS
Great climbers, these creatures have been found on top of cliffs.

Lifestyles of the RICH and FURRY

OUTRAGEOUS WAYS TO PAMPER YOUR PET

From canine country clubs to tabby tiaras, pets today are living in the lap of luxury. In 2016, pet owners in the U.S. and U.K. spent about $73 billion on supplies and services to pamper their pets.

"Pets improve our lives," says Bob Vetere of the American Pet Products Association. "So we want to improve theirs." *NG Kids* tracks just how far some owners go to give their pets the royal treatment.

WHAT TO WEAR

When Selena Gomez and Amanda Seyfried need fashion for their dogs, they don't have to look far. That's because many stores now cater exclusively to the pampered pet. At Fifi & Romeo (left) in Los Angeles, dogs in handmade cashmere sweaters and colorful raincoats are considered fashionable, not funny-looking, and are sure to please the most finicky pooch.

Will your pet be less happy if you don't shower it with expensive stuff?

Absolutely not! "As long as your pet has food, comfort, and friendship, that's what's most important," says pet psychologist John C. Wright.

60

IN THE HOUSE

Skeeter the cairn terrier hangs out in a two-story doghouse with floor-to-ceiling windows, and heated floors. It's just one of many custom-made cribs owners are building for their pets. "One owner asked for a cat house with a separate dining room, litter box room, and bedroom," says Michelle Pollak of La Petite Maison, which builds luxury pet homes (above). "Some pet owners spare nothing to make sure their pets are comfortable and happy."

KENNEL—OR VACATION?

Sampson the Yorkshire terrier loves a good massage. His sister, Delilah, likes to get her toenails painted. They can do it all at the Olde Towne Pet Resort in Virginia, U.S.A. (below), one of many "pet spas" around the country that act more like luxury hotels than kennels.

CHOW TIME

Plain old dog chow just won't do for some canines. Gourmet pet food has become all the rage. Places like Three Dog Bakery offer biscuits made of carob chips, apples, oatmeal, and peanut butter, and cats munch on Alaskan salmon bites.

Pampering your pet could cost you an arm and a paw!

LUXURY SUITE AT PET SPA	$110 A NIGHT
PROFESSIONAL MASSAGE	$35
CUSTOM-BUILT DOGHOUSE	$10,000
HAND-KNITTED SWEATER	$280
GOURMET DOG TREATS	$6.99

PET TECH

Think you're tech-savvy? With all the gadgets owners are buying for their pets, some animals may have you beat. Some owners set up webcams so their pets can watch them at work. And Petzila, a company dedicated to connecting pets with their owners, offers a device that allows away-from-home owners to see, talk to, and surprise a pet with a treat—all through Wi-Fi and the click of an app.

NauGHty PETS

CAUGHT ON CAMERA

I ENJOY BIRD-WATCHING ... ESPECIALLY AT DINNERTIME.

BEST. CHEW TOY. EVER.

NAME **Bruno**

FAVORITE ACTIVITY
Testing out new chew toys

FAVORITE TOY **Rubber ducky**

PET PEEVE **Stinky feet**

NAME **Mumford**

FAVORITE ACTIVITY **Making a list of birds to chase—um, watch**

FAVORITE TOY **Birdhouse scratching post**

PET PEEVE **Rainy days**

THE PIANO ALWAYS SOUNDS BEST WHEN EVERYONE IS ASLEEP.

I FOUND MY COSTUME FOR NEXT HALLOWEEN: KING PUP THE MUMMY!

NAME **Elton**

FAVORITE ACTIVITY
Composing piano *meow*-sic

FAVORITE TOY **Piano pedals**

PET PEEVE **Keyboard cover**

NAME **Iggy**

FAVORITE ACTIVITY **Playing dress-up in household supplies**

FAVORITE TOY **Toilet plunger—a stick and a chew toy in one!**

PET PEEVE **Wipes**

Bet you didn't know

7 facts about pet rodents to **nibble on**

1 A **golden hamster's** **cheek pouches** extend all the way to its hips.

2 **Gerbils** can **recognize each other** by the **taste** of their **saliva.**

3 A **gerbil** ▶ may **stomp its feet** to communicate.

4 A rat's front **teeth** can grow **five** up to (12.7 cm) **inches a year.**

5 In **Switzerland** it's illegal to own just one guinea pig— **you must have** at least **two.**

6 A **baby mouse** is called a **pinky.**

7 Guinea pigs often **sleep** with their **eyes open.**

FAMOUS PETS OF HISTORY

History is full of legendary leaders, great thinkers— and famous fur balls. People have kept pets for thousands of years, and many have gained stardom for everything from saving lives to simply being supercute. Check out this timeline of famous pets.

1300s B.C.

The star status of Ta-mit the cat is literally written in stone. Ta-mit's owner, Prince Thutmose (the son of Egyptian pharaoh Amenhotep III), adored his pet so much that he ordered pictures of her carved into her limestone sarcophagus, or coffin, along with hieroglyphics demonstrating the prince's affection toward his pet. Most felines during this time were mummified and buried as part of rituals to celebrate gods. But Ta-mit, or "she-cat" in ancient Egyptian, was given a special sarcophagus simply because she was such a precious pet.

100s

Chinese emperor Ling of the Eastern Han loved his dog (which was possibly a Pekingese) so much that he gave it the rank of a senior court official. This meant that the dog was treated as royalty. The pooch supposedly was assigned a bodyguard to protect and wait on it, um, paw and foot. The dog ate the best quality rice and meat, and slept on cushy carpets. Ling even gave his dog a special hat to wear.

1600s

A PORTRAIT OF NEWTON PUTTING OUT FLAMES SET BY DIAMOND

DIAMOND

Physicist Isaac Newton set the world on fire with his revolutionary experiments on the force of gravity. The scientist's dog, Diamond, became famous for setting real flames. Legend has it that when Newton left Diamond home alone one night, the mischievous pooch jumped on a desk and knocked over a candle, igniting and destroying stacks of Newton's research. The notes may have been destroyed, but the dog's reputation lived on: The story of Diamond has appeared in several books and magazine articles.

1700s

Russian ruler Peter the Great might not have been quite so great without his horse Lisette. In fact, the horse may have saved her owner's life during the Great Northern War, an 18th-century conflict between Russia and the empire of Sweden. The leader was seated on Lisette on the battlefield when a bullet was fired in his direction. Hearing the shot, Lisette quickly backed up so that the bullet hit her saddle rather than her owner. They were both unharmed, and the horse's act won her a place in history—plus plenty of treats from her grateful owner.

1800s

PORTRAIT OF LORY

Queen Victoria, whose reign in the United Kingdom lasted 63 years, owned two birds that were real rock stars. The queen loved her parrot Lory so much that she had an artist create a portrait of the bird, which today is part of the Royal Collection. And the queen's African gray parrot Coco was taught how to sing the British national anthem. Coco became famous for supposedly belting out the patriotic tune most mornings.

1900s

Lump the dachshund cuddled his way into his caretaker's heart—and art. The affectionate pooch lived in France with Pablo Picasso, a renowned 20th-century artist who helped develop a new painting style called cubism. Picasso adored Lump so much he featured the dog in many of his paintings. The artist also drew a picture of Lump on a dinner plate, which is now thought to be worth up to $90,000. While Picasso's paintings of Lump are expensive, the real dog was clearly priceless.

PICASSO AND LUMP

2000s

BO (LEFT) AND SUNNY CHILL OUT ON THE WHITE HOUSE LAWN.

Photographers were always snapping pics of U.S. president Barack Obama's pooches, Bo and Sunny. While the Portuguese water dogs didn't mind posing for the camera, they preferred roaming the White House lawn or taking naps in their historic home. They even had some duties, such as going to hospitals to cheer up patients and greeting world leaders who had come to visit. Being first dogs also meant getting cuddles from the commander in chief, even after Bo chewed up the president's gym shoes.

Prehistoric TIMELINE

HUMANS HAVE WALKED on Earth for some 200,000 years, a mere blip in the planet's 4.5-billion-year history. A lot has happened during that time. Earth formed, and oxygen levels rose in the millions of years of the Precambrian time. The productive Paleozoic era gave rise to hard-shelled organisms, vertebrates, amphibians, and reptiles.

Dinosaurs ruled the Earth in the mighty Mesozoic. And 64 million years after dinosaurs became extinct, modern humans emerged in the Cenozoic era. From the first tiny mollusks to the dinosaur giants of the Jurassic and beyond, Earth has seen a lot of transformation.

THE PRECAMBRIAN TIME

4.5 billion to 542 million years ago

- The Earth (and other planets) formed from gas and dust left over from a giant cloud that collapsed to form the sun. The giant cloud's collapse was triggered when nearby stars exploded.
- Low levels of oxygen made Earth a suffocating place.
- Early life-forms appeared.

THE PALEOZOIC ERA

542 million to 251 million years ago

- The first insects and other animals appeared on land.
- 450 million years ago (m.y.a.), the ancestors of sharks began to swim in the oceans.
- 430 m.y.a., plants began to take root on land.
- More than 360 m.y.a., amphibians emerged from the water.
- Slowly, the major landmasses began to come together, creating Pangaea, a single supercontinent.
- By 300 m.y.a., reptiles had begun to dominate the land.

What Killed the Dinosaurs?

It's a mystery that's boggled the minds of scientists for centuries: What happened to the dinosaurs? While various theories have bounced around, a new study confirms that the most likely culprit is an asteroid or comet that created a giant crater. Researchers say that the impact set off a series of natural disasters like tsunamis, earthquakes, and temperature swings that plagued the dinosaurs' ecosystem and disrupted their food chain. This, paired with intense volcanic eruptions that caused drastic climate changes, is thought to be why half of the world's species—including the dinosaurs—died in a mass extinction.

DINO TIMES

THE MESOZOIC ERA

251 million to 65 million years ago

The Mesozoic era, or the age of the reptiles, consisted of three consecutive time periods (shown below). This is when the first dinosaurs began to appear. They would reign supreme for more than 150 million years.

TRIASSIC PERIOD

251 million to 199 million years ago

- Appearance of the first mammals. They were rodent-size.
- The first dinosaur appeared.
- Ferns were the dominant plants on land.
- The giant supercontinent of Pangaea began breaking up toward the end of the Triassic.

JURASSIC PERIOD

199 million to 145 million years ago

- Giant dinosaurs dominated the land.
- Pangaea continued its breakup, and oceans formed in the spaces between the drifting landmasses, allowing sea life, including sharks and marine crocodiles, to thrive.
- Conifer trees spread across the land.

CRETACEOUS PERIOD

145 million to 65 million years ago

- The modern continents developed.
- The largest dinosaurs developed.
- Flowering plants spread across the landscape.
- Mammals flourished, and giant pterosaurs ruled the skies over small birds.
- Temperatures grew more extreme. Dinosaurs lived in deserts, swamps, and forests from the Antarctic to the Arctic.

THE CENOZOIC ERA—TERTIARY PERIOD

65 million to 2.6 million years ago

- Following the dinosaur extinction, mammals rose as the dominant species.
- Birds continued to flourish.
- Volcanic activity was widespread.
- Temperatures began to cool, eventually ending in an ice age.
- The period ended with land bridges forming, which allowed plants and animals to spread to new areas.

Who Ate What?

Herbivores
- Primarily plant-eaters
- Weighed up to 100 tons (91 t)—the largest animals ever to walk on Earth
- Up to 1,000 blunt or flat teeth to grind vegetation
- Many had cheek pouches to store food.
- Examples: *Styracosaurus, Mamenchisaurus*

Carnivores
- Meat-eaters
- Long, strong legs to run faster than plant-eaters; ran up to 30 miles an hour (48 km/h)
- Most had good eyesight, strong jaws, and sharp teeth.
- Scavengers and hunters; often hunted in packs

- Grew to 45 feet (14 m) long
- Examples: *Velociraptor, Gigantoraptor, Tyrannosaurus rex*

TYRANNOSAURUS REX

GIGANTORAPTOR

What if dinos hadn't gone extinct?

If dinos still roamed Earth, they'd likely be the world's most dominant animals. And it's possible that they'd have picked up a few more skills. For instance, some species might have learned to use simple tools. (After all, types of birds—the dinosaur's closest living relatives—developed the ability to use tools such as sticks and leaves to dig or "fish" for food.) If humans were around in a dino-filled world, we'd need to avoid getting eaten by carnivorous dinosaurs. And plant-eating dinos would gobble up lots of leafy greens, leaving us with way less to eat. If these guys still existed, it would be anything but *dino*-mite.

DID YOU KNOW?

Tyrannosaurus means "tyrant lizard." At about 40 feet (12 m) long and about 15 to 20 feet (4.6 to 6 m) tall, the *T. rex* was one of the largest meat-eating dinosaurs that ever lived. If it roamed the Earth today, its bite would be strong enough to dent a car.

VELOCIRAPTOR

SINOSAUROPTERYX

MAMENCHISAURUS

PARASAUROLOPHUS

ERKETU

Machairoceratops cronusi

A Great Discovery!

Researchers in Utah, U.S.A., recently discovered a horned, plant-eating creature as long as a pickup truck and weighing about as much as a rhino. Named *Machairoceratops cronusi*, the dino is thought to have lived about 77 million years ago. The creature's crowning glory? Two massive curved spikes sticking out of the top of its head that may have been used to attract potential mates.

Bet you didn't know

Giant prehistoric snakes sometimes preyed upon dinosaur eggs and hatchlings.

TUOJIANGOSAURUS

STYRACOSAURUS

MONONYKUS

DINO Classification

Classifying dinosaurs and all other living things can be a complicated matter, so scientists have devised a system to help with the process. Dinosaurs are put into groups based on a very large range of characteristics.

Scientists put dinosaurs into two major groups: the bird-hipped ornithischians and the lizard-hipped saurischians.

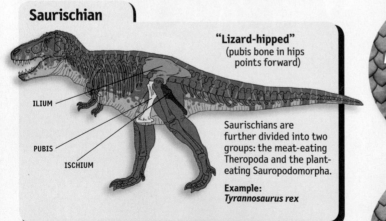

Ornithischian

ILIUM

PUBIS

ISCHIUM

"Bird-hipped"
(pubis bone in hips points backward)

Ornithischians have the same-shaped pubis as birds of today, but today's birds are actually more closely related to the saurischians.

Example: *Styracosaurus*

Saurischian

ILIUM

PUBIS

ISCHIUM

"Lizard-hipped"
(pubis bone in hips points forward)

Saurischians are further divided into two groups: the meat-eating Theropoda and the plant-eating Sauropodomorpha.

Example:
Tyrannosaurus rex

Within these two main divisions, dinosaurs are then separated into orders and then families, such as Stegosauria. Like other members of the Stegosauria, *Stegosaurus* had spines and plates along the back, neck, and tail.

SOME DINOSAURS **HAD** 1,000 **TEETH.**

ALL DINOSAURS **WALKED ON THEIR TOES.**

LIKE BABY HUMANS, *PSITTACOSAURUS* **CRAWLED** BEFORE IT **WALKED.**

MOST DINOSAURS COULD SWIM.

3 NEWLY DISCOVERED DINOS

Humans have been searching for—and discovering—dinosaur remains for hundreds of years. In that time, at least 1,000 species of dinos have been found all over the world, and thousands more may still be out there waiting to be unearthed. Recent discoveries include *Savannasaurus elliottorum*. Found in Australia, it measured about half the length of a basketball court. For more exciting dino discoveries, read on.

1 *Timurlengia euotica* (Saurischian)

Named After: Timur Lenk, a 14th-century Central Asian warlord

Length: 10 to 13 feet (3 to 4 m)

Time Range: Late Cretaceous

Where: Uzbekistan

2 *Savannasaurus elliottorum* (Saurischian)

Named After: Savanna landscape where it was found

Length: 40 to 50 feet (12 to 15 m)

Time Range: Late Cretaceous

Where: Queensland, Australia

3 *Zuul crurivastator* (Ornithischian)

Named After: Zuul, a demon in the 1984 movie *Ghostbusters*

Length: 20 feet (6 m)

Time Range: Cretaceous

Where: Montana, U.S.A.

DINOSAUR FAMILY TREE

Dinosaurs evolved 230 million years ago from small, two-legged, meat-eating reptiles. The earliest dinosaurs soon branched off into two groups, Ornithischia and Saurischia. The groups are based on dinosaurs' hip bones (see p. 70). These groups kept branching as dinosaurs developed and changed to live in almost every environment on Earth.

HETERODONTOSAURS

THYREOPHORANS

ORNITHISCHIANS
Bird-hipped dinosaurs

DINOSAURIA

SAUROPODS

SAUROPODOMORPHS

SAURISCHIANS
Lizard-hipped dinosaurs

THEROPODS

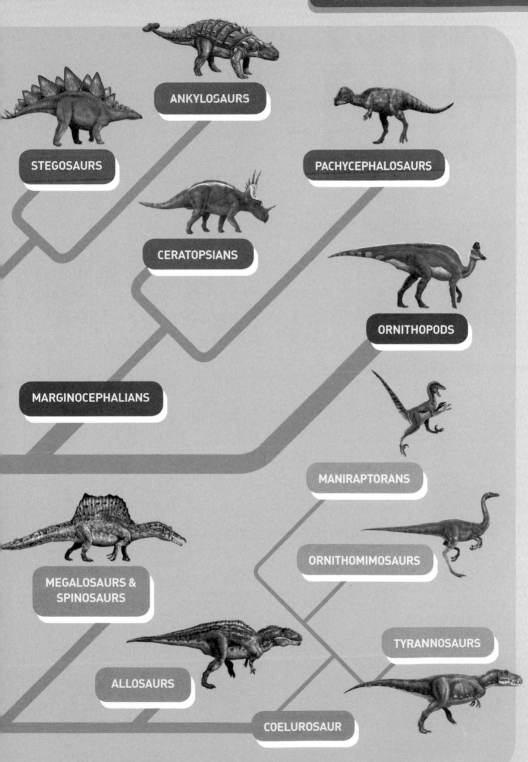

ANKYLOSAURS

STEGOSAURS

PACHYCEPHALOSAURS

CERATOPSIANS

ORNITHOPODS

MARGINOCEPHALIANS

MANIRAPTORANS

ORNITHOMIMOSAURS

MEGALOSAURS & SPINOSAURS

TYRANNOSAURS

ALLOSAURS

COELUROSAUR

QUIZ WHIZ

How much do you know about all things animal? Quiz yourself!

Write your answers on a piece of paper. Then check them below.

1 **True or false?** Jaguar jaws are strong enough to crush turtle shells.

2 Which one of these animals is an invertebrate?
a. sponge
b. mollusk
c. spider
d. all of the above

3 Chinstrap penguins nest in crowded communities called _____, home to hundreds of thousands of birds.
a. neighborhoods
b. colonies
c. flocks
d. parties

4 **True or false?** Queen Victoria's pet parrot could sing the British national anthem.

5 Scientists are using which type of gadgets to seek out polar bear dens in the wild?
a. virtual reality glasses
b. video games
c. drones
d. smartphones

Not **STUMPED** yet? Check out the *NATIONAL GEOGRAPHIC KIDS QUIZ WHIZ* collection for more crazy **ANIMAL** questions!

ANSWERS: 1. True : 2. d; 3. b; 4. True; 5. c

HOMEWORK HELP

Wildly Good Animal Reports

Beluga whale

Your teacher wants a written report on the beluga whale. Not to worry. Use these organizational tools so you can stay afloat while writing a report.

STEPS TO SUCCESS: Your report will follow the format of a descriptive or expository essay (see p. 199 for "How to Write a Perfect Essay") and should consist of a main idea, followed by supporting details and a conclusion. Use this basic structure for each paragraph as well as the whole report, and you'll be on the right track.

1. Introduction
State your **main idea.**
The beluga whale is a common and important species of whale.

2. Body
Provide **supporting points** for your main idea.
The beluga whale is one of the smallest whale species.
It is also known as the "white whale" because of its distinctive coloring.
These whales are common in the Arctic Ocean's coastal waters.

Then **expand** on those points with further description, explanation, or discussion.
The beluga whale is one of the smallest whale species.
Belugas range in size from 13 to 20 feet (4 to 6.1 m) in length.
It is also known as the "white whale" because of its distinctive coloring.
Belugas are born gray or brown. They fade to white at around five years old.
These whales are common in the Arctic Ocean's coastal waters.
Some Arctic belugas migrate south in large herds when sea ice freezes over.

3. Conclusion
Wrap it up with a **summary** of your whole paper.
Because of its unique coloring and unusual features, belugas are among the most familiar and easily distinguishable of all the whales.

KEY INFORMATION

Here are some things you should consider including in your report:

What does your animal look like?
To what other species is it related?
How does it move?
Where does it live?
What does it eat?
What are its predators?
How long does it live?
Is it endangered?
Why do you find it interesting?

SEPARATE FACT FROM FICTION: Your animal may have been featured in a movie or in myths and legends. Compare and contrast how the animal has been portrayed with how it behaves in reality. For example, penguins can't dance the way they do in *Happy Feet.*

PROOFREAD AND REVISE: As with any great essay, when you're finished, check for misspellings, grammatical mistakes, and punctuation errors. It often helps to have someone else proofread your work, too, as he or she may catch things you have missed. Also, look for ways to make your sentences and paragraphs even better. Add more descriptive language, choosing just the right verbs, adverbs, and adjectives to make your writing come alive.

BE CREATIVE: Use visual aids to make your report come to life. Include an animal photo file with interesting images found in magazines or printed from websites. Or draw your own! You can also build a miniature animal habitat diorama. Use creativity to help communicate your passion for the subject.

THE FINAL RESULT: Put it all together in one final, polished draft. Make it neat and clean, and remember to cite your references.

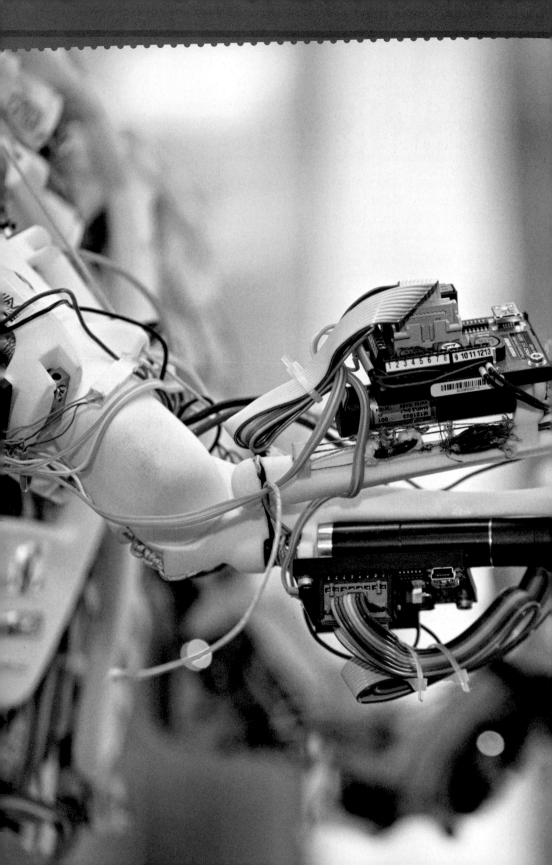

Science and Technology

Roboy, a robot developed by the University of Zurich Artificial Intelligence Lab in Switzerland, shakes hands with a human.

COOL inventions

SOUPED-UP SNOWMOBILE

With this turbocharged vehicle, getting around powder-packed slopes will be, uh, *snow* problem. The Snowcrawler snowmobile is designed with two skis under its front end. Beneath its back end is a pair of tracks, or rubber belts wrapped around a set of wheels. (It's a smaller version of what you see on many bulldozers.) Hop inside the snug, heated interior and rev up the engine, which activates the wheels that turn the tracks. Each track has grooves that grip uneven and slippery surfaces to easily glide over difficult terrain. Let it snow!

TRACKS

SMART SOLES

GO RIGHT!

This might take shoes in a new direction. The Lechal company created shoe insoles that "tell" wearers how to get from one place to another. How do they work? Slip the cushions into your sneakers. The insoles have built-in devices that vibrate. And these devices connect wirelessly to your smartphone. Pull up the Lechal app on your phone and type in your destination. The app uses GPS to map out the quickest path for you to walk. Every time you need to take a left or right, the app signals the corresponding sole to vibrate so you know which direction to turn. That's one amazing feat.

THESE TELL YOU WHEN TO TURN!

SMART WHEEL

GENIUS WHEEL

With the FlyKly bicycle wheel, you'll be on a roll. This motorized wheel propels your bike forward, making for an easy ride. Just swap the back wheel of your bike for the FlyKly wheel. Then use your smartphone to launch the FlyKly app, which controls how fast the wheel goes. Pick your pace, then start pedaling. The app will signal the wheel to accelerate to your desired speed. During the ride you'll still pedal, but not very hard—the FlyKly does most of the work. That sounds *wheel*-y great!

FLYKLY APP

FLOATING **FURNITURE**

It's easy to drift off in the Zerobody bed. This comfy contraption features a plastic, water-filled mattress that's designed to mold to the shape of the person lying on it. Simply kick off your shoes and climb onto the bed. As you stretch out, the mattress will mold to your body. Meanwhile, the water in the mattress will gently rock you from side to side. It's a similar feeling to floating on your back in a pool. The mattress even heats up to make you extra cozy. Now that's a dream bed.

LIE HERE

WHAT, YOU'VE NEVER SEEN A HUMAN WITH FINS BEFORE?

WACKY **WET SUIT**

The Aqua Lung Oceanwings wet suit looks a little fishy. Modeled after a manta ray's fins, the suit has flaps of fabric that stretch between the arms and legs on each side. This allows divers to glide along the ocean current just like the fish. The heavy suit also helps undersea explorers sink to greater depths; to resurface, divers simply inflate the suit's built-in balloon-like device, which pulls them back up. And after a short rest, wet-suit wearers can dive right back into the fun!

You're playing at the park when you hear a buzz in the air. You look up and see a miniature flying saucer hovering above you. It's a drone, one of millions sold around the world in recent years. And whether they're used for toys or top-secret missions, it seems like drones are everywhere.

The Buzz on DRONES

DRONE DETAILS

Equipped with high-tech cameras, microphones, and sensors, drones can capture scenes from unique angles. They've proven to be useful in emergencies, like natural disasters, because they can be flown into unstable areas to provide instant feedback on damage and search for survivors. Drones are also used as an "eye in

HIGH-TECH DIGITAL VIDEO CAMERA

the sky" for sporting events like the Olympics and professional golf and soccer games, giving fans at home a closer-than-ever view of key plays and their favorite players. They're key in science, too: Researchers use drones for everything from studying critically endangered Sumatran orangutans high in the treetops of Indonesia to discovering ancient ruins in hard-to-reach locations.

NO-DRONE ZONE

But not everyone is flying high over drones. Crashing drones have injured people on the ground, and there have been reports of people using them to peep on private residences. They can also pose a huge threat to airplanes and helicopters. There have been many near misses in the sky due to drones flying dangerously close to aircraft.

Because of the risk they cause, many cities around the world have banned the buzzing drones. Police in the Netherlands have trained a bald eagle to fly to the gadget, clasp it in its claws, and bring it down to the ground. In Tokyo, Japan, where drones are forbidden in certain parts of the city, cops are attaching a 10-foot (3-m) net to their own drones to nab illegal flyers. Want to fly a drone in India? You must first get a license, like you'd need to drive a car or pilot a plane.

So will drones be as popular as smartphones and iPods one day? Possibly. But the hope is that a focus on laws and flying smart will keep the sky—and those below it—safe.

ROBOTICS

Robots may soon reboot the entire way you live. Over the past 50 years, these machines have mainly been used by NASA, or in places such as factories. But scientists are developing humanlike bots that can do so much more. Check out the science behind three awesome robots.

BENEBOT

WHAT IT'S WIRED FOR:
Storing information

Benebot operates by connecting through Wi-Fi to the cloud. The cloud uses the Internet to access networks of computer servers to perform tasks like storing data and supporting video chats. Benebot is able to share things with you that are kept on the cloud—for instance, information about products.

HOW IT WILL CHANGE YOUR LIFE:
Not sure which video game to buy while shopping at the electronics store? Using data from the cloud, Benebot will give you the scoop about each of your options so you can make a decision. It'll also stream videos of cool new items.

CHIMP

WHAT IT'S WIRED FOR:
Moving around obstacles

CHIMP uses a system called LIDAR to find objects and move around them. As the machine moves, it shoots pulses of light from its head. These beams bounce off objects back to CHIMP's built-in sensors, and it then measures how long the light takes to return to figure out the distance of objects and how to navigate around them.

HOW IT WILL CHANGE YOUR LIFE: The five-foot (1.5-m)-tall, 400-pound (181-kg) droid was designed to aid people affected by disasters such as tornadoes. CHIMP could use its navigation skills to deliver supplies to disaster victims. Or, if something were broken in your house, someday CHIMP might swing into handyman mode and fix it.

PR2

WHAT IT'S WIRED FOR:
Recognizing patterns

When PR2 comes across a rumpled piece of clothing, it uses pattern-recognition to search for similar shapes programmed into its database. If it finds a match, it receives steps on how to fold it.

HOW IT WILL CHANGE YOUR LIFE: In addition to folding your laundry, PR2 can use its pattern recognition technology for other tasks such as tying shoelaces. With its agile hands, PR2 can even pour pancake batter into a frying pan and flip flapjacks.

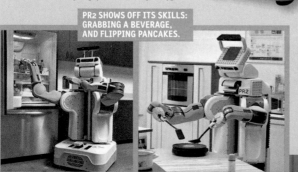

PR2 SHOWS OFF ITS SKILLS: GRABBING A BEVERAGE, AND FLIPPING PANCAKES.

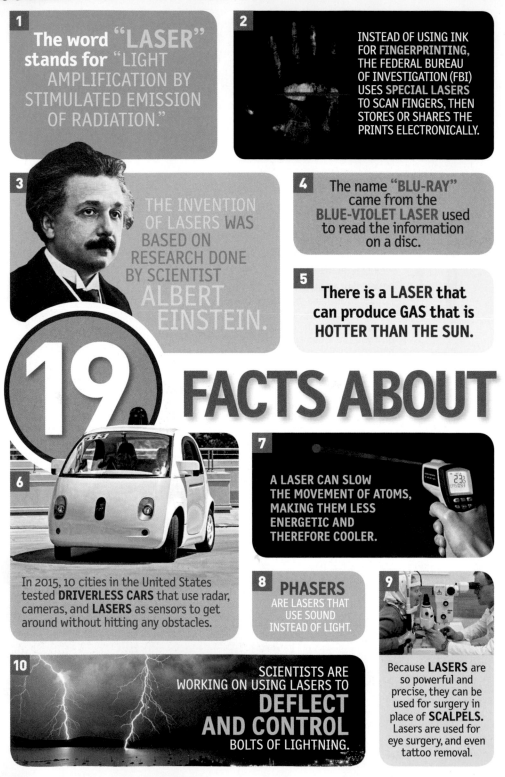

1 The word **"LASER"** stands for "LIGHT AMPLIFICATION BY STIMULATED EMISSION OF RADIATION."

2 INSTEAD OF USING INK FOR FINGERPRINTING, THE FEDERAL BUREAU OF INVESTIGATION (FBI) USES SPECIAL LASERS TO SCAN FINGERS, THEN STORES OR SHARES THE PRINTS ELECTRONICALLY.

3 THE INVENTION OF LASERS WAS BASED ON RESEARCH DONE BY SCIENTIST ALBERT EINSTEIN.

4 The name **"BLU-RAY"** came from the **BLUE-VIOLET LASER** used to read the information on a disc.

5 There is a **LASER** that can produce **GAS** that is **HOTTER THAN THE SUN.**

19 FACTS ABOUT

6 In 2015, 10 cities in the United States tested **DRIVERLESS CARS** that use radar, cameras, and **LASERS** as sensors to get around without hitting any obstacles.

7 A LASER CAN SLOW THE MOVEMENT OF ATOMS, MAKING THEM LESS ENERGETIC AND THEREFORE COOLER.

8 PHASERS ARE LASERS THAT USE SOUND INSTEAD OF LIGHT.

9 Because **LASERS** are so powerful and precise, they can be used for surgery in place of **SCALPELS.** Lasers are used for eye surgery, and even tattoo removal.

10 SCIENTISTS ARE WORKING ON USING LASERS TO **DEFLECT AND CONTROL** BOLTS OF LIGHTNING.

11 **Pointing a LASER BEAM at an airplane or helicopter is ILLEGAL.** The beam can reach all the way to the aircraft and make it hard for the pilot to see.

12

Lasers are used to ENGRAVE materials, cutting designs or words INTO the surface.

13 THE MARS ROVER CURIOSITY HAS A **LASER** FOR **ZAPPING MARTIAN ROCKS** TO FIGURE OUT WHAT THE ROCKS ARE MADE OF.

14 **LASERS** CAN BE USED FOR **HAIR REMOVAL.** THE LASERS ZAP THE HAIR WITH POWERFUL LIGHT AND SOON STOP THE HAIR FROM GROWING.

15 LASERS ARE A LOT LIKE THE **BEAM** OF A FLASHLIGHT, ONLY THE LIGHT IS FOCUSED TO ONE TINY POINT SO THAT

IT IS **POWERFUL** ENOUGH TO **CUT THROUGH** MATERIALS.

LASERS

16 Some **laser beams** are **INVISIBLE** **in the air** but can be seen in smoke.

17

POLICE OFFICERS USE LASERS TO CLOCK THE **SPEED OF CARS** BY MEASURING THE TIME IT TAKES THE LIGHT TO HIT A **REFLECTIVE SURFACE** ON THE CAR AND BOUNCE BACK.

18 IN AN EFFORT TO STOP THE SPREAD OF MALARIA, A SCIENTIST INVENTED A **MOSQUITO-KILLING LASER GUN** CALLED THE **DEATH STAR** THAT TRACKS AND KILLS **MOSQUITOES.**

19 **LASER LIGHT SHOWS** USE SPECIAL LASER BEAMS, PROJECTORS, AND MIRRORS TO PUT ON SPECTACULAR EVENTS, OFTEN SET TO MUSIC.

History's Greatest Hits

George Washington Carver

George Washington Carver's quest for knowledge made him a world-famous scientist and inventor. Find out about the groundbreaking life of this American hero.

START

Around 1864

George Washington Carver is born into slavery on a farm in Missouri, U.S.A. When slavery is abolished in 1865, his former owners, Moses and Susan Carver, decide to raise the orphaned George as their son.

1891 to 1896

Carver becomes the first black student accepted at Iowa State University, where he studies agriculture, the science of farming.

SPUD SPRAY

MASHED MOSQUITOES

1896

Carver becomes a teacher at Tuskegee University in Alabama, U.S.A. He invents hundreds of products, including new kinds of paints and insecticides (chemicals used to kill insects).

PEANUT POWER

1906

Discovering more than 300 ways to use peanut plants, Carver turns the nuts into glue, medicine, and paper. He shares his knowledge with farmers. (Fun fact: Carver did not invent peanut butter.)

NO, TEDDY, I SAID MORE WATER, NOT LESS.

WHOOPS.

1915

Carver becomes famous for his farming smarts, and even advises former U.S. president Theodore Roosevelt on agricultural matters.

1943

By the end of his career, Carver is a symbol of the important contributions of African Americans and inspires people all over, no matter what their skin color is.

ACCIDENTS
Happen

BUT SOMETIMES THEY RESULT IN AMAZING DISCOVERIES.

THE INVENTION: THE POPSICLE

THE MOMENT OF "OOPS": Overnight freezing

THE DETAILS: When 11-year-old Frank Epperson left a glass of powdered soda mix overnight on his porch in Oakland, California, U.S.A., he made snack history. The next morning, he discovered that his drink had frozen after an unusually cold night, the mixing stick still propped up in the glass. Hoping to salvage his soda after failing to pull it out of the glass, Epperson ran the cup under warm water. Pop! The primitive Popsicle slid out, complete with the stirrer stick as a handle. Twenty years later, Epperson patented his idea, calling it the Popsicle.

THE INVENTION: THE SLINKY

THE MOMENT OF "OOPS": Falling objects

THE DETAILS: In 1943, engineer Richard James was at his desk in Pittsburgh, Pennsylvania, U.S.A., when a box of shipbuilding supplies on a nearby shelf suddenly tipped over. Startled, James looked up from his work. In the middle of everything falling, he noticed a metal spring slink to the ground. As he watched it walk over itself down some books stacked on the ground, he was struck with an idea: It might make a great toy! The Slinky—named by James's wife, Betty—was an instant hit, with the first 400 selling out in 90 minutes.

HOW TO FACE FAILURE

Some people might hate hearing the word "failure." But we say it's not so bad. Follow these tips to make failure fantastic.

FAILURE IS THE BEST TEACHER.

Embrace the teaching power of screwing up. Fill in your teammates on your embarrassment on the soccer field. They'll learn how to avoid making the same mistake themselves.

SUCCESS IS NOTHING WITHOUT FAILURE.

When you fell off your bike, you weren't a failure, because you didn't stay on the ground. You hopped back on the seat and kept trying. Failing first makes success feel extra sweet!

FAILURE STINGS— AND THAT'S OK!

Don't ignore a flunked test or a missed pop fly because they're painful. Do better next time by studying harder and practicing more. But most important, just move on.

WHAT IS LIFE?

This seems like such an easy question to answer. Everybody knows that singing birds are alive and rocks are not. But when we start studying bacteria and other microscopic creatures, things get more complicated.

SO WHAT EXACTLY IS LIFE?
Most scientists agree that something is alive if it can do the following: reproduce; grow in size to become more complex in structure; take in nutrients to survive; give off waste products; and respond to external stimuli, such as increased sunlight or changes in temperature.

KINDS OF LIFE
Biologists classify living organisms by how they get their energy. Organisms such as algae, green plants, and some bacteria use sunlight as an energy source. Animals (like humans), fungi, and some Archaea use chemicals to provide energy. When we eat food, chemical reactions within our digestive system turn our food into fuel.

Living things inhabit land, sea, and air. In fact, life also thrives deep beneath the oceans, embedded in rocks miles below the Earth's crust, in ice, and in other extreme environments. The life-forms that thrive in these challenging environments are called extremophiles. Some of these draw directly upon the chemicals surrounding them for energy. Since these are very different forms of life than what we're used to, we may not think of them as alive, but they are.

HOW IT ALL WORKS
To try and understand how a living organism works, it helps to look at one example of its simplest form—the single-celled bacterium called *Streptococcus.* There are many kinds of these tiny organisms, and some are responsible for human illnesses. What makes us sick or uncomfortable are the toxins the bacteria give off in our bodies.

A single *Streptococcus* bacterium is so small that at least 500 of them could fit on the dot above this letter *i*. These bacteria are some of the simplest forms of life we know. They have no moving parts, no lungs, no brain, no heart, no liver, and no leaves or fruit. Yet this life-form reproduces. It grows in size by producing long chain structures, takes in nutrients, and gives off waste products. This tiny life-form is alive, just as you are alive.

What makes something alive is a question scientists grapple with when they study viruses, such as the ones that cause the common cold and smallpox. They can grow and reproduce within host cells, such as those that make up your body. Because viruses lack cells and cannot metabolize nutrients for energy or reproduce without a host, scientists ask if they are indeed alive. And don't go looking for them without a strong microscope— viruses are a hundred times smaller than bacteria.

Scientists think life began on Earth some 3.9 to 4.1 billion years ago, but no fossils exist from that time. The earliest fossils ever found are from the primitive life that existed 3.6 billion years ago. Other life-forms, some of which are shown below, soon followed. Scientists continue to study how life evolved on Earth and whether it is possible that life exists on other planets.

MICROSCOPIC ORGANISMS*

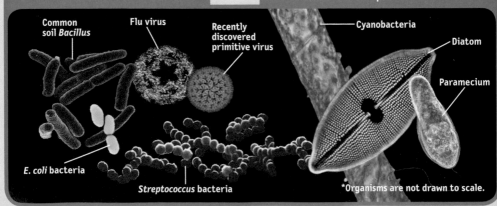

Common soil *Bacillus*

Flu virus

Recently discovered primitive virus

Cyanobacteria

Diatom

Paramecium

E. coli bacteria

Streptococcus bacteria

*Organisms are not drawn to scale.

The Three Domains of Life

Biologists divide all living organisms into three domains: Bacteria, Archaea, and Eukarya. Archaean and Bacterial cells do not have nuclei, and they are so different from each other that they belong to different domains. Since human cells have a nucleus, humans belong to the Eukarya domain.

1 BACTERIA

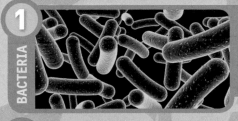

Domain Bacteria: These single-celled microorganisms are found almost everywhere in the world. Bacteria are small and do not have nuclei. They can be shaped like rods, spirals, or spheres. Some of them are helpful to humans, and some are harmful.

2 ARCHAEA

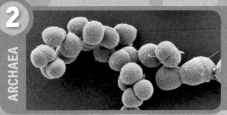

Domain Archaea: These single-celled micro-organisms are often found in extremely hostile environments. Like Bacteria, Archaea do not have nuclei, but they have some genes in com-mon with Eukarya. For this reason, scientists think the Archaea living today most closely resemble the earliest forms of life on Earth.

3 EUKARYA

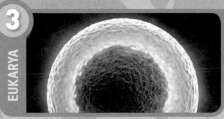

Domain Eukarya: This diverse group of life-forms is more complicated than Bacteria and Archaea, as Eukarya have one or more cells with nuclei. These are the tiny cells that make up your whole body. Eukarya are divided into four groups: fungi, protists, plants, and animals.

What is a domain? Scientifically speaking, a domain is a major taxonomic division into which natural objects are classified (see p. 30 for "What Is Taxonomy?").

FYI

FUNGI

Kingdom Fungi (about 100,000 species): Mainly multicellular organisms, fungi cannot make their own food. Mushrooms and yeast are fungi.

PROTISTS

Protists (about 250,000 species): Once considered a kingdom, this group is a "grab bag" that includes unicellular and multicellular organisms of great variety.

PLANTS

Kingdom Plantae (about 300,000 spe-cies): Plants are multicellular, and many can make their own food using photosyn-thesis (see p. 88 for "Photosynthesis").

ANIMALS

Kingdom Animalia (about 1,000,000 species): Most animals, which are multi-cellular, have their own organ systems. Animals do not make their own food.

HOW DOES YOUR GARDEN GROW?

The plant kingdom is more than 300,000 species strong, growing all over the world: on top of mountains, in the sea, in frigid temperatures— everywhere. Without plants, life on Earth would not be able to survive. Plants provide food and oxygen for animals and humans.

Three characteristics make plants distinct:

1. Most have chlorophyll (a green pigment that makes photosynthesis work and turns sunlight into energy), while some are parasitic.

2. They cannot change their location on their own.

3. Their cell walls are made from a stiff material called cellulose.

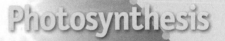

Photosynthesis

Plants are lucky—they don't have to hunt or shop for food. Most use the sun to produce their own food. In a process called photosynthesis, a plant's chloroplast (the part of the plant where the chemical chlorophyll is located) captures the sun's energy and combines it with carbon dioxide from the air and nutrient-rich water from the ground to produce a sugar called glucose. Plants burn the glucose for energy to help them grow. As a waste product, plants emit oxygen, which humans and other animals need to breathe. When we breathe, we exhale carbon dioxide, which the plants then use for more photosynthesis—it's all a big, finely tuned system. So the next time you pass a lonely houseplant, give it thanks for helping you live.

Weird but true

Check out these outrageous facts.

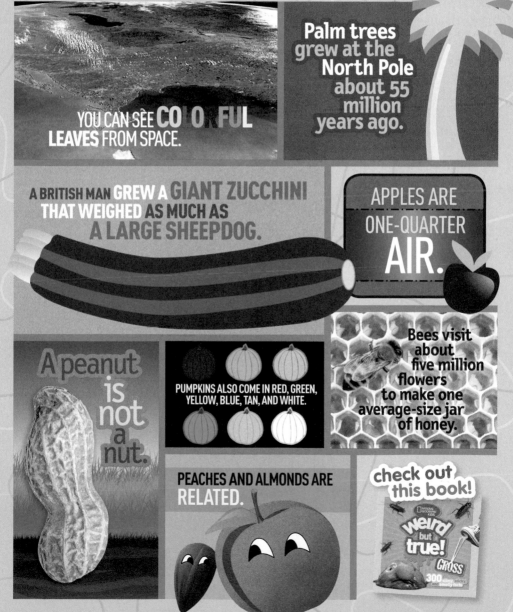

YOU CAN SEE **COLORFUL LEAVES** FROM SPACE.

Palm trees grew at the **North Pole** about 55 million years ago.

A BRITISH MAN **GREW A GIANT ZUCCHINI** THAT WEIGHED **AS MUCH AS A LARGE SHEEPDOG.**

APPLES ARE ONE-QUARTER **AIR.**

A peanut is not a nut.

PUMPKINS ALSO COME IN RED, GREEN, YELLOW, BLUE, TAN, AND WHITE.

Bees visit about five million flowers to make one average-size jar of honey.

PEACHES AND ALMONDS ARE RELATED.

check out this book!

weird but true! GROSS

300

GROW YOUR OWN BIOFILM

SOUP + DIRT + WARMTH = BIOFILM

CONCEPTS
MICROBIAL BIOLOGY, DECOMPOSITION

What's biofilm? It's a colony of bacteria that forms on a surface— a pond, a bowl, a boat in the ocean. The bacteria form a thin film, spreading out to make the most of the food source.

Biofilm is also known as scum or slime.

If it smells awful, you've probably met your goal of achieving biofilm.

WHAT YOU NEED
a cup of soup (low-sodium chicken soup works best)
pinch of dirt
food coloring
water
plastic container
measuring cup

HOW LONG IT TAKES
three days to one week

WHAT TO DO

DAY ONE:

1 POUR A CUP (.25 L) OF SOUP into the container and add the dirt.

2 LEAVE THE CONTAINER in a warm place, uncovered, for four to five days. The ideal temperature is 98.6°F (37°C)—body temperature. You may need to leave it out longer if it's cooler.

DAY TWO AND ON:

3 WATCH FOR A CHANGE in the liquid. When it begins to cloud, biofilm is forming.

LAST DAY:

4 DUMP OUT THE LIQUID and gently rinse the container with water. No scrubbing. No soap.

5 DRIP THE FOOD COLORING down the inside walls of the container. Swirl it round to coat the bottom and sides. Wait 15 minutes, swirling the color again every few minutes.

6 FILL THE CONTAINER with water, then dump out the colored water.

7 THE SMALL SPOTS of color on the walls of the container are the biofilm.

WHAT TO EXPECT The biofilm will form a ring around the container. It will be difficult to rinse it from the container even with soap, water, and some scrubbing.

WHAT'S GOING ON? Bacteria are tiny organisms that live in two ways: motile (moving freely) and sessile (in a group on a surface). Some motile bacteria become sessile, settling down near a food source that can keep them fed even if they quit moving. A biofilm is a colony of bacteria that live on a surface. If you provide bacteria with a food source, a biofilm may form.

The dirt provided the start-up for the biofilm. One teaspoon (5 mL) of dirt can harbor between 100 million and 1 billion bacteria. In the container, bacteria grow best at the boundary of air and liquid.

YOU AND YOUR CELLS

Your body is made up of microscopically tiny structures called cells—many trillions of them!

Every living thing—from the tiniest bug to the biggest tree—is made up of cells, too. Cells are the smallest building blocks of life. Some living things, such as an amoeba, are made up of just one cell. Other living things contain many more. Estimates for an adult human, for example, range from 10 trillion to 100 trillion cells!

An animal cell is a bit like the world's tiniest water balloon. It's a jellylike blob surrounded by an oily "skin" called a cell membrane. The membrane works to let some chemicals into the cell and keep others out. The "jelly" on the inside is called cytoplasm. It's speckled with tiny cell parts, called organelles. Some organelles make energy. Others take apart and put together various chemicals, which become ingredients for different body functions such as growth and movement.

CHECK OUT THE BOOK!

ULTIMATE BODY-PEDIA

SEEING CELLS

The first microscope that clearly showed anything smaller than a flea was invented in the late 1500s. Later, people tinkered with microscopes and lenses to make them even more powerful. One of these people was the English scientist Robert Hooke.

Hooke designed a microscope of his own and drew detailed pictures of what he saw. In 1665, he published his illustrations in a book called *Micrographia*, which means

"little pictures." One picture shows boxy spaces in a slice of cork from a tree. Hooke called the spaces "cells" because they looked like little rooms. It would be another 200 years before scientists realized that cells make up all living things.

YOU HAVE A LOT OF NERVE!

Different parts of your brain control different activities, but how does your brain tell all the parts of your body what to do?

And, in return, how do your eyes, ears, and nose tell your brain what they see, hear, and smell? The answer is your nerves!

Nerves—thin, threadlike structures— carry messages between your brain and the rest of your body, in both directions. Nerves run down your spine and branch out all the way to your fingers and toes. This system of nerves controls your body, tells your muscles to move, and lets you experience the wonderful world around you. Nerves are part of your nervous system, which also includes your brain and spinal cord.

Your nerves are made of cells called neurons. Neurons send and receive messages between your brain and the other parts of your body by sending out alternating electrical and chemical signals.

Messages flash from neuron to neuron along your nerves and inside your brain. Signals from your eyes might tell the brain, "There's my school bus." The brain then sends signals that zoom from cell to cell making sense of the message. Then the brain sends signals back down to the nerves connected to your leg muscles to say, "Run to the bus stop!"

TOUR A NEURON

Neurons have four parts:

CELL BODY Contains the nucleus, which controls the activity of the cell and contains its DNA, or deoxyribonucleic acid

AXON Fiber that transmits impulses from the cell body to another nerve cell

DENDRITE Branchlike fiber extending from the cell body that receives signals from other neurons

MYELIN A fatty covering around the axons that insulates the axon, giving the white matter its characteristic color

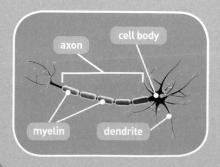

axon

cell body

myelin

dendrite

Your Amazing Ears

OUTER EAR

INNER EAR

COCHLEA

MIDDLE EAR

EARDRUM

Listen up! Your ears are so much more than just two funny-looking things stuck to the side of your head. Here's an earful on all that's cool about these awesome organs.

Your entire inner ear can fit inside the tip of your pinkie.

Some people can hear their own eyeballs move.

TRIPLE PLAY. The ears are made up of three sections: the outer ear, the middle ear, and the inner ear. Each part plays a separate and equally important role to keep your hearing sharp. Here's how sound travels through your ears.

OUTER EAR: The part you can see and feel, the outer ear consists of the pinna and the ear canal. Sound waves enter here and travel down the ear canal to the eardrum.

MIDDLE EAR: Sound waves create vibrations that strike the eardrum, causing the three tiny bones located here to move. The movement amplifies the sound and delivers it to the inner ear.

INNER EAR: Sound vibrations enter the cochlea, the small, snail-shaped, liquid-filled tube that's lined with tiny hairs. The vibrations make the tiny hairs wave back and forth and tickle the nerve cells. This causes the nerve cells to send messages to your brain that are interpreted as sound.

BETTER BALANCE. Your ears don't just let you hear—they keep you balanced, too. How? Above the cochlea in the inner ear is a set of three fluid-filled canals, called the semicircular canals. When you move your head, tiny hair cells in the canals move too, sending nerve impulses to the brain that tell you where you are. And that dizzy feeling you get when you've spun around in circles one too many times? That happens because the fluid in the semicircular canals continues to swish around even after you stop, confusing your brain into thinking that you're still spinning.

DRUM ROLL. Despite its name, the eardrum has nothing to do with percussion. Rather, this tiny piece of skin located between the outer and middle ear is called a "drum" because it's such a tightly stretched membrane. Bad ear infections or trauma can cause it to tear, or perforate, but the eardrum usually heals itself within a few months.

WAX ON. It's sticky, it's icky, and it can smell funky. So what's the point of earwax, anyway? The yellowish brown stuff is packed with dead skin cells and chemicals that fight off infections. And it traps dirt and dust, too, keeping your middle and inner ears sparkly clean. So while it may be gunky, it keeps you healthy. And that's not just a ball of wax!

Sense of Smell

Pee-ew! Mammals use their sense of smell to seek out food, avoid predators, and find a mate. But some are better sniffers than others, and the mammals that reign supreme have more olfactory receptors dedicated to smelling. The amount of receptors is determined by the number of scent genes in an animal's DNA—the more you have, the better you sniff! Check out the number of genes devoted to smell in these mammals to see who takes the best whiff.

AFRICAN ELEPHANT
1,948

GUINEA PIG
796

RAT
1,207

DOG
811

Some sharks can smell one drop of blood in **25 million** drops of ocean.

A polar bear can smell a seal on the ice from **20 miles** away. (32 km)

HUMAN
396

The human brain can detect more than **10,000** different smells.

ORANGUTAN
296

HORSE
1,066

Your Amazing
brain

Inside your body's supercomputer

Y
ou carry around a three-pound (1.4-kg) mass of wrinkly material in your head that controls every single thing you will ever do. From enabling you to think, learn, create, and feel emotions to controlling every blink, breath, and heartbeat—this fantastic control center is your brain. It is a structure so amazing that a famous scientist once called it the "most complex thing we have yet discovered in our universe."

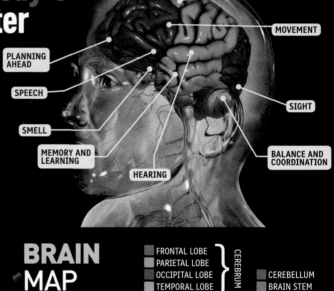

TOUCH

MOVEMENT

PLANNING AHEAD

SPEECH

SIGHT

SMELL

MEMORY AND LEARNING

BALANCE AND COORDINATION

HEARING

BRAIN MAP

■ FRONTAL LOBE
■ PARIETAL LOBE
■ OCCIPITAL LOBE
■ TEMPORAL LOBE

CEREBRUM

■ CEREBELLUM
■ BRAIN STEM

THE BIG QUESTION

WHAT TAKES UP TWO-THIRDS OF YOUR BRAIN'S WEIGHT AND ALLOWS YOU TO SWIM, EAT, AND SPEAK?

Answer: The huge hunk of your brain called the cerebrum. It's definitely the biggest part of the brain. The four lobes of the cerebrum house the centers for memory, the senses, movement, and emotion, among other things.

The cerebrum is made up of two hemispheres—the right and the left. Each side controls the muscles of the opposite side of the body.

CHECK YOUR MEMORY

How much can your brain remember? Put it to the test.

CHALLENGE

Take 30 seconds. Memorize as many of these pictures as you can. Cover the pictures. Now get a pencil and a piece of paper. Write down the pictures you remember. How many did you get right?

WHAT EXACTLY IS HAPPENING?

Looking at pictures actually helps your brain to remember better. Short-term memory, also called working memory, relies heavily on the visual cortex. Words that are read are processed very quickly by our brains. They don't stick around for very long. But recording a picture in your brain takes longer. The more time spent looking at the picture, the better the memory. Saying a word out loud does the same thing. It takes longer to speak a word than it does to read it. That's why you remember it better when you say it aloud. The lesson? When you are doing last-minute cramming for a test, look at pictures and speak things out loud. Your memory—and your test score—will thank you.

CHECK OUT THE BOOK!

BRAIN GAMES

THE MIND-BLOWING SCIENCE OF YOUR AMAZING BRAIN

YOUR SHORT-TERM MEMORY CAN HOLD ONLY ABOUT SEVEN THINGS AT ONE TIME.

THE GENE SCENE

NATURE'S BLUEPRINT

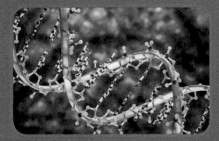

Genetics is the study of heredity, or how traits from parents are passed along to their children. And genes are the elements we inherit from each of our parents that combine to make us the individuals we are. By studying genes, scientists have been able to learn not only what makes us similar to and different from one another, but also the causes of certain diseases that are inherited (passed down) from one generation to another.

Amazingly, advances in research have helped scientists discover that there are "disease genes"—genes that indicate that a person who is carrying them may be more likely to get a specific disease. Researchers are also developing ways to test people to see if they have these genes. They are digging deeper into the genetics behind more and more diseases, such as cancer and heart disease, to see which healthy patients could be at risk in the future. Doctors are now even able to know in advance whether a patient will respond well to a particular treatment (medicine) based on their genetic code! Going forward, researchers are working to make genome sequencing (studying a person's unique genetic makeup) more widely available so many people can have access to this amazing medical care. One day we may be able to fix these broken genes.

In 2003, after more than a decade of hard work, scientists completed a very ambitious task called the Human Genome Project. They mapped the entire "sequence" of human DNA—our hereditary "code" containing tens of thousands of genes. DNA is nature's blueprint for human beings, and it makes up the building blocks of life.

Would it surprise you to know that, despite how different individual people seem from one another, more than 99 percent of DNA is the same in all people? It's true! Though there are definite physical and other differences we can identify—such as eye color, hair color, height, and skin color—humans are genetically mostly the same.

ADD IT UP

Ten years ago, the number of human genes was thought to be 100,000. Since then, scientists have learned more and revised that number down to between 20,000 and 25,000.

LIMBS FROM
LIMBS

ARMED AND BRAVE

You might have heard of organ transplants, in which a person receives a new organ on the inside of their body, but did you know that some people can receive transplants on the *outside* of their bodies?

In 2012 a U.S. Army soldier who had lost all four limbs after being injured by a roadside bomb in 2009 received a rare double-arm transplant—one of only a small number of people to successfully undergo this risky surgery. In a 13-hour operation, a team of 16 surgeons joined the bone, muscles, blood vessels, nerves, and skin of donor arms with those of former sergeant Brendan Marrocco. With time and physical therapy, these replacement arms have helped Marrocco do many of the things he did before, such as drive a car.

SMART PARTS

A DOLPHIN'S TALE

Maja Kazazic had become used to living with pain—and feeling different. As a teen, Maja lost her leg after she was injured in the Bosnian civil war. Her artificial limb—called a prosthesis—made every movement painful.

Maja's life changed when she met Winter, a dolphin at Clearwater Marine Aquarium in Florida, U.S.A. (above). Winter had lost her tail in a crab trap as a baby. When Winter got a high-tech tail to help her swim, Maja wondered if a similar device could help her be pain free. The aquarium put Maja in touch with the company that had made Winter's prosthesis. Maja received a new leg out of the same materials that helped Winter. Soon the pair were swimming together—one with a new leg, the other with a new tail.

QUIZ WHIZ

Discover your tech-savvy smarts by taking this quiz!

Write your answers on a piece of paper. Then check them below.

1 **True or false?** Anyone can fly a drone in India.

2 **What's the main purpose of earwax?**
a. It helps fight off infections and keeps your ears clean.
b. It helps you hear better.
c. It's used to make candles.
d. It has no purpose.

3 **The human brain can detect more than _____ different smells.**
a. 10
b. 100
c. 1,000
d. 10,000

4 **True or false?** In surgery, doctors sometimes use powerful lasers in place of scalpels.

5 **Genes play a role in determining which of our physical characteristics?**
a. height
b. hair color
c. eye color
d. all of the above

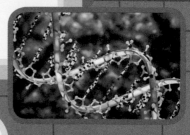

Not **STUMPED** yet? Check out the *NATIONAL GEOGRAPHIC KIDS QUIZ WHIZ* collection for more crazy **TECHNOLOGY** questions!

ANSWERS:
1. False. In India, you must first get a license, like you would need to drive a car; 2. a; 3. d; 4. True; 5. d

HOMEWORK HELP

This Is How It's Done!

Sometimes, the most complicated problems are solved with step-by-step directions. These "how to" instructions are also known as a process analysis essay. While scientists and engineers use this tool to program robots and write computer code, you also use process analysis every day, from following a recipe to putting together a new toy or gadget. Here's how to write a basic process analysis essay.

Step 1: Choose Your Topic Sentence

Pick a clear and concise topic sentence that describes what you're writing about. Be sure to explain to the reader why the task is important—and how many steps there are to complete it.

Step 2: List Materials

Do you need specific ingredients or equipment to complete your process? Mention these right away so the readers will have all they need to do this activity.

Step 3: Write Your Directions

Your directions should be clear and easy to follow. Assume that you are explaining the process for the first time, and define any unfamiliar terms. List your steps in the exact order the reader will need to follow to complete the activity. Try to keep your essay limited to no more than six steps.

Step 4: Restate Your Main Idea

Your closing idea should revisit your topic sentence, drawing a conclusion relating to the importance of the subject.

EXAMPLE OF A PROCESS ANALYSIS ESSAY

Downloading an app is a simple way to enhance your tablet. Today, I'd like to show you how to search for and add an app to your tablet. First, you will need a tablet with the ability to access the Internet. You'll also want to ask your parents' permission before you download anything onto your tablet. Next, select the specific app you're seeking by going to the app store on your tablet and entering the app's name into the search bar. Once you find the app you're seeking, select "download" and wait for the app to load. When you see that the app has fully loaded, tap on the icon and you will be able to access it. Now you can enjoy your app and have more fun with your tablet.

Wind turbines stand behind a solar power park near Werder, Germany.

Going Green

5 Animals Threatened by Climate Change

1

Polar Bear

WHERE IT LIVES: Canada, Greenland, Russia, Norway, and Alaska, U.S.A.

WHY IT'S THREATENED: Due to shrinking amounts of sea ice in the Arctic, polar bears are losing their habitat—and changing sea temperatures are reducing the prey that polar bears rely on for food.

HOPE FOR THE FUTURE: Areas of the Arctic have been declared nature preserves, and work is being done to conserve dens and other important habitat areas used by polar bears.

2

Adélie Penguin

WHERE IT LIVES: Antarctica

WHY IT'S THREATENED: By 2099, 58 percent of the habitat where Adélie penguins lay their eggs could be too warm and too wet to host colonies.

HOPE FOR THE FUTURE: Research shows that Adélie penguins have endured the warmer temperatures in East Antarctica's Cape Adare peninsula, which may be a sign that they can survive the threat of global warming.

American Pika

3

WHERE IT LIVES: Mountaintops of the western U.S. and southwestern Canada

WHY IT'S THREATENED: Rising temperatures are causing changes in vegetation in the pika's range, making it difficult for the animal to find food.

HOPE FOR THE FUTURE: Scientists have observed that some pikas have adapted by changing their diets. Pikas that eat unusual foods such as moss might be able to remain in cool, rocky areas at lower elevations year-round.

Orange-Spotted Filefish

4

WHERE IT LIVES: Indo-Pacific coral reefs

WHY IT'S THREATENED: Not only are coral reefs—the fish's habitat—in decline, but filefish are especially sensitive to warmer waters.

HOPE FOR THE FUTURE: Conservationists are working together to save the coral reefs (and all the animals that thrive off them), by expanding marine protected areas and taking steps to reverse global warming.

5

Gila Monster

WHERE IT LIVES: Southwestern U.S., northwest Mexico

WHY IT'S THREATENED: Hotter, drier conditions in the deserts means this colorful lizard is not getting enough water to survive, causing a decline in its numbers.

HOPE FOR THE FUTURE: Conservationists urge people to set aside a special Gila monster habitat in higher regions of the Southwest where there is more rainfall.

THE ARCTIC'S
DISAPPEARING ICE

In the past few decades, sea ice cover in the Arctic has shrunk because of global climate change. Arctic sea ice freezes up and expands in the winter and melts and shrinks in the summer. It typically reaches its smallest size every September. Scientists call this the "Arctic sea ice minimum." This minimum has shrunk from 3.02 million square miles (7.83 million sq km) in 1980 to about 1.7 million square miles (4.41 million sq km) in 2015. The change is so significant that cartographers at the *National Geographic Atlas of the World* redrew the map of the Arctic to reflect the smaller sea ice coverage. So what's behind this ice loss in the Arctic? Scientists point to a phenomenon known as the "positive feedback loop."

Sea ice's bright surface reflects sunlight back into space. This means icy areas absorb less solar energy and remain cool. But when air and ocean temperatures rise over time and more sea ice melts, fewer bright surfaces reflect sunlight back into space. The ice and exposed seawater absorb more solar energy, and this causes a feedback loop of more melting and more warming.

If the ice loss continues at the current rate, scientists are concerned the Arctic will become ice free during the summer at some point within this century. As the ice melts, it's essential that we find ways to protect the indigenous people and animals—such as polar bears and seals—that rely on the Arctic's ice for food and survival.

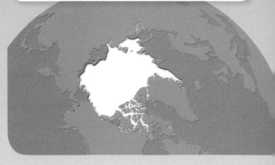

ARCTIC SEA ICE MINIMUM IN 1980

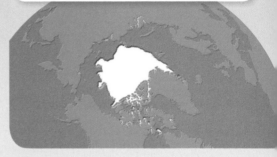

ARCTIC SEA ICE MINIMUM IN 2015

COMPARISON OF ARCTIC SEA ICE MINIMUMS

Arctic sea ice minimum in 1980

Arctic sea ice minimum in 2015

A MELTING WORLD

If all the ice on Earth melted, the world's oceans would rise 216 feet (66 m). But how high is that exactly? Check this chart to see out what might end up underwater.

THE STATUE OF LIBERTY 305 feet (93 m)

12 GIRAFFES 216 feet (66 m)

5 SCHOOL BUSES 200 feet (61 m)

6 ORCAS 192 feet (59 m)

107

Pollution

Cleaning Up Our Act

So what's the big deal about a little dirt on the planet? Pollution can affect animals, plants, and people. In fact, some studies show that more people die every year from diseases linked to air pollution than from car accidents. And right now nearly one billion of the world's people don't have access to clean drinking water.

A LITTLE POLLUTION = BIG PROBLEMS

You can probably clean your room in a couple of hours. (At least we hope you can!) But you can't shove air and water pollution under your bed or cram them into the closet. Once released into the environment, pollution—whether it's oil leaking from a boat or chemicals spewing from a factory's smokestack—can have a lasting environmental impact.

KEEP IT CLEAN

It's easy to blame things like big factories for pollution problems. But some of the mess comes from everyday activities. Exhaust fumes from cars and garbage in landfills can seriously trash the Earth's health. We all need to pitch in and do some house-cleaning. It may mean bicycling more and riding in cars less. Or not dumping water-polluting oil or household cleaners down the drain. Look at it this way: Just as with your room, it's always better not to let Earth get messed up in the first place.

What a Prince!

The heir to the British throne is doing his part to save Earth's oceans. Working to combat both overfishing and the amount of plastic that lands in the ocean every year—8.8 million tons (8 million t) by some estimates—Prince Charles is leading a charitable drive to protect the seas, with a focus on sustainable fishing. We'd say that's a quite a royal effort.

Declining Biodiversity

Saving All Creatures, Great and Small

Earth is home to a huge mix of plants and animals—millions and possibly billions of species—and scientists have officially identified and named only about 1.9 million so far! Scientists call this healthy mix biodiversity.

THE BALANCING ACT

The bad news is that half of the planet's plant and animal species may be on the path to extinction, mainly because of human activity. People cut down trees, build roads and houses, pollute rivers, overfish, and overhunt. The good news is that many people care. Scientists and volunteers race against the clock every day, working to save wildlife before time runs out. By building birdhouses, planting trees, and following the rules for hunting and fishing, you can be a positive force for preserving biodiversity, too. Every time you do something to help a species survive, you help our planet to thrive.

Green sea turtle

Habitats Threatened

Living on the Edge

Even though tropical rain forests cover only about 7 percent of the planet's total land surface, they are home to half of all known species of plants and animals. Because people cut down so many trees for lumber and firewood and clear so much land for farms, hundreds of thousands of acres of rain forest disappear every year.

SHARING THE LAND

Wetlands are also important feeding and breeding grounds. People have drained many wetlands, turning them into farm fields or sites for industries. More than half the world's wetlands have disappeared within the past century, squeezing wildlife out. Balancing the needs of humans and animals is the key to lessening habitat destruction.

Toucan

109

1 Recycling a million cell phones can recover about 50 pounds (23 kg) of gold.

2 *NATIONAL GEOGRAPHIC KIDS* MAGAZINE ONCE COLLECTED 16,407 SNEAKERS TO BE RECYCLED.

3 BRITISH ECO-ADVENTURER DAVID DE ROTHSCHILD SAILED THE PACIFIC ON A BOAT MADE FROM **12,500 RECYCLED PLASTIC BOTTLES.**

4 Recycling one aluminum can saves enough energy to listen to a full album on your iPod.

19

REUSABLE FACTS ABOUT

5 GLASS IS 100 PERCENT RECYCLABLE AND CAN BE RECYCLED AN ENDLESS NUMBER OF TIMES.

6 In Finland, **94 percent** of plastic bottles are recycled.

7 ONE ARTIST USES SATELLITE DISHES, REMOTE CONTROLS, CABLES, AND OTHER ITEMS FOUND IN RECYCLING CENTERS TO CREATE LARGE ART INSTALLATIONS.

8 ADIDAS MAKES SNEAKERS that are made out of fishing nets and recycled ocean waste.

9 35 percent of trash generated in the United States is recycled or composted.

10 Residents of Vancouver, Canada, CAN FACE FINES FOR FAILING TO RECYCLE.

11 ONE TON (0.9 t) OF RECYCLED PAPER CAN SAVE 17 TREES.

12 You can buy boxes of recycled crayons that are made from broken and mismatched ones.

13 MEMBERS OF THE **RECYCLED ORCHESTRA,** IN CATEURA, PARAGUAY, ARE FAMOUS FOR PLAYING INSTRUMENTS MADE COMPLETELY OUT OF RECYCLED MATERIALS.

14 An artist in New Orleans, Louisiana, U.S.A., creates mosaics out of Mardi Gras beads and trash found throughout the city.

RECYCLING

15 One company uses items like old playing cards to make ball gowns.

16 AMERICANS THROW AWAY ENOUGH OFFICE PAPER EACH YEAR TO BUILD A WALL FROM SEATTLE TO NEW YORK.

17 In one hour, a group of students in Hong Kong collected 2,528 pounds, 11 ounces (1,147 kg) of glass bottles to be recycled—a world record.

18 THE INSULATION IN ONE ECO-FRIENDLY HOUSE IN BRIGHTON, ENGLAND, U.K., IS MADE OF THOUSANDS OF TOOTHBRUSHES, DVD CASES, AND DENIM WASTE.

19 IN SWEDEN, RECYCLING STATIONS MUST BE NO MORE THAN 984 FEET (300 m) FROM ANY RESIDENTIAL AREA FOR EASY ACCESS.

By the Numbers
TRASH BREAKDOWN

After you toss out a banana peel, a soda can, or a smelly sock, it's out of sight, but it's still around— sometimes for weeks, and other times for hundreds of years! Here's a timeline of how long it takes everyday trash to decompose— or completely break down—in a landfill.

BANANA PEEL
2–5 WEEKS

APPLE CORE
2 MONTHS

WOOL SOCKS
1–5 YEARS

PLASTIC BAG
10–20 YEARS

LEATHER
50 YEARS

RUBBER BOOT SOLE
50–80 YEARS

ALUMINUM CAN
80–200 YEARS

GLASS BOTTLE
1 MILLION YEARS OR MORE

PLASTIC FISHING LINE
600 YEARS

Here's some food for thought: Around the world, approximately 3.97 million tons (3.6 million t) of fruits, veggies, and other food waste is tossed away every day.

And plenty of those scraps—especially produce—is perfectly good to eat. In fact, the amount of food that winds up wasted could feed two billion hungry people around the world. On top of food scraps, imperfect produce also often ends up in landfills, contributing to food waste, which, in turn, is a major source of greenhouse gas emissions. That's why advocates like Tristram Stuart are trying to change the way we look at imperfect food. From misshapen melons to bruised bananas, Stuart says it's just fine to fill up on ugly food.

Ugly
FOOD

And he's demonstrating just that through his Feeding the 5,000 campaign—free public feasts made entirely of orphaned food. He's also encouraging major food corporations and grocery stores to stop throwing away so-called "ugly" fruits and veggies. "Today, there are major food corporations agreeing that it's unacceptable to throw so much away, and the United States recently announced a food waste reduction goal, calling for a 50 percent reduction by 2030," says Stuart. "In the United Kingdom, food waste has been reduced by 21 percent."

Even better news? You can help, too. "Anyone can take that slightly brown banana and turn it into a smoothie instead of tossing it," says Stuart. "But you also have the power to call the industry into account as well. It can be as easy as going into your local grocery store and asking about how much they are throwing away." Another simple step: Sign Stuart's pledge to reduce food waste (check it out at feedbackglobal.org) and share it with your friends and family to let them know that eating ugly food can be a beautiful thing.

QUIZ WHIZ

What's your eco-friendly IQ? Find out with this quiz!

Write your answers on a piece of paper. Then check them below.

1 Tropical rain forests are home to _____ of all known species of plants and animals.

a. a quarter
b. a third
c. half
d. three-quarters

2 **True or false?** An aluminum can could take 200 years to decompose.

3 **What is causing a decline among Gila monsters?**

a. hotter, drier conditions in the deserts
b. hunting
c. a deadly fungus
d. all of the above

4 **True or false?** Residents of Vancouver, Canada, can face fines for using plastic grocery bags.

5 Approximately how much food is tossed out around the world each day?

a. 3.97 million tons (3.6 million t)
b. 3,000 pounds (1,361 kg)
c. 30,000 tons (27,215 t)
d. 750 pounds (340 kg)

Not **STUMPED** yet? Check out the *NATIONAL GEOGRAPHIC KIDS QUIZ WHIZ* collection for more crazy **ENVIRONMENT** questions!

ANSWERS:
1. c; 2. True; 3. a; 4. False. They can face fines for failing to recycle; 5. a

Write a Letter That Gets Results

Knowing how to write a good letter is a useful skill. It will come in handy anytime you want to persuade someone to understand your point of view. Whether you're emailing your congressperson or writing a letter for a school project or to your grandma, a great letter will help you get your message across. Most important, a well-written letter leaves a good impression.

Check out the example below for the elements of a good letter.

Your address

Date

Salutation
Always use "Dear" followed by the person's name; use Mr., Mrs., Ms., or Dr. as appropriate.

Introductory paragraph
Give the reason you're writing the letter.

Body
The longest part of the letter, which provides evidence that supports your position. Be persuasive!

Closing paragraph
Sum up your argument.

Complimentary closing
Sign off with "Sincerely" or "Thank you."

Your signature

Abby Jones
1204 Green Street
Los Angeles, CA 90045

March 31, 2019

Dear Mr. School Superintendent,

I am writing to you about how much excess energy our school uses and to offer a solution.

Every day, we leave the computers on in the classroom, the TVs are plugged in all the time, and the lights are on all day. All of this adds up to a lot of wasted energy, which is not only harmful for the Earth, as it increases the amount of harmful greenhouse gas emissions into the environment, but is also costly to the school. In fact, I read that schools spend more on energy bills than on computers and textbooks combined!

I am suggesting that we start an Energy Patrol to monitor the use of lighting, air-conditioning, heating, and other energy systems within our school. My idea is to have a group of students dedicated to figuring out ways we can cut back on our energy use in the school. We can do room checks, provide reminders to students and teachers to turn off lights and computers, replace old lightbulbs with energy-efficient products, and even reward the classrooms that do the most to save energy.

Above all, I think our school could help the environment tremendously by cutting back on how much energy we use. Let's see an Energy Patrol at our school soon. Thank you.

Sincerely,

Abby Jones

Abby Jones

COMPLIMENTARY CLOSINGS

Sincerely, Sincerely yours, Thank you, Regards, Best wishes, Respectfully,

Jack-o'-lanterns—carved pumpkins illuminated by candles—glow on Halloween night. The name comes from an Irish folktale character called Stingy Jack.

Culture Connection

1

Some believe **KEEPING GOATS** close helps keep **EVIL AWAY.**

2 A Nigerian superstition says that if you **KISS A BABY** on the lips it will **DROOL** as an adult.

4 The **NUMBER 13** is notoriously believed to bring **BAD LUCK.** Many hotels and apartments skip number 13 when numbering floors, going from 12 to 14.

5 A **WEDDING RING** hanging from a string and held over a pregnant woman's belly is often said to **PREDICT** the sex of a baby.

3 Some people believe that if you catch a **FALLING LEAF** on the first day of autumn you will go all winter without catching **A COLD.**

(19) GOOD AND BAD FACTS ABOUT

6 **BANANAS** and **SUITCASES** are not allowed on board most crab-fishing boats because they are believed to bring bad luck.

7 A Japanese superstition says that the person in the middle of a **PHOTOGRAPH** will have BAD LUCK.

8 It is supposedly bad luck to **SPILL SALT,** but if you throw a pinch of salt over your **LEFT SHOULDER,** you can reverse the bad luck.

9 ACCORDING TO TRADITION, A FOUR-LEAF CLOVER BRINGS GOOD LUCK TO ITS FINDER, ESPECIALLY IF FOUND ACCIDENTALLY.

10 A FRENCH-CANADIAN superstition says that if a pregnant woman does not eat fish, her baby will be born with a FISH HEAD.

11 A company called KNOCK ON WOOD sells wooden blocks so that believers of the superstition can always have a piece of wood handy.

12 Barbershops in India will close on Tuesday because a HINDU superstition considers Tuesday haircuts BAD LUCK.

13 NAPOLEON BONAPARTE was superstitious and had a fear of cats—believing them to be BAD LUCK. Black cats are often associated with luck—good and bad.

14 An old superstition says that opening an UMBRELLA indoors will bring a STORM of bad luck.

SUPERSTITIONS

15 WHISTLING or saying the word "PIG" on a ship is believed to bring BAD WEATHER.

16 A scientist once proved that 75 percent of a study group of PIGEONS became superstitious, believing that nodding their head a certain way meant they would get fed.

17 Ancient Greeks believed that ROSEMARY helped keep away EVIL SPIRITS.

18 A superstition dating back to ANCIENT TIMES says that you will stay young if you CARRY ACORNS in your pockets.

19 The EARLIEST known ideas of superstitions date back to ANCIENT GREECE. An early idea was to cross one's fingers for luck, as a cross marks the coming together of GOOD SPIRITS.

119

MONEY Around the World!

Jordan's HALF-DINAR COIN has seven sides.

A **$3 BILL** is used in the Bahamas.

THE CENTRAL BANK OF THE BAHAMAS

$3

THE CENTRAL BANK OF THE BAHAMAS

THREE DOLLARS

A481546

A British businessman created his own currency —named the **PUFFIN**— for an island he owned off of England.

IN ARGENTINA, **"MANGO"** IS SLANG FOR **"PESO."**

BANCO CENTRAL DE CHILE
FA6876603
20 MIL PESOS
20000
VEINTE MIL PESOS
2006

A **20,000**-PESO BANKNOTE FROM CHILE CONTAINS INK THAT CHANGES **COLOR** WHEN TILTED.

The INCA called gold **"THE SWEAT OF THE SUN"** and silver **"THE TEARS OF THE MOON."**

A PORCUPINE APPEARED ON A COLLECTIBLE **50-TENGE COIN** FROM KAZAKHSTAN.

I KNEW I SHOULD'VE TRIED A FAKE ATM INSTEAD.

IN 2002, A MAN OPENED A FAKE BANK AND TOOK IN **$650,000** BEFORE HE WAS CAUGHT.

In Spain, **"PASTA"** is a slang term for "money."

A 1913 U.S. LIBERTY HEAD NICKEL—ONE OF THE ONLY FIVE IN EXISTENCE— **SOLD AT** AUCTION FOR MORE THAN **$3.1 MILLION.**

THE PHRASE **"BRING HOME THE BACON"** STARTED AFTER A 12TH-CENTURY PRIEST REWARDED A MARRIED COUPLE **WITH A SIDE OF BACON.**

BRICKS OF COMPRESSED TEA LEAVES WERE ONCE USED AS CURRENCY IN SIBERIA, MONGOLIA, AND CHINA.

MONEY TIP!

ANY TIME YOU BUY SOMETHING **ON SALE,** PUT WHAT YOU SAVED IN YOUR PIGGY BANK.

121

CHEW ON THIS

MANGO LASSI

India's version of the smoothie can be mixed with fruit or spices, but it's almost always blended with yogurt. It's a favorite refreshment in the summertime, when India's temperatures can hit triple digits. Sip up these facts about the mango lassi's ingredients.

Some people chew **CARDAMOM** pods to fight bad breath.

A **MANGO** tree can grow up to 100 feet (30 m) tall.

In the 11th century, German peasants paid for goods with **HONEY.**

LIME juice has been used to clean the walls of the Taj Mahal, India's most famous landmark.

YOGURT was once thought to bring a long life and good looks to those who ate it.

CHECK OUT THE BOOK!

NATIONAL GEOGRAPHIC KIDS **COOK BOOK**

COOL THINGS ABOUT INDIA

Many buildings in the village of Shani Shingnapur have no doors.

India has more post offices than any other country.

The game of chess was likely invented in India.

Cows—considered sacred by many in India—are often seen roaming city streets.

The country's national bird is the peacock.

SWEDISH MEATBALLS

Swedish meatballs, or *köttbullar* (pronounced SHUT-boo-lahr), are a favorite in Sweden. Smaller than Italian meatballs, they're sometimes eaten plain as a snack. But the most famous Swedish meatball dish is *köttbullar med gräddsås*, or meatballs with cream sauce. Often served with noodles, jam, and mashed potatoes, the meal has become the country's unofficial national dish.

The British gave the **ALLSPICE** tree its name when they couldn't figure out what spice it produced.

Over 600 pasta shapes—including the **egg noodle**—are produced around the world.

Ancient Egyptians worshipped the **ONION,** believing the vegetable contained magic.

NUTMEG oil is used to treat toothaches in some parts of the Middle East.

PANKO, a Japanese-style bread crumb, is made from bread without crusts.

COOL THINGS ABOUT SWEDEN

One of the most popular flavors of ice cream in Sweden is *salmiakki,* or salty licorice.

Sweden was the first country in Europe to establish a national park.

Stockholm, the capital of Sweden, is spread across 14 islands.

The world's first ice hotel was built in Jukkasjärvi, Sweden, in the 1980s.

In the summer, parts of Sweden have 24 hours of daylight.

Food That FOOLS YOU

COOL TOPPING

Whipped cream has too much air to hold up for long. So this banana split is topped with whipped topping. Some stylists use sour cream or—*yum!*—shaving cream.

Does this banana split look good enough to eat? Hold on to your spoon, because things aren't exactly as they appear.

In the two hours it takes to do a photo shoot, ice cream melts, bananas turn brown, whipped cream sags, and the cherry slides right off. What to do? Call in the experts.

"Real food starts to look yucky after sitting out for a while," food stylist Linda Garrido says. Garrido's job is to make food look great for the camera. This could mean substituting something that *looks* like food for the real thing. Or it could mean "doctoring" the real food to make it look better longer.

Keep in mind, though: If it's a specific food being advertised, then that food has to be real. "A soup company once put marbles in the soup to prop up the vegetables," food photographer Taran Z says. "You can't do that." But if the food is not being advertised, then anything goes.

National Geographic Kids got the inside scoop on the tricks of the trade. So go ahead and dig into this banana split— just beware of the vegetable shortening and lemon juice!

JAM SESSION

Food stylists create strawberry ice cream by stirring strawberry jam into the vanilla ice-cream mixture.

SOUR SOLUTION

No one wants a bruised-looking banana. So this banana is painted with lemon juice to keep the fruit from turning brown.

 2 p.m.

 2:05 p.m.

 2:20 p.m.

STICK 'EM UP

It's tough being at the top. That's why this cherry is held in place by a toothpick to keep it from sliding off. If the cherry's not perfect, red lipstick can be used for touch-ups.

NUTCASE

Each hand-selected nut is carefully placed with tweezers. Sometimes nuts are touched up with a brown eyebrow pencil.

"ICING" CREAM

What appears to be chocolaty frozen goodness is really store-bought chocolate cake icing that was thickened with powdered sugar.

PLAIN VANILLA

Nothing's worse than mushy ice cream. This vanilla is a mixture of vegetable shortening, corn syrup, and powdered sugar. It'll look real for days.

FLYING SAUCES

Real chocolate, caramel, and strawberry sauces slide to the bottom of the bowl. But *these* sauces are thickened with corn syrup. That makes them less drippy so they stay put.

awes8me FASHION

When it comes to funky fashion, some people really wear it well! From far-out facial hair to gowns made from garbage, here's a roundup of some of the most awesome looks out there!

1. FRUIT FEET Talk about sweet shoes. These heels, designed by a Japanese artist, look almost good enough to eat. Just don't *really* try to snack on them—the sugary treats are totally fake.

2. BEACHY KEEN Need a new look for the spring? Consider a blue-hued style for your locks. Surf's up—and so is your do!

TORCH

SOCCER FIELD

3. PROPER TOPPERS The bigger the hat, the better? That's the case at a horse race in Ascot, England, where headpieces called fascinators are a must.

4. (RE)WORK IT A Dutch designer reused materials from previous collections to create this weird look that used techniques such as embroidery. Recycling is so in.

5. FOR THE BIRDS The wife of the creator of the video game *Angry Birds* showed her support in a gown resembling the game's main character, Red. What's next, a *Minecraft* tuxedo?

6. FACE-OFF The facial hair competition gets fierce at the World Beard and Moustache Championships, where contestants mold their strands into masterpieces.

7. IN THE FRAME Slip on silly-looking specs—like these from the Paris Fashion Week runway—to see the world in a funkier light.

8. HAIR APPARENT Wonder if she's feeling camera shy? A pop singer strikes a mysterious pose by hiding behind a wall of blond hair.

CELEBRATIONS

1 CHINESE NEW YEAR
February 5
Also called Lunar New Year, this holiday marks the new year according to the lunar calendar. Families celebrate with parades, feasts, and fireworks. Young people may receive gifts of money in red envelopes.

2 HOLI
March 21
This festival in India celebrates spring and marks the triumph of good over evil. People cover one another with powdered paint, called *gulal,* and douse one another with buckets of colored water.

3 DAY OF THE SEA
March 23
Bolivia may be a landlocked country, but it boasts a navy, which it honors every March. On this day, also known as *Día del Mar,* people march through the streets carrying model ships and pictures of the ocean.

4 EASTER
April 21
A Christian holiday that honors the resurrection of Jesus Christ, Easter is celebrated by giving baskets filled with gifts, decorated eggs, or candy to children.

5 QINGMING FESTIVAL
April 5
Also known as "Grave Sweeping Day," this Chinese celebration calls on people to return to the graves of their deceased loved ones. There, they tidy up the graves, as well as light firecrackers, burn fake money, and leave food as an offering to the spirits.

6 KONINGSDAG
April 27
Orange you glad it's King's Day? People across the Netherlands celebrate the monarchy with street parties and by wearing all things orange.

7 RAMADAN AND EID AL-FITR
May 5*–June 5**
A Muslim holiday, Ramadan is a month long, ending in the Eid Al-Fitr celebration. Observers fast during this month— eating only after sunset. People pray for forgiveness and hope to purify themselves through observance.

8 SCARLET SAILS CELEBRATION
June 21
The end of the school year in St. Petersburg, Russia, is celebrated in this event, during which huge ships with bright red sails travel down the Neva River. Fireworks, concerts, and water shows also highlight this festive occasion.

9 TANABATA
July 7
To commemorate this Star Festival, people in Japan first write wishes on colorful strips of paper. Then they hang the paper on bamboo branches in their yards and around their homes in the hope that their wishes will come true.

10 BASTILLE DAY
July 14
The French call this day *La Fête Nationale,* as it is the celebration of the start of the French Revolution in 1789. In Paris, fireworks light up the night skies while dance parties spill into the streets.

*Begins at sundown.
**Dates may vary slightly by location.

Around the World

11 LAS BOLAS DE FUEGO
August 31

This annual event in Nejapa, El Salvador, marks the anniversary of a volcanic eruption that once forced an evacuation of the tiny town. Residents—dressed in protective clothing—light balls made with rags soaked in kerosene, then throw them into the air before partying well into the night.

12 NAG PANCHAMI
August 5

In Nepal and India, Hindus worship snakes—and keep evil spirits out of their homes—by sticking images of serpents on their doors and making offerings to the revered reptiles.

13 ROSH HASHANAH
September 29*–October 1

A Jewish holiday marking the beginning of a new year on the Hebrew calendar. Celebrations include prayer, ritual foods, and a day of rest.

14 HANUKKAH
December 22*–30

This Jewish holiday is eight days long. It commemorates the rededication of the Temple in Jerusalem. Hanukkah celebrations include the lighting of menorah candles for eight days and the exchange of gifts.

15 CHRISTMAS DAY
December 25

A Christian holiday marking the birth of Jesus Christ, Christmas is usually celebrated by decorating trees, exchanging presents, and having festive gatherings.

JANUARY
S	M	T	W	T	F	S
		1	2	3	4	5
6	7	8	9	10	11	12
13	14	15	16	17	18	19
20	21	22	23	24	25	26
27	28	29	30	31		

FEBRUARY
S	M	T	W	T	F	S
					1	2
3	4	5	6	7	8	9
10	11	12	13	14	15	16
17	18	19	20	21	22	23
24	25	26	27	28		

MARCH
S	M	T	W	T	F	S
					1	2
3	4	5	6	7	8	9
10	11	12	13	14	15	16
17	18	19	20	21	22	23
24	25	26	27	28	29	30
31						

APRIL
S	M	T	W	T	F	S
	1	2	3	4	5	6
7	8	9	10	11	12	13
14	15	16	17	18	19	20
21	22	23	24	25	26	27
28	29	30				

MAY
S	M	T	W	T	F	S
			1	2	3	4
5	6	7	8	9	10	11
12	13	14	15	16	17	18
19	20	21	22	23	24	25
26	27	28	29	30	31	

JUNE
S	M	T	W	T	F	S
						1
2	3	4	5	6	7	8
9	10	11	12	13	14	15
16	17	18	19	20	21	22
23	24	25	26	27	28	29
30						

JULY
S	M	T	W	T	F	S
	1	2	3	4	5	6
7	8	9	10	11	12	13
14	15	16	17	18	19	20
21	22	23	24	25	26	27
28	29	30	31			

AUGUST
S	M	T	W	T	F	S
				1	2	3
4	5	6	7	8	9	10
11	12	13	14	15	16	17
18	19	20	21	22	23	24
25	26	27	28	29	30	31

SEPTEMBER
S	M	T	W	T	F	S
1	2	3	4	5	6	7
8	9	10	11	12	13	14
15	16	17	18	19	20	21
22	23	24	25	26	27	28
29	30					

OCTOBER
S	M	T	W	T	F	S
		1	2	3	4	5
6	7	8	9	10	11	12
13	14	15	16	17	18	19
20	21	22	23	24	25	26
27	28	29	30	31		

NOVEMBER
S	M	T	W	T	F	S
					1	2
3	4	5	6	7	8	9
10	11	12	13	14	15	16
17	18	19	20	21	22	23
24	25	26	27	28	29	30

DECEMBER
S	M	T	W	T	F	S
1	2	3	4	5	6	7
8	9	10	11	12	13	14
15	16	17	18	19	20	21
22	23	24	25	26	27	28
29	30	31				

What's Your Chinese Horoscope?
Locate your birth year to find out.

In Chinese astrology the zodiac runs on a 12-year cycle, based on the lunar calendar. Each year corresponds to one of 12 animals, each representing one of 12 personality types. Read on to find out which animal year you were born in and what that might say about you.

RAT
1972, '84, '96, 2008, '20
Say cheese! You're attractive, charming, and creative. When you get mad, you can have really sharp teeth!

HORSE
1966, '78, '90, 2002, '14
Being happy is your "mane" goal. And while you're smart and hardworking, your teacher may ride you for talking too much.

OX
1973, '85, '97, 2009, '21
You're smart, patient, and as strong as an ... well, you know what. Though you're a leader, you never brag.

SHEEP
1967, '79, '91, 2003, '15
Gentle as a lamb, you're also artistic, compassionate, and wise. You're often shy.

TIGER
1974, '86, '98, 2010
You may be a nice person, but no one should ever enter your room without asking—you might attack!

MONKEY
1968, '80, '92, 2004, '16
No "monkey see, monkey do" for you. You're a clever problem-solver with an excellent memory.

RABBIT
1975, '87, '99, 2011
Your ambition and talent make you jump at opportunity. You also keep your ears open for gossip.

ROOSTER
1969, '81, '93, 2005, '17
You crow about your adventures, but inside you're really shy. You're thoughtful, capable, brave, and talented.

DRAGON
1976, '88, 2000, '12
You're on fire! Health, energy, honesty, and bravery make you a living legend.

DOG
1970, '82, '94, 2006, '18
Often the leader of the pack, you're loyal and honest. You can also keep a secret.

SNAKE
1977, '89, 2001, '13
You may not speak often, but you're very smart. You always seem to have a stash of cash.

PIG
1971, '83, '95, 2007, '19
Even though you're courageous, honest, and kind, you never hog all the attention.

3 Fun Kits for Mom & Dad

On Mother's Day or Father's Day, give the gift of family time together. Make these cool kits as presents and have tons of family fun!

1 Herb Garden

YOU WILL NEED: SMALL HERB PLANTS SUCH AS THYME, BASIL, AND ROSEMARY • SANDWICH BAG FULL OF SMALL STONES • POTTING SOIL • TROWEL OR LARGE SPOON • HOMEMADE LABELS FOR HERBS (WE MADE THEM BY GLUING CRAFT FOAM ONTO WOODEN SKEWERS) • GARDENING GLOVES • LARGE FLOWERPOT TO DISPLAY ALL THE ITEMS

HOW TO GROW YOUR HERB GARDEN: Cover the bottom of the flowerpot with stones for drainage. Fill the pot partway with soil. Carefully remove the plants from their containers and position them in the larger pot, leaving some space between each plant. Fill in soil around the plants. Water until the soil is damp, then place the flowerpot in a sunny spot. Water the herbs when the soil dries out—about once a week. Then watch your garden grow.

2 Car Wash

YOU WILL NEED: PAPER TOWELS • SPONGE • OLD TOWELS TO USE AS RAGS • INGREDIENTS FOR HOMEMADE CAR SHAMPOO (DISHWASHING LIQUID, POWDERED LAUNDRY DETERGENT, BELOW) • SPRAY BOTTLE OF WINDOW CLEANER • HOMEMADE CAR AIR FRESHENER (BELOW) • NICE BUCKET TO DISPLAY ALL THE ITEMS

HOW TO MAKE CAR SHAMPOO: In a bucket, mix one-third cup (80 mL) of dishwashing liquid, one-quarter cup (50 g) of powdered laundry detergent, and one gallon (3.8 L) of water.

HOW TO MAKE AN AIR FRESHENER Trace the shape of a cookie cutter onto craft foam, then cut out the shape. With an adult's permission, spray the foam with perfume or cologne several times. Let dry. Punch a hole at the top and tie a string through the hole. Then hang the air freshener from the car's rearview mirror.

3 Movie Night

ADMIT ONE
93274
Movie Night!

Fill a basket with DVDs, bags of microwave popcorn, candy, and a blanket for curling up on the couch. Include homemade movie tickets for each member of your family.

12 Ways to Say Friend

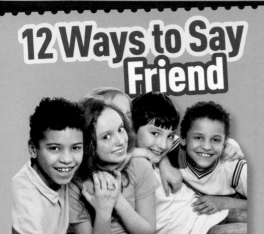

1. **AFRIKAANS:** **vriend** (male) / **vriendin** (female)
2. **CANTONESE:** **pung yau**
3. **GERMAN:** **Freund** (male) / **Freundin** (female)
4. **HAWAIIAN:** **hoaloha**
5. **HINDI:** **dost**
6. **ICELANDIC:** **vinur** (male) / **vinkona** (female)
7. **MALAY:** **kawan**
8. **SPANISH:** **amigo** (male) / **amiga** (female)
9. **SWAHILI:** **rafiki**
10. **TAGALOG** (Filipino): **kaibigan**
11. **AKUAPIM TWI** (Ghana): **adamfo**
12. **WELSH:** **ffrind**

LANGUAGES IN PERIL

TODAY, there are more than 7,000 languages spoken on Earth. But by 2100, more than half of those may disappear. In fact, experts say one language dies every two weeks, due to the increasing dominance of larger languages, such as English, Spanish, and Mandarin. So what can be done to keep dialects from disappearing? Efforts like National Geographic's Enduring Voices Project are now tracking down and documenting the world's most threatened indigenous languages, such as Tofa, spoken only by people in Siberia, and Magati Ke, from Aboriginal Australia. The hope is to preserve these languages— and the cultures they belong to.

10 LEADING LANGUAGES

Approximate population of first-language speakers (in millions)

1. Chinese*	1,197
2. Spanish	414
3. English	335
4. Hindi	260
5. Arabic	237
6. Portuguese	203
7. Bengali	193
8. Russian	167
9. Japanese	122
10. Javanese	83

Some languages have only a few hundred speakers, while Chinese has nearly one billion two hundred million native speakers worldwide. That's about triple the next largest group of language speakers. Colonial expansion, trade, and migration account for the spread of the other most widely spoken languages. With growing use of the Internet, English is becoming the language of the technology age.

*Includes all forms of the language.

By the Numbers

HIT THE BOOKS

Got a minute?

If you spend a little time reading each day, by the time you reach high school you'll be a reading wizard. Check out how many times you can read *Harry Potter and the Sorcerer's Stone* if you read a little—or a lot—every day.

IF YOU READ **1 HOUR** EVERY DAY

EVERY YEAR, A SIXTH GRADER WILL HAVE READ: **3,285,000** words

THAT'S THE SAME AS READING *HARRY POTTER AND THE SORCERER'S STONE:* **42** times

FROM KINDERGARTEN THROUGH HIGH SCHOOL GRADUATION, YOU'LL HAVE READ FOR NEARLY: **198** days

IF YOU READ **20 MINUTES** EVERY DAY

EVERY YEAR, A SIXTH GRADER WILL HAVE READ: **1,095,000** words

THAT'S THE SAME AS READING *HARRY POTTER AND THE SORCERER'S STONE:* **14** times

FROM KINDERGARTEN THROUGH HIGH SCHOOL GRADUATION, YOU'LL HAVE READ FOR NEARLY: **66** days

IF YOU READ **5 MINUTES** EVERY DAY

EVERY YEAR, A SIXTH GRADER WILL HAVE READ: **273,750** words

THAT'S THE SAME AS READING *HARRY POTTER AND THE SORCERER'S STONE:* **3.5** times

FROM KINDERGARTEN THROUGH HIGH SCHOOL GRADUATION, YOU'LL HAVE READ FOR NEARLY: **14** days

MONSTER MYTHS

5 TERRIFYING TALES DEBUNKED

BUSTED!

Are monsters more than just the stuff of freaky films? Some people think so. They believe that big, bad beasts—hairy giants, pterodactyl-like brutes, and more—lurk just out of sight in areas around the world. Luckily, scientists have explanations that bust these tales. Check out five monster myths that have been defanged.

The Nepali name for Mount Everest in the Himalaya means "Forehead of the Sky."

MYTH 1

THE **LOVELAND FROG,** A BIG AMPHIBIOUS CREATURE, PROWLS AN OHIO, U.S.A., TOWN.

HOW IT MAY HAVE STARTED
This slimy, froglike beast is said to stand four feet (1.2 m) tall and walk on two legs. In 1972 a police officer claimed he caught sight of it on a roadside while driving through Loveland, Ohio, U.S.A., at night. When another officer also reported seeing the freaky frog, the rumor took off.

WHY IT'S NOT TRUE
An investigation by local police found no evidence of the creature. Later, one of the police officers stated that he didn't actually believe that he had seen a monster, and that people had exaggerated his story. It's probable that the Loveland Frog was actually an escaped pet monitor lizard—some types can stretch 10 feet (3 m).

MYTH 2

SHAGGY-HAIRED BEASTS CALLED **YETIS** ROAM ASIA'S PEAKS.

HOW IT MAY HAVE STARTED
Yetis are allegedly hairy ogres that look like a human-bear hybrid with jagged fangs. The legend of the yeti probably originated in Tibet, a territory nestled near Asia's Himalaya mountain range. Sherpas, a once nomadic people from the area, may have spread the myth during their travels in the 16th century. People still claim to see yetis today.

WHY IT'S NOT TRUE
In 2014 scientists did DNA tests on strands of hair found where yetis were supposedly spotted. Results showed that the hairs came not from an unknown beast, but from a rare subspecies of brown bear that lives in the area. It's likely that those who claimed to have seen a yeti really just saw this bear.

MYTH 3

THE DOBHAR-CHÚ—PART DOG, PART OTTER, ALL MONSTER— LURKS IN IRELAND.

HOW IT MAY HAVE STARTED

An otter-dog mix, the Dobhar-chú (Gaelic for "water hound") supposedly inhabits Ireland's lakes. It's known for unleashing eerie whistles and having an appetite for humans. No one knows where the legend of this beast came from, but it dates back to at least the 1700s, when a carved image of the creature appeared on the tombstone of one of its alleged victims.

WHY IT'S NOT TRUE

It's more likely that Dobhar-chú is a Eurasian otter. The animal is found in Ireland's rivers and lakes and often whistles to communicate.

> Lough Corrib, a huge lake in western Ireland, contains more than 360 islands.

MYTH 4

> The wetlands of Lake Bangweulu in Zambia are home to roughly 390 species of birds.

THE KONGAMATO, A FLYING REPTILIAN MONSTER, ATTACKS BOATERS IN AFRICA.

HOW IT MAY HAVE STARTED

Reportedly seen soaring over southern and central African swamps, the Kongamato is said to have leathery wings, sharp teeth, and a bad habit of swooping down to smash boats that paddle into its territory. Some say the creature is a pterodactyl—a prehistoric flying reptile. Although the myth has circulated for about a century, its origins are unknown.

WHY IT'S NOT TRUE

Scientists know the Kongamato couldn't be a long-extinct pterodactyl. It's more likely a swamp-dwelling hammerhead bat, the largest bat in Africa. It could also be a big type of stingray that tips boats as it leaps from the water.

MYTH 5

IN THE AMERICAS, THE BEASTLY CHUPACABRA DRINKS THE BLOOD OF FARM ANIMALS.

HOW IT MAY HAVE STARTED

When several goats and chickens in areas of Puerto Rico turned up dead with their blood seemingly drained in the 1990s, rumors spread that the culprit was a vampire-like monster with fangs, a forked tongue, and quills running down its back. A rash of similar deaths that occurred a few years later in Texas were also blamed on the Chupacabra (which roughly translates to "goat sucker" in Spanish).

WHY IT'S NOT TRUE

Investigators looking into the deaths of chickens in Texas found no real evidence that the animals' blood had been drained, making the possibility of a vampire-like slayer way less likely. And sightings of the Chupacabra have usually turned out to be sickly coyotes or dogs suffering from mange, a skin condition that gives them a sinister appearance.

World Religions

Around the world, religion takes many forms. Some belief systems, such as Christianity, Islam, and Judaism, are monotheistic, meaning that followers believe in just one supreme being. Others, like Hinduism, Shintoism, and most native belief systems, are polytheistic, meaning that many of their followers believe in multiple gods.

All of the major religions have their origins in Asia, but they have spread around the world. Christianity, with the largest number of followers, has three divisions—Roman Catholic, Eastern Orthodox, and Protestant. Islam, with about one-fifth of all believers, has two main divisions—Sunni and Shiite. Hinduism and Buddhism account for almost another one-fifth of believers. Judaism, dating back some 4,000 years, has more than 13 million followers, less than one percent of all believers.

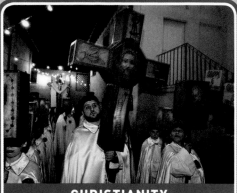

CHRISTIANITY

Based on the teachings of Jesus Christ, a Jew born some 2,000 years ago in the area of modern-day Israel, Christianity has spread worldwide and actively seeks converts. Followers in Switzerland (above) participate in an Easter season procession with lanterns and crosses.

BUDDHISM

Founded about 2,400 years ago in northern India by the Hindu prince Gautama Buddha, Buddhism spread throughout East and Southeast Asia. Buddhist temples have statues, such as the Mihintale Buddha (above) in Sri Lanka.

HINDUISM

Dating back more than 4,000 years, Hinduism is practiced mainly in India. Hindus follow sacred texts known as the Vedas and believe in reincarnation. During the festival of Navratri, which honors the goddess Durga, the Garba dance is performed (above).

📷 CLOSE-UP

Technology Meets Tradition

It has been 1,200 years since the bishop of Rome became known as the pope. Pope Francis became the head of the Roman Catholic Church in 2013 and has embraced technology as a way to reach Catholics around the globe. He's the first pope to pose for a selfie and has more than 25 million Twitter followers.

ISLAM

Muslims believe that the Koran, Islam's sacred book, records the words of Allah (God) as revealed to the Prophet Muhammad beginning around A.D. 610. Believers (above) circle the Kaaba in the Haram Mosque in Mecca, Saudi Arabia, the spiritual center of the faith.

JUDAISM

The traditions, laws, and beliefs of Judaism date back to Abraham (the Patriarch) and the Torah (the first five books of the Old Testament). Followers pray before the Western Wall (above), which stands below Islam's Dome of the Rock in Jerusalem.

QUIZ WHIZ

How vast is your knowledge about the world around you? Quiz yourself!

Write your answers on a piece of paper. Then check them below.

1 **True or false?** According to Chinese astrology, 2019 is the Year of the Rat.

2 **Whistling or saying the word "pig" on a ship is supposed to bring _____?**
a. good weather
b. bad weather
c. abundant fish
d. mermaids

3 **What is the Swahili word for friend?**
a. vriend
b. adamfo
c. rafiki
d. jambo

4 **In the summer, parts of Sweden have 24 hours of _____.**

5 **According to myth, a flying reptilian monster named the Kongamato attacks _____.**
a. boaters in Africa
b. hikers in the Himalaya
c. farm animals in Texas
d. swimmers in Ireland

Not **STUMPED** yet? Check out the *NATIONAL GEOGRAPHIC KIDS QUIZ WHIZ* collection for more crazy **CULTURE** questions!

ANSWERS:
1. False. 2019 is the Year of the Pig; 2. b; 3. c; 4. daylight; 5. a

Explore a New Culture

STAMPS OF
SOUTH AFRICA

You're a student, but you're also a citizen of the world. Writing a report on a foreign nation or your own country is a great way to better understand and appreciate how different people live. Pick the country of your ancestors, one that's been in the news, or one that you'd like to visit someday.

CURRENCY
AND COINS OF
SOUTH AFRICA

Passport to Success

A country report follows the format of an expository essay because you're "exposing" information about the country you choose.

THE FLAG OF
SOUTH AFRICA

Simple Steps

1. **RESEARCH** Gathering information is the most important step in writing a good country report. Look to Internet sources, encyclopedias, books, magazine and newspaper articles, and other sources to find important and interesting details about your subject.

2. **ORGANIZE YOUR NOTES** Put the information you gathered into a rough outline. For example, sort everything you found about the country's system of government, climate, etc.

3. **WRITE IT UP** Follow the basic structure of good writing: introduction, body, and conclusion. Remember that each paragraph should have a topic sentence that is then supported by facts and details. Incorporate the information from your notes, but make sure it's in your own words. And make your writing flow with good transitions and descriptive language.

4. **ADD VISUALS** Include maps, diagrams, photos, and other visual aids.

5. **PROOFREAD AND REVISE** Correct any mistakes, and polish your language. Do your best!

6. **CITE YOUR SOURCES** Be sure to keep a record of your sources.

Space and Earth

NASA astronaut Karen Nyberg conducts an eye health exam on herself in the Destiny laboratory of the Earth-orbiting International Space Station.

THE UNIVERSE BEGAN WITH A BIG BANG

Clear your mind for a minute and try to imagine this: All the things you see in the universe today—all the stars, galaxies, and planets—are not yet out there. Everything that now exists is concentrated in a single, incredibly hot, dense state that scientists call a singularity. Then, suddenly, the basic elements that make up the universe flash into existence. Scientists say that actually happened about 13.8 billion years ago, in the moment we call the big bang.

For centuries scientists, religious scholars, poets, and philosophers have wondered how the universe came to be. Was it always there? Will it always be the same, or will it change? If it had a beginning, will it someday end, or will it go on forever?

These are huge questions. But today, because of recent observations of space and what it's made of, we think we may have some of the answers. Everything we can see or detect around us in the universe began with the big bang. We know the big bang created not only matter but also space itself. And scientists think that in the very distant future, stars will run out of fuel and burn out. Once again the universe will become dark.

POWERFUL PARTICLE

It's just one tiny particle, but without it the world as we know it would not exist. That's what scientists are saying after the recent discovery of the Higgs boson particle, a subatomic speck related to the Higgs field, which is thought to give mass to everything around us. Without the Higgs boson, all the atoms created in the big bang would have zipped around the cosmos too quickly to collect into stars and planets. So you can think of it as a building block of the universe—and of us!

EARLY LIFE ON EARTH

About 3.5 billion years ago
Earth was covered by one gigantic reddish ocean. The color came from hydrocarbons.

The first life-forms on Earth were Archaea that could live without oxygen. They released large amounts of methane gas into an atmosphere that would have been poisonous to us.

About 3 billion years ago
erupting volcanoes linked together to form larger landmasses. And a new form of life appeared—cyanobacteria, the first living things that used energy from the sun.

Some 2 billion years ago
the cyanobacteria algae filled the air with oxygen, killing off the methane-producing Archaea. Colored pools of greenish brown plant life floated on the oceans. The oxygen revolution that would someday make human life possible was now under way.

About 530 million years ago
the Cambrian explosion occurred. It's called an explosion because it's the time when most major animal groups first appeared in our fossil records. Back then, Earth was made up of swamps, seas, a few active volcanoes, and oceans teeming with strange life.

More than 450 million years ago
life began moving from the oceans onto dry land. About 200 million years later dinosaurs began to appear. They would dominate life on Earth for more than 150 million years.

1 ONE OF THE BIGGEST **TELESCOPE MIRRORS** IS 330 INCHES (8.4 M) ACROSS. TO MAKE THE MIRROR, A REFLECTIVE METAL SURFACE WAS LAID ON A GIANT, **SOLID-GLASS BASE.**

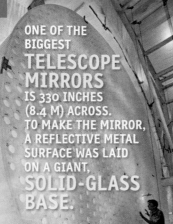

2 **CELL PHONES AND CAMERAS** can be clamped to the eyepiece of a telescope to take **PHOTOS OF SPACE.**

3 ALMA, THE WORLD'S BIGGEST RADIO TELESCOPE OBSERVATORY, HAS 66 MOVABLE RADIO ANTENNAS.

4 DIFFERENT TELESCOPES CAN "SEE" DIFFERENT TYPES OF ENERGY FROM SPACE: RADIO WAVES, VISIBLE LIGHT, X-RAYS, GAMMA RAYS, AND OTHER HIGH-ENERGY PARTICLES.

(19) FACTS ABOUT

5 Through **GALILEO'S TELESCOPES** people saw that stars and planets move in patterns, which helped them figure out that **EARTH ORBITS THE SUN,** rather than the other way around.

6 A TELESCOPE CALLED NUSTAR ALLOWS ASTRONOMERS TO SEE THE X-RAY-LACED WINDS BLASTING OUT OF SUPERMASSIVE BLACK HOLES. THE WINDS COME OUT IN THE SHAPE OF A SPHERE.

7 WHEN THE GIANT **MAGELLAN TELESCOPE** IS BUILT in 2021, IT WILL BE ABLE TO VIEW OBJECTS SUCH AS THESE "PILLARS OF CREATION" in the Eagle Nebula some 7,000 light-years away.

8 An inventor created a telescope that **CONVERTS LIGHT INTO SOUND,** giving viewers a multisensory experience.

9 THE HUBBLE TELESCOPE HAS TRAVELED MORE THAN **THREE BILLION MILES** (4.8 BILLION KM).

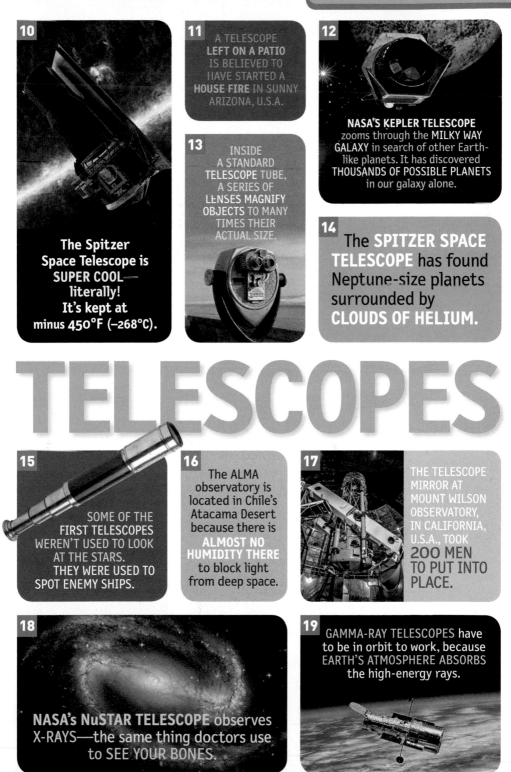

10 The Spitzer Space Telescope is SUPER COOL— literally! It's kept at minus 450°F (–268°C).

11 A TELESCOPE LEFT ON A PATIO IS BELIEVED TO HAVE STARTED A HOUSE FIRE IN SUNNY ARIZONA, U.S.A.

12 NASA'S KEPLER TELESCOPE zooms through the MILKY WAY GALAXY in search of other Earth-like planets. It has discovered THOUSANDS OF POSSIBLE PLANETS in our galaxy alone.

13 INSIDE A STANDARD TELESCOPE TUBE, A SERIES OF LENSES MAGNIFY OBJECTS TO MANY TIMES THEIR ACTUAL SIZE.

14 The SPITZER SPACE TELESCOPE has found Neptune-size planets surrounded by CLOUDS OF HELIUM.

TELESCOPES

15 SOME OF THE FIRST TELESCOPES WEREN'T USED TO LOOK AT THE STARS. THEY WERE USED TO SPOT ENEMY SHIPS.

16 The ALMA observatory is located in Chile's Atacama Desert because there is ALMOST NO HUMIDITY THERE to block light from deep space.

17 THE TELESCOPE MIRROR AT MOUNT WILSON OBSERVATORY, IN CALIFORNIA, U.S.A., TOOK 200 MEN TO PUT INTO PLACE.

18 NASA's NuSTAR TELESCOPE observes X-RAYS—the same thing doctors use to SEE YOUR BONES.

19 GAMMA-RAY TELESCOPES have to be in orbit to work, because EARTH'S ATMOSPHERE ABSORBS the high-energy rays.

PLANETS

MERCURY

VENUS

EARTH

MARS

CERES

JUPITER

SUN

MERCURY

Average distance from the sun:
35,980,000 miles (57,900,000 km)
Position from the sun in orbit: 1st
Equatorial diameter: 3,030 miles (4,878 km)
Length of day: 59 Earth days
Length of year: 88 Earth days
Surface temperatures: -300°F (-184°C)
to 800°F (427°C)
Known moons: 0
Fun fact: The planet Mercury is made
mostly of metals.

VENUS

Average distance from the sun:
67,230,000 miles (108,200,000 km)
Position from the sun in orbit: 2nd
Equatorial diameter: 7,520 miles (12,100 km)
Length of day: 243 Earth days
Length of year: 224.7 Earth days
Average surface temperature: 864°F (462°C)
Known moons: 0
Fun fact: Venus is sometimes known as
Earth's "twin sister" because the planets
are similar in size and mass.

EARTH

Average distance from the sun:
93,000,000 miles (149,600,000 km)
Position from the sun in orbit: 3rd
Equatorial diameter: 7,900 miles (12,750 km)
Length of day: 24 hours
Length of year: 365 days
Surface temperatures: -126°F (-88°C)
to 136°F (58°C)
Known moons: 1
Fun fact: Our planet, Earth, is about
4.55 billion years old.

MARS

Average distance from the sun:
141,633,000 miles (227,936,000 km)
Position from the sun in orbit: 4th
Equatorial diameter: 4,221 miles (6,794 km)
Length of day: 25 Earth hours
Length of year: 1.9 Earth years
Surface temperatures: -270°F (-168°C)
to 80°F (27°C)
Known moons: 2
Fun fact: There were once superhot and
explosive volcanoes on Mars.

This artwork shows the eight planets and five dwarf planets in our solar system. The relative sizes and positions of the planets are shown but not the relative distances between them.

SATURN

URANUS

NEPTUNE

PLUTO

HAUMEA

MAKEMAKE

ERIS

JUPITER
Average distance from the sun:
  483,682,000 miles (778,412,000 km)
Position from the sun in orbit: 6th
Equatorial diameter: 88,840 miles (142,980 km)
Length of day: 9.9 Earth hours
Length of year: 11.9 Earth years
Average surface temperature: -235°F (-148°C)
Known moons: 69*
Fun fact: Jupiter's moon Europa has a deep, ice-covered ocean.

SATURN
Average distance from the sun:
  890,800,000 miles (1,433,500,000 km)
Position from the sun in orbit: 7th
Equatorial diameter: 74,900 miles (120,540 km)
Length of day: 10.7 Earth hours
Length of year: 29.5 Earth years
Average surface temperature: -218°F (-139°C)
Known moons: 62*
Fun fact: Saturn's outermost ring is made up of fine dust particles and rocks the size of soccer balls.

URANUS
Average distance from the sun:
  1,784,000,000 miles (2,870,970,000 km)
Position from the sun in orbit: 8th
Equatorial diameter: 31,760 miles (51,120 km)
Length of day: 17.2 Earth hours
Length of year: 84 Earth years
Average surface temperature: -323°F (-197°C)
Known moons: 27
Fun fact: Uranus receives less than 0.3 percent of the sun's energy that Earth gets.

NEPTUNE
Average distance from the sun:
  2,795,000,000 miles (4,498,250,000 km)
Position from the sun in orbit: 9th
Equatorial diameter: 30,775 miles (49,528 km)
Length of day: 16 Earth hours
Length of year: 164.8 Earth years
Average surface temperature: -353°F (-214°C)
Known moons: 14*
Fun fact: Neptune has storms with winds whipping around at 1,600 miles an hour (402 km/h).

*Includes provisional moons, which await confirmation and naming from the International Astronomical Union.

For information about dwarf planets—Ceres, Pluto, Haumea, Makemake, and Eris—see p. 148.

DWARF PLANETS

Haumea

Eris

Pluto

Thanks to advanced technology, astronomers have been spotting many never-before-seen celestial bodies with their telescopes. One new discovery? A population of icy objects orbiting the sun beyond Pluto. The largest, like Pluto itself, are classified as dwarf planets. Smaller than the moon but still massive enough to pull themselves into a ball, dwarf planets nevertheless lack the gravitational "oomph" to clear their neighborhood of other sizable objects. So, while larger, more massive planets pretty much have their orbits to themselves, dwarf planets orbit the sun in swarms that include other dwarf planets as well as smaller chunks of rock or ice.

So far, astronomers have identified five dwarf planets: Ceres, Pluto, Haumea, Makemake, and Eris. There is also a newly discovered dwarf planet beyond Neptune that will need additional study before it is named. Astronomers are observing hundreds of newly found objects in the frigid outer solar system. As time and technology advance, the family of known dwarf planets will surely continue to grow.

CERES
Position from the sun in orbit: 5th
Length of day: 9.1 Earth hours
Length of year: 4.6 Earth years
Known moons: 0

PLUTO
Position from the sun in orbit: 10th
Length of day: 6.4 Earth days
Length of year: 248 Earth years
Known moons: 5

HAUMEA
Position from the sun in orbit: 11th
Length of day: 3.9 Earth hours
Length of year: 282 Earth years
Known moons: 2

MAKEMAKE
Position from the sun in orbit: 12th
Length of day: 22.5 Earth hours
Length of year: 305 Earth years
Known moons: 1*

ERIS
Position from the sun in orbit: 13th
Length of day: 25.9 Earth hours
Length of year: 561 Earth years
Known moons: 1

*Includes provisional moons, which await confirmation and naming from the International Astronomical Union.

DESTINATION SPACE

BLACK HOLE

This is your most dangerous mission yet. You've traveled to the galaxy M82 to get a close-up view of one of the strangest and deadliest things in the universe: a black hole. This one is called M82 X-1.

Most black holes are born when a giant star runs out of nuclear fuel and implodes, causing an explosion. After that, the black hole's gravity is so strong that it pulls in anything that gets too close. Nothing can escape a black hole's intense gravity—not even light, the fastest thing in the universe.

You want to get a better look, so you put on a special space suit and exit your spacecraft. When you're 943 miles (1,518 km) away from the black hole, you notice something strange. Your legs are becoming longer and skinnier. Oh no! You're being "spaghettified." The black hole's gravity is stretching your body like a long noodle. You fire up your suit's rockets and zoom away from the black hole before it can tear you apart and swallow you up. You don't want to spend your life looking like spaghetti.

Scientists now think that almost every galaxy has a big black hole in its center. Our galaxy, the Milky Way, has a black hole called Sagittarius A*. (A* is scientist code for "A-star.") At 26,000 light-years from Earth, it's much too far away to be dangerous to humans.

Destination
The black hole M82 X-1

Location
The galaxy M82

Distance
12 million light-years from Earth (a light-year is the distance light travels in one year)

Time to reach
325 billion years

Weather
Superheated gas clouds and bright x-rays

BLACK HOLE TIME TRAVEL

The intense gravity near a black hole makes time behave in strange ways. If an astronaut left his spacecraft to explore a black hole up close, he'd see the hands on his watch ticking at normal speed. But if anyone back on the spacecraft could observe the spacewalker's watch from far away, they'd see its hands slow down as the spacewalker got closer to the black hole. When the spacewalker returned to the spaceship after an hour, years would have passed for those aboard the spacecraft.

Someday humans may be able to use black holes to travel forward in time. An astronaut could take a short trip near a black hole and return to Earth after years, decades, or even centuries had passed there. A black hole time machine could allow a time traveler to find out what the world will be like in the future.

Sky Calendar 2019

Jupiter

Partial solar eclipse

Leonid meteor shower

January 3–4 Quadrantids Meteor Shower Peak. Featuring up to 40 meteors an hour, it is the first meteor shower of every new year.

January 21 Total Lunar Eclipse. Visible throughout most of North America, South America, far western Europe and Africa, and the eastern Pacific Ocean.

January 21 Supermoon, Full Moon. The moon will be full and at a close approach to Earth, likely appearing bigger and brighter than usual. This is one of three supermoons in 2019. The others are February 19 and March 21.

February 27 Mercury at Greatest Eastern Elongation. Visible low in the western sky just after sunset, Mercury will be at its highest point above the horizon.

May 6–7 Eta Aquarids Meteor Shower Peak. View about 30 to 60 meteors an hour.

July 9 Saturn at Opposition. Your best chance to view Saturn in 2019. The planet will appear bright in the sky and be visible throughout the night.

August 12–13 Perseid Meteor Shower Peak. One of the best! Up to 60 meteors an hour. Best viewing is in the direction of the constellation Perseus.

October 21–22 Orionid Meteor Shower Peak. View up to 20 meteors an hour. Look toward the constellation Orion for the best show.

November 11 Transit of Mercury Across the Sun. As Mercury moves directly between the sun and Earth, Mercury can be seen as a dark disk moving across the sun. Be sure to use telescopes and approved solar filters to safely observe the event. This rare occurrence won't happen again until 2039! Visible in South and Central America, parts of North America, Europe, Africa, and the Middle East.

November 17–18 Leonid Meteor Shower Peak. View up to 15 meteors an hour.

November 24 Conjunction of Venus and Jupiter. Look for these two bright planets close together in the western sky just after sunset.

December 13–14 Geminid Meteor Shower Peak. A spectacular show! Up to 120 multicolored meteors an hour.

Various dates throughout 2019 View the International Space Station. Visit spotthestation.nasa.gov to find out when the ISS will be flying over your neighborhood.

Dates may vary slightly depending on your location. Check with a local planetarium for the best viewing time in your area.

Bet you didn't know

6 stellar facts about stars

1 Our galaxy, known as the **Milky Way**, contains an estimated **200 to 400 billion** stars.

2 The **fastest spinning** star ever discovered, VFTS 102, rotates at a **million miles** an hour (1.6 million km/h).

3 A "**zombie star**" is a surviving fragment of a **star** that **exploded**.

4 **Scientists** have created pieces of **white dwarf stars** in a **lab**.

5 **Harry Potter** characters **Sirius Black** and **Bellatrix Lestrange** were named after **stars**.

6 The star **VY Canis Majoris** is so **large** a **plane** would **take** more than a thousand years to orbit it.

ROCK STARS

The world is full of rocks—some big, some small, some formed deep within the Earth, and some formed at the surface. While they may look similar, not all rocks are created equal. Look closely, and you'll see differences between every boulder, stone, and pebble. Here's more about the three top varieties of rocks.

Igneous

Named for the Greek word meaning "from fire," igneous rocks form when hot, molten liquid called magma cools. Pools of magma form deep underground and slowly work their way to the Earth's surface. If they make it all the way, the liquid rock erupts and is called lava. As the layers of lava build up, they form a mountain called a volcano. Typical igneous rocks include obsidian, basalt, and pumice, which is so chock-full of gas bubbles that it actually floats in water.

OBSIDIAN   **PUMICE**

Metamorphic

Metamorphic rocks are the masters of change! These rocks were once igneous or sedimentary, but thanks to intense heat and pressure deep within the Earth, they have undergone a total transformation from their original form. These rocks never truly melt; instead, the heat twists and bends them until their shapes substantially change. Metamorphic rocks include slate as well as marble, which is used for buildings, monuments, and sculptures.

MARBLE   **SLATE**

Sedimentary

When wind, water, and ice constantly wear away and weather rocks, smaller pieces called sediment are left behind. These are sedimentary rocks, also known as gravel, sand, silt, and clay. As water flows downhill, it carries the sedimentary grains into lakes and oceans, where they get deposited. As the loose sediment piles up, the grains eventually get compacted or cemented back together again. The result is new sedimentary rock. Sandstone, gypsum, limestone, and shale are sedimentary rocks that have formed this way.

SANDSTONE   **GYPSUM**

A LOOK INSIDE

The **CRUST** includes tectonic plates, landmasses, and the ocean. Its thickness varies from 3 to 62 miles (5 to 100 km).

The **MANTLE** is about 1,800 miles (2,897 km) of hot, thick, solid rock.

The **OUTER CORE** is liquid molten lava made mostly of iron and nickel.

The **INNER CORE** is a solid center made mostly of iron and nickel.

The distance from Earth's surface to its center is 3,963 miles (6,378 km) at the Equator. There are four layers: a thin, rigid crust; the rocky mantle; the outer core, which is a layer of molten iron; and finally the inner core, which is believed to be solid iron.

What if you could dig to the other side of Earth?

Got a magma-proof suit and a magical drill that can cut through any surface? Then you're ready to dig some 8,000 miles (12,875 km) to Earth's other side. First you'd need to drill about 25 miles (40 km) through the planet's ultra-tough crust to its mantle. The heat and pressure at the mantle are intense enough to turn carbon into diamonds—and to, um, crush you. If you were able to survive, you'd still have to bore 1,800 more miles (2,897 km) to hit Earth's Mars-size core that can reach 11,000°F (6093°C). Now just repeat the journey in the opposite order to resurface on the planet's other side. But exit your tunnel quickly. A hole dug through Earth would quickly close as surrounding rock filled in the empty space. The closing of the tunnel might cause small earthquakes, and your path home would definitely be blocked. Happy digging!

What Is a Volcano?

IT'S SERIOUSLY HOT 4,000 MILES (6,437 KM) DOWN AT THE CENTER OF THE EARTH.
The temperature there ranges from 9032°F to 12,632°F (5000°C to 7000°C). That kind of heat melts rock into liquid, or molten, form. Sometimes molten rock gushes up and bursts through an opening in Earth's surface—a volcano—in a fiery flow of lava. Sometimes a volcano takes the shape of a mountain. Sometimes it even forms underwater.

MAGMA AND LAVA
Magma is molten rock before it reaches Earth's surface. Lava is molten rock after it reaches the surface. When lava erupts from a volcano, it can be liquid, semiliquid, or solid rock, depending on its temperature. The outer layer of rock can cool within minutes, but thick lava can take years to cool completely.

BUBBLING AND BOILING
Mud pots like these bubble and steam at the base of some volcanic mountains.

The Karymsky volcano in Russia is the most active volcano in its region. It's been actively erupting for more than 500 years. The volcano produces a fine, powdered rock called ash, which looks like black smoke.

TRY THIS!

LAVA LAMP

To make a groovy lava lamp, first you'll need a tall jar.

1 Pour about 6 inches (15 cm) of water into the jar.

2 Add 2/3 cup (158 mL) of vegetable oil.

3 Wait until the oil rises to the top. Then add two drops of red food coloring to the oil.

4 To make your oily "lava" flow, shake some salt into the jar. Continue adding salt for as long as you want to make the bubbles sink and float in the water. Place the jar in front of a lamp for best results.

WHAT JUST HAPPENED?

Your lava lamp doesn't contain real lava—it just looks like it. Here's how it works. The oil floats on the water because it is less dense. The salt is denser, so it sinks to the bottom, pulling some oil along with it. As the salt dissolves, the oil floats back to the top. Now you have a cool lava flow that won't burn your hands!

Great Heights

Mauna Loa volcano in Hawaii, U.S.A.

30,080 feet (9,170 m) is the height of Mauna Loa volcano, which makes up part of Hawaii. It begins below the ocean.

19,340 feet (5,895 m) is the height of Kilimanjaro, the tallest mountain in Africa. It is also a volcano.

19 miles (30 km) is the height reached by the ash cloud over the volcano Hekla, in Iceland, in a 1947 eruption.

1,640 feet (500 m) is the height to which some lava fountains rose in the eruption of Askja, a volcano in Iceland.

THE WORLD'S LARGEST SALT FLAT CREATES AN OUT-OF-THIS-WORLD ILLUSION.

FAKE LAKE

FLAMINGOS SEARCH FOR FOOD IN THE SALAR DE UYUNI.

Seeing someone who appears to be walking on a cloud might sound like a dream. But this surreal scene exists in the South American country of Bolivia: It is called the Salar de Uyuni (Sah-LAR DAY Uh-YOO-nee). The walking-on-air effect is actually caused by something totally ordinary: A reflection in a rain puddle. And this astounding optical illusion is just one of the things that makes the Salar de Uyuni so bizarre.

HIGH AND DRY

Some 40,000 years ago, towering mountain ranges trapped rainfall and prevented water runoff in a region of the Andes Mountains called the Altiplano. The result? A huge lake loaded with the plateau's natural salt deposits. When climate change reduced the amount of rainfall in the area, the lake dried up, leaving a deep layer of salt behind. Today the salar sprawls about 4,000 square miles (10,360 sq km)—roughly the size of Jamaica.

WHITE OUT

Because of its dry climate, the salar is a hard-crusted wasteland for most of the year. Seasonal rain occasionally submerges the salt under a superwide puddle. At most a couple of inches deep, the water layer is too thin to make any waves, which explains its endless-looking mirror surface.

SIGNS OF LIFE

Although the region can seem empty, the "sea" of salt does have some inhabitants. Creatures like the Andean fox live on stony outcrops—technically the tip-tops of buried

Bolivia has 37 official languages, but Spanish is the most common.

The national animal of Bolivia is the llama.

A CLOSE-UP LOOK AT THE SALT FLAT DURING ITS DRY SEASON

AN ANDEAN FOX, ALSO CALLED A CULPEO, EXPLORES THE SALT FLAT.

Bolivia has two capital cities: La Paz and Sucre.

HOW THE SALT FLAT TOOK SHAPE

1 ABOUT 40,000 YEARS AGO ...

Some 40,000 years ago, a giant prehistoric lake called Lago Minchin covered 4,000 square miles (10,360 sq km) of what is now southwest Bolivia in South America. The lake was completely surrounded by mountains on all sides.

2 ABOUT 25,000 YEARS AGO ...

Over time, the massive lake shrank into smaller, separate lakes. As the lakes continued to shrink, they leached, or drew out, salt deposits from the surrounding mountains.

3 ABOUT 10,000 YEARS AGO ...

The lakes dried out approximately 10,000 years ago, leaving behind the salt deposits. Today, Salar de Uyuni is the world's largest salt flat.

volcanoes. Migrating flamingos also fly in to breed and chow down on the algae that grow in the water.

BURIED TREASURE

With about 10 billion tons (9.1 billion t) of salt lying around, it's no surprise that salt production in the salar is a big business. But the real gold mine lies beneath the surface, where lithium, which is used to make batteries in cell phones, can be found. This untapped resource could be worth a whopping trillion dollars.

But for many visitors, this strange place's most valuable feature will always be the mind-blowing scenery. This seemingly endless mirror is an unforgettable sight—and a reflection of nature's true beauty.

NORTH AMERICA
ATLANTIC OCEAN
SOUTH AMERICA
PACIFIC OCEAN
BOLIVIA

PERU
La Paz
BOLIVIA
Sucre
Salar de Uyuni
PACIFIC OCEAN
PARAGUAY
CHILE
ARGENTINA

157

HOT SPOT

FOUNTAINS OF SUPERHEATED WATER CREATE A WEIRD LANDMARK.

A bizarre blob of steaming fountains bursts with water and color from the barren landscape. It may look like a scene from another planet, but the surreal Fly Geyser unexpectedly gushes up from the Nevada, U.S.A., desert. The mounds stand 12 feet (3.7 m) tall, spouting scalding water 5 feet (1.5 m) higher. At first glance, Fly Geyser seems to be a natural wonder, but it's not quite natural. It's technically not a geyser either. It's an accident.

BIRTH OF FLY GEYSER Although Fly Geyser is powered by nature, it got a kick start from humans. The fountains spew water that continuously flows from a single underground hole, which was drilled by workers about 50 years ago. They had hoped to strike water that was so hot it could power an electrical plant with geothermal energy. The boiling water spurting from the Fly Geyser originates deep below the surface, where it is heated by shallow magma—hot, liquid rock. This wet zone is covered by a hard layer of rock, which traps the hot water. Because it can't escape as steam, the pressurized water's temperature rises far above the normal boiling point. The artificial, drilled hole gives the water a way out, like the opening of a soda bottle.

IT'S ALIVE! Even though the water spewing from Fly Geyser tops 200°F (93°C), the temperature turned out to be too low for a geothermal plant. The hole was plugged, but the hot water eventually forced its way up. Minerals that dissolved in the exiting water gradually built the mounds and surrounding terraces.

Fly Geyser's mounds and terraces aren't only alive with color—they're literally alive. The brilliant reds, yellows, and greens are caused by organisms called thermophiles, or "heat lovers." They are the only life-forms that can survive in such high, deadly temperatures. Different colors of thermophiles live in water at different temperatures, creating Fly Geyser's changing colors.

THEY'RE GONNA BLOW!

Natural geysers are more complicated than Fly Geyser. The world's most famous geyser, Wyoming's Old Faithful in Yellowstone National Park, in the U.S.A., doesn't spray continuously like Fly Geyser. Instead, it erupts about 16 times a day, shooting a steamy torrent of water more than 130 feet (40 m) into the air. What makes Old Faithful and other natural geysers different from Fly Geyser is their complex plumbing systems. The hot water's path to the surface becomes constricted, and the pressure builds. The heated water begins to bubble, and then explodes up and out. "It's like a volcano," explains U.S. Geological Survey researcher Shaul Hurwitz. "Once it starts erupting, all the stored water is released rapidly."

HOT PURSUIT Fly Geyser wasn't hot enough to support a geothermal plant, but it was a necessary step in a hit-or-miss process. Other heat-seeking holes in the area tapped into hotter water and were put to use. That water makes steam that cranks big machines to create electricity. Most power plants use steam, but geothermal ones don't burn coal or gas to make it, so they're much cleaner.

QUIZ WHIZ

Are your space and Earth smarts out of this world? Take this quiz!

Write your answers on a piece of paper. Then check them below.

1 **True or false?** Earth is about 4.55 million years old.

2 **What does Earth's crust contain?**
a. tectonic plates
b. landmasses
c. oceans
d. all of the above

3 **True or false?** You can take photos of space by clamping your cell phone camera to a telescope's eyepiece.

4 **Salar de Uyuni, the world's largest salt flat, is located in which South American country?**
a. Peru
b. Colombia
c. Bolivia
d. Brazil

5 **It can take a few _____ for lava to completely cool.**
a. years
b. hours
c. seconds
d. centuries

Not **STUMPED** yet? Check out the *NATIONAL GEOGRAPHIC KIDS QUIZ WHIZ* collection for more crazy **SPACE AND EARTH** questions!

ANSWERS:
1. False. It is about 4.55 billion years old; 2. d; 3. True; 4. c; 5. a

ACE YOUR SCIENCE FAIR

You can learn a lot about science from books, but to really experience it firsthand, you need to get into the lab and "do" some science. Whether you're entering a science fair or just want to learn more on your own, there are many scientific projects you can do. So put on your goggles and lab coat, and start experimenting.

Most likely, the topic of the project will be up to you. So remember to choose something that is interesting to you.

Bonus!

Take your project one step further. Your school may have an annual science fair, but there are also local, state, regional, and national science fair competitions. Compete with other students for awards, prizes, and scholarships!

THE BASIS OF ALL SCIENTIFIC INVESTIGATION AND DISCOVERY IS THE SCIENTIFIC METHOD. CONDUCT YOUR EXPERIMENT USING THESE STEPS:

Observation/Research—Ask a question or identify a problem.

Hypothesis—Once you've asked a question, do some thinking and come up with some possible answers.

Experimentation—How can you determine if your hypothesis is correct? You test it. You perform an experiment. Make sure the experiment you design will produce an answer to your question.

Analysis—Gather your results, and use a consistent process to carefully measure the results.

Conclusion—Do the results support your hypothesis?

Report Your Findings—Communicate your results in the form of a paper that summarizes your entire experiment.

EXPERIMENT DESIGN
There are three types of experiments you can do.

MODEL KIT—a display, such as an "erupting volcano" model. Simple and to the point.

DEMONSTRATION—shows the scientific principles in action, such as a tornado in a wind tunnel.

INVESTIGATION—the home run of science projects, and just the type of project for science fairs. This kind demonstrates proper scientific experimentation and uses the scientific method to reveal answers to questions.

FUN and GAMES

Find the HIDDEN ANIMALS

ANIMALS OFTEN BLEND IN with their environments for protection. Find the animals listed below in the photographs. Write the letter of the correct photo on a separate sheet of paper. **ANSWERS ON PAGE 338**

1. walking leaf insect
2. flounder
3. walruses
4. island fox
5. cowrie*
6. leaf-tailed gecko

***HINT:** A cowrie is a sea snail.

A

B

C

D

E

F

What in the World?

MAGIC SHOW These photos show close-up views of magic trick props. On a separate sheet of paper, unscramble the letters to identify what's in each picture. Bonus: Use the highlighted letters to solve the puzzle below.

ANSWERS ON PAGE 338

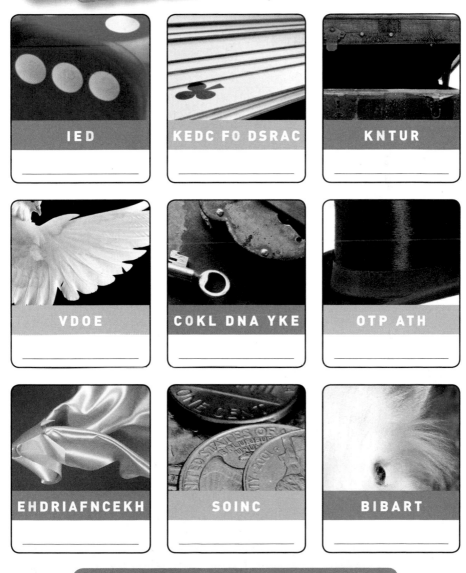

IED

_____

KEDC FO DSRAC

_____

KNTUR

_____

VDOE

_____

COKL DNA YKE

_____

OTP ATH

_____

EHDRIAFNCEKH

_____

SOINC

_____

BIBART

_____

HINT: What do you call an owl that can do magic tricks?

ANSWER: __ __ __ – __ I __ __ __

165

Lucky Break

A leprechaun is down on his luck and can't find the pot of gold. Help him get through the magical forest to his fortune. Then find 10 lucky shamrocks hidden in the maze. HINT: To reach the pot of gold, you can try crossing logs and bridges, climbing ladders and ropes, or taking a boat ride.

ANSWER ON PAGE 338

START

END

FUNNY FILL-IN

HAPPY BIRTHDAY

Ask a friend to give you words to fill in the blanks in this story and write them on a separate sheet of paper. Then read the story out loud and fill in the words for a laugh.

Dear Aunt _____ ,
          name

Thank you so much for my _____ birthday gift. When the mail carrier
                          adjective

delivered the package, it was covered in _____ and was making a(n)
                                         something sticky

_____ sound. I set aside the box to eat my _____-flavored
animal noise ending in -ing   something gross

birthday cake. But suddenly the box started to _____ . "_____ !" we all said as
                                               verb   exclamation

we ran over to it. I _____ opened the box and peeled back some _____
                     adverb ending in -ly   adjective

_____ . It was a chemistry set—but the _____ and _____
noun, plural   liquid   baking ingredient, plural

had gotten mixed up, creating a brand-new creature! It was _____ , covered
                                                          color

in _____ , and had _____ _____ . I love my new pet,
   noun, plural   large number   body part, plural

_____ ! Thank you again for the _____ !
vegetable, plural   noun

Sincerely,

_____
      your name

CHECK OUT THIS BOOK!

NATIONAL GEOGRAPHIC KIDS

Thank you cards

Creative Activities, Cool Tips, Amazing Photos and 30 CARDS to Show Your Gratitude

167

Color Coded

Some items on this Hawaiian beach have mysteriously changed color. Find 12 things that are the wrong color.

ANSWERS ON PAGE 338

FRESH FRUIT FOR SALE

Brain Bogglers

The most amazing thing about your brain is that the more you use it, the stronger it gets. Play these games and puzzles to hit the mental gym and bulk up your brainpower!

ANSWERS ON PAGE 338

Beastly Phrases

A rebus is a riddle made up of letters, pictures, and symbols. Can you solve these four animal-themed rebuses?

[🐝 - EE] + 🟤

🐎 + 🪙

A 🐆 🥫 +T 🪙

its ⚅

🌳 of the 👫

Out of the Box

The answers to these riddles require some extra thought. Examine each word carefully and try to think of other ways it might be used when thinking about the solutions.

When the dog sits on a railroad, his owner's friend receives money. What is the friend doing?

The police officer told the adult to move away from the saw so the kids could play with it. Where are they?

Mr. Martin and Ms. Duncan just finished building the tallest building in the city. Just as everyone cheered this great accomplishment, a dog came along and with one swipe of its tail destroyed the building. How could this happen?

Flip Out

Why don't bats need good eyesight? To find out, flip two letters from the top line to the bottom and three letters from the bottom line to the top without moving any letters to the left or right. It's OK if there are spaces between letters in the same word.

U THR   SORNI

  L   EAA   INCG

THESE PUZZLES ARE DRIVING ME BATTY!

169

What in the World?

DIGGING FOR DIAMONDS

These photographs show views of diamond shapes. On a separate sheet of paper, unscramble the letters to identify what's in each picture. **Bonus:** Use the highlighted letters to solve the puzzle below.

ANSWERS ON PAGE 338

ISKET

SETUHILGOH

REFWA OIEKCOS

SOIERMAKEN

RIENSRGA

LEAASBBL DIDONMA

ADISNTE SLGSA

EGRALY WEASTRE

CFENE

HINT: What is a diamond's food?

ANSWER: __ __ __ A __ __ .

Hyena

Just Joking

SPECIAL GROSS EDITION

KNOCK, KNOCK.

Who's there?
Police.
Police who?
Police brush your teeth—your breath is awful!

Q What Spanish city is full of people with the flu?

A Barf-elona

TONGUE TWISTER!

Freshly fried fat frogs

Q What kind of monster can you find in a tissue?

A The boogie man

You've got to be joking ...

Q What do you get if you cross a **pig** and a **portable bathroom?**

A A pork-a-potty

CHECK OUT THE BOOK!

Just Joking GROSS

SIGNS
OF THE TIMES

Seeing isn't always believing. Two of these funny signs are not real. Can you figure out which two are fake?

ANSWER ON PAGE 338

1

2 FATIGUE ZONE
KEEP PLAYING TRIVIA - IT MAY SAVE YOUR LIFE

3 SOFT SHOULDER

4 LOST ST DOLLAR ST

5 READLYN "857 friendly people AND ONE OLD GRUMP"

6 HAM SANDWICH 3 ½

7 HUGS 25¢

Laugh Out Loud

"GUESS WHO GOT GROUNDED AGAIN?"

"DON'T YOU KNOW 'GO FISH' IS A CARD GAME?"

"HOW MANY TIMES HAVE I TALKED TO YOU ABOUT EATING TOO MUCH JUNK FOOD?"

"DID YOU REMEMBER TO ZIP UP THE TENT, BOBBY?"

"... AND SPANKY DID THAT ONE!"

Funny FILL-IN
Crash Course

Ask a friend to give you words to fill in the blanks in this story and write them on a separate sheet of paper. Then read the story out loud and fill in the words for a laugh.

My family decided to go mini-golfing this past weekend. We grabbed the long metal

_____ and walked up to the first hole. I took a big swing, aiming the ball straight

noun, plural

for the _____ . "_____!" I yelled at the top of my _____ . The ball

noun   silly word   body part, plural

bounced off a(n) _____ dinosaur and went _____ through the air.

color   verb ending in -ing

My family scrambled to hide behind the _____ as the ball zipped past them.

noun

It hit _____ on the top of the _____ and smacked into a fake

relative's name   another body part

_____ . Finally, the ball _____ down a _____ and landed with

animal   past-tense verb   noun

a(n) _____ in the pond. As the ball sank to the bottom, everyone started to

funny noise

_____ . _____ joked that I needed putting lessons from a professional

verb   another relative's name

_____ before we got to the hole with the _____ _____ mill.

noun   adjective   noun

PLAY
Funny FILL-IN
AND MORE!
natgeokids.com/ffi

SPLASH DOWN!

Crazy stuff is happening at the water park. Find at least 15 things that are wrong in the scene. **ANSWERS ON PAGE 338**

What in the World?

BEING NOSY

These photos show close-up views of animal noses. On a separate sheet of paper, unscramble the letters to identify what's in each picture. **Bonus:** Use the highlighted letters to solve the puzzle below.

ANSWERS ON PAGE 338

GRTIE

SNAIA NEPLATEH

GDO

ILAMNRDL

ESA ILNO

WTO-DOTE HOLST

INCAAM

NSOOIP TRDA ORFG

KSIA EDRE

HINT: What does a nose say to be polite?

ANSWER: __ __ __ __ __ Z __ __ __ __ __ __ __ __ Y __ U .

Funny FILL-IN
Spaced Out

Ask a friend to give you words to fill in the blanks in this story and write them on a separate sheet of paper. Then read the story out loud and fill in the words for a laugh.

Welcome to the year 30 _____ . It was my first day as Intergalactic Space
<u>number between 0 and 99</u>

Sheriff, so I decided to patrol Planet _____ . I jumped into my space
<u>friend's name</u>

_____ , turned on the antigravity _____ , and traveled at _____
<u>type of transportation</u>   <u>noun</u>   <u>adjective</u>

speed toward the planet. When I stepped onto the _____ surface, I came face-to-face
<u>adjective</u>

with an alien. He was the size of a(n) _____ and looked like a giant _____ lump
<u>noun</u>   <u>color</u>

of _____ . "_____ ," I said to him, the galactic word for "hello." But the
<u>type of food, plural</u>   <u>silly word</u>

alien didn't respond. Instead, he pulled out his laser _____ , _____ my
<u>noun</u>   <u>past-tense verb</u>

vehicle, then tried to _____ me. Quickly, I activated my defense _____ . The laser
<u>verb</u>   <u>noun</u>

beam hit the alien on the _____ . "_____ !" yelled the alien as he turned
<u>body part</u>   <u>exclamation</u>

into a big puddle of _____ . Exhausted, I teleported back to the space station
<u>something icky</u>

near _____ . This job is going to be tougher than I thought.
<u>name of a planet in our solar system</u>

PLAY
Funny FILL-IN
AND MORE!
natgeokids.com/ffi

Laugh Out Loud

"OH, GOOD ... MY FAVORITE TV SHOW IS ON!"

"IT CAN SPOT A LEOPARD SEAL A MILE AWAY!"

"WHERE'S THE FIRE? I CLOCKED YOU GOING OVER TWO MILES A DAY!"

"I QUIT STORING MINE IN TREES YEARS AGO."

CRITTER CHAT

If wild animals used social media, what would they say? Follow this prairie dog's day as it updates its feed.

BLACK-TAILED PRAIRIE DOG
PlainsPup

Lives in: Grasslands of Canada, the United States, and Mexico
Likes: Digging and dozing

FRIENDS

Coyote
CoolCanine

Burrowing Owl
UnderOwl

Western Diamond-back Rattlesnake
SnakeRattleNRoll

---

6 a.m.

PlainsPup
Ugh, that was an early alarm! But I'm on dirt-moving duty today. Got to keep my colony's burrow entrances clean—all 70 of them!

SnakeRattleNRoll
Hey, thanks! It's so thoughtful of you to clear out the house from time to time since I like to hang out in abandoned prairie dog holes.

PlainsPup
You're such a den crasher.

CoolCanine
At least **SnakeRattleNRoll** doesn't move in and then cover the entrance with dung from other animals! *Cough ...* **UnderOwl** *... cough ...*

UnderOwl
Only when I'm nesting! It's not like I can leave my eggs, so I use the poo to lure dung beetles to my door. It's like ordering dinner in!

11:35 a.m.

PlainsPup
HAWK! HAWK! Run for cover! #WatchDog

SnakeRattleNRoll
Slither for your lives!

11:37 a.m.

PlainsPup
PREDATOR UPDATE: It was just a very hawk-shaped cloud.

SnakeRattleNRoll
I nearly shook my rattle off! It usually shakes about 60 times a second to scare predators, but I think it just broke a hundred!

UnderOwl
Us too! My chicks can imitate **SnakeRattleNRoll's** sound when they feel threatened. It sounded like the burrow was a snake shack!

5:45 p.m.

PlainsPup
Aw, man! My sister ate my dinner again. Living with family can be rough. I have to share everything—my burrow, my food.

SnakeRattleNRoll
At least you don't live in that prairie dog colony that has, like, 400 MILLION members!

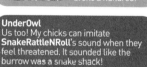

CoolCanine
400 million pack mates? That sounds *awooooooo*-ful. Get it? #CoyotePuns

UnderOwl
But with so many members maybe it would be a party *owl* the time. #OwlPunsAreBetterThanCoyotePuns

A woman on a zip line soars over Lignon Hill in Legazpi, Philippines.

Awesome Exploration

Munazza Alam spends most of her evenings staring at the stars. As an astronomer—and National Geographic explorer-in-residence—she stays up all night to make observations on things like brown dwarfs, exoplanets, and other celestial bodies. Here are 19 things Munazza can't work without.

1 SKY CHART
"WE MAKE SKY CHARTS OF WHERE EACH TARGET WILL BE IN THE SKY AND AT WHAT TIME DURING THE DAY IT WILL BE UP—AND THEN PLAN AROUND THAT."

2 FLASHLIGHT
"OBSERVATORIES ARE DARK LOCATIONS, SO I KEEP ONE ON ME AT ALL TIMES."

3 MEDICINE
"Since observatories are located on mountains and other high-altitude locations, I try to be prepared with medicines to help with headaches, nausea, and other symptoms of altitude sickness."

4 EXTERNAL HARD DRIVE
"WE COLLECT SO MUCH DATA, SO I HAVE TO BE SURE IT'S **SAFE AND BACKED UP** IN MULTIPLE LOCATIONS."

(19) THINGS IN AN EXPLORER'S

5 LAPTOP
"I use my computer to download, process, and analyze the data from the telescope. You'll never find me working without it!"

6 OBSERVING LOGS
"THESE WORKSHEETS ARE A GREAT WAY TO **KEEP ORGANIZED NOTES** ON EACH OBJECT THAT WE OBSERVE THROUGHOUT THE NIGHT."

7 TEA
"A little caffeine in my system helps me stay up to observe."

8 GAMES
"Sometimes we set **'long exposures'**— or observations in which the telescope is taking data for an extended period of time. So my team and I like to play fun games to pass the time while our data comes in."

9 PEN & PAPER
"I ALWAYS KEEP A PEN AND PAPER HANDY, JUST IN CASE I NEED TO DO A QUICK CALCULATION."

10

CAMERA
"OBSERVATORIES OFFER SOME OF THE BEST VIEWS OF THE NIGHT SKY, SO I LOVE DOING SOME ASTROPHOTOGRAPHY IN MY DOWNTIME WHILE OBSERVING."

11

COOKIES
"They give me a great energy boost when I try to stay up all night observing."

12

MUSIC
"LISTENING TO MUSIC HELPS ME TO STAY AWAKE—AND PASS THE TIME—WHILE WE OBSERVE AT NIGHT."

13

BINOCULARS
"I use these to check the weather and cloud conditions outside. "

14

CHAPSTICK
"WE SPEND A LOT OF TIME IN DRY PLACES, SO I TRY MY BEST TO KEEP MY SKIN MOISTURIZED."

LABORATORY

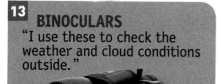

15

LUNCH
"I always pack a night lunch to enjoy during the middle of the night. Observing is hard work, and it makes me hungry."

16

JACKET AND GLOVES
"IN CASE I NEED TO BUNDLE UP IF IT GETS COLD AT THE OBSERVATORY SITE AT NIGHT."

17

BLANKET
"I'll wrap one around me as I work in the telescope control room—it can get pretty cold in there, too."

18

WATER BOTTLE
"IT'S IMPORTANT TO STAY HYDRATED WHEN WE'RE OUT THERE IN THE DESERT."

19

TARGET LIST
"THIS IS A LIST OF ALL OUR TARGETS—LIKE STARS, PLANETS, OR GALAXIES—THAT WE WILL OBSERVE AT NIGHT. WE'LL INCLUDE THEIR COORDINATES IN THE SKY, THEIR BRIGHTNESS, AND SOME OTHER KEY INFORMATION THAT WILL MAKE THEM EASIER TO FIND."

DARE to EXPLORE

Do you have what it takes to be a great explorer? Read these stories of four adventurers, and see how you can get started on the exploration path.

DEE BOERSMA
Biologist

WANT TO BE A BIOLOGIST?
STUDY: Math, science, and technology
WATCH: The documentary *March of the Penguins*
READ: *Galápagos George* by Jean Craighead George

"No matter what you end up doing with your life, try to make the world a better place."

Conservation biologist Dee Boersma talks about working in remote locations to study penguins and sharing the planet with other animals.

"When I first went to the Galápagos Islands off the coast of Ecuador over 40 years ago to study the penguins that lived there, I camped by myself for two weeks to see what I could discover. Rats, venomous snakes, and three-foot (0.9-m)-long iguanas were everywhere. No other humans were with me on the island, so it could get a little lonely. But I would talk to the sea lions that slept on the beach outside my tent—they snore so loud!

"The lives of penguins aren't so different from our own: They raise families and take care of their loved ones. What we humans need to do is protect their habitats so they can thrive. Each one of us can do something to make life better for other creatures."

DEE BOERSMA OBSERVES MAGELLANIC PENGUINS IN ARGENTINA.

GALÁPAGOS PENGUIN

PENGUINS SWIM UP TO 3,100 MILES (5,000 KM) IN A YEAR.

CORY RICHARDS
Adventure photographer

WANT TO BE A **PHOTOGRAPHER?**

STUDY: Photography, anthropology, and geology

WATCH: The documentary *Cave People of the Himalaya*

READ: *Banner in the Sky* by James Ramsey Ullman

RICHARDS SCALES A PEAK IN THE ROCKY MOUNTAINS IN CANADA ON A PHOTO EXPEDITION.

"Don't let **obstacles** discourage you from reaching your **goals.** Anything is **possible** if you put your **heart** into it."

RICHARDS'S STUNNING PHOTOGRAPHY

CANADA

EUROPE'S CRIMEAN PENINSULA

"One time I was rappelling, or descending by rope, down a seaside cliff in Spain to photograph some climbers. Suddenly the rock that my rope was anchored to at the top of the cliff broke away. My stomach lurched as I went into a free fall, plummeting 50 feet (15 m) into the ocean. Once I hit the water, the heavy camera equipment strapped to my body dragged me under the waves. With my heart hammering, I freed myself from the gear and swam to the surface. My cameras were ruined, but I was alive.

"Working as a photographer can be a nonstop adventure. My career has taken me to every terrain imaginable, from icy peaks in Asia to the vast plains of Africa to coral reefs in the South Pacific Ocean. I've snapped pictures of people scaling mountains, diving, and skiing across Antarctica. I love using photography to show the incredible things humans are capable of doing.

"Getting the right shot involves creativity and sometimes danger. Stay open to new experiences, and you'll never be disappointed."

IN EXTREME COLD, CAMERAS CAN PACK UP WITH ICE.

STEVE BOYES
Conservation scientist

WANT TO BE A CONSERVATION SCIENTIST?

STUDY: Biology, math, and photography

WATCH: *Hi Duma*, about a boy and his cheetah cub pal

READ: *Okavango: Africa's Last Eden* by Frans Lanting

"Never think that the world's questions have all been answered. Questions still exist for us to investigate."

STEVE BOYES EXPLORES THE RIVER IN A MOKORO, OR DUGOUT CANOE, TO OBSERVE AND PHOTOGRAPH ANIMALS LIKE THE ONES AT LOWER RIGHT.

OK981

AFRICAN WILD DOG

CAPE BUFFALO

MEYER'S PARROT

CONSERVATION BIOLOGIST STEVE BOYES SHARES SOME OF HIS *WILD* ADVENTURES IN AFRICA.

"One day my team and I were floating down the 648-mile (1,043-km) Okavango River in Africa in dugout canoes called *mokoros* when suddenly a hippopotamus's face was rushing up at me! The hippo blasted out of the water, toppled over my canoe, and sent me flying into the air before I splashed back down in the river. My boat started to sink, and the hippo wasn't going anywhere. A teammate set off a flare to distract the animal so I could swim away. After that, we all paid very close attention to every single ripple in the river.

"When you're this deep into the wilderness, you don't have a lot of resources. We often used canoes because there weren't many roads. We had to deal with thorny bushes everywhere and hungry ants that were constantly biting us.

"But wilderness areas like the Okavango are disappearing. That's why I've committed myself not only to observing these beautiful places but to protecting them, too. It's my privilege to do it."

HIPPOPOTAMUSES ARE CLOSELY RELATED TO DOLPHINS.

JENNY DALTRY
Herpetologist

WANT TO BE A HERPETOLOGIST?
STUDY: Biology, geography, and other sciences
WATCH: *Avatar*
READ: *Not Your Typical Book About the Environment* by Elin Kelsey

"It doesn't matter who you are or where you're from. You have the potential to accomplish amazing things. Stay positive and focused, and you'll reach your goals."

Herpetologist Jenny Daltry has come face-to-fangs with venomous snakes and toothy crocodiles. Here, she talks about warming up to cold-blooded animals.

"One time while on the Caribbean island of Montserrat, I was observing amphibians near the top of a volcano that hadn't erupted in over 350 years. Suddenly, I heard a tremendous roar and spun around to see a column of smoke shooting into the air. The volcano was erupting! I turned to run. Luckily, I found a path away from the rumbling mountain and made it to safety.

"Fleeing a lava-spewing volcano is one of many unforgettable moments I've had on the job. Another is helping to preserve the Antiguan racer—a small, harmless snake found on the island of Antigua. Twenty years ago only 50 were left on Earth, and today, over 1,200 Antiguan racers now exist. Helping to bring animals back from the brink of extinction makes you realize just how much is possible. Every single person has the power to make a difference."

ORIENTAL VINE SNAKE

SIAMESE CROCODILE

ANTIGUAN SPOTTED ANOLE

A CROCODILE CAN'T STICK ITS TONGUE OUT.

What Kind of Explorer Are You?

Take this quiz and mark your answers on a piece of paper to find out the type of adventurous occupation that's the perfect fit for you!

1 It's a beautiful day out! What tops your list of things to do?

A. taking a walk down to your neighborhood pond to look for turtles and ducks
B. grabbing your camera and snapping some pictures of the birds in your backyard
C. digging around your yard and looking for cool stones and creatures living underground
D. going for a hike

2 What's your dream vacation?

A. snorkeling with tropical fish in Tahiti
B. watching wildlife on a safari in Africa
C. digging for dinosaur bones in Argentina
D. climbing Mount Fuji in Japan

4 **What's your favorite subject in school?**

A. biology
B. visual arts
C. history
D. gym

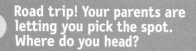

5 **Road trip! Your parents are letting you pick the spot. Where do you head?**

A. the beach
R. the zoo
C. a museum
D. a state park

3 **What's your idea of the perfect pet?**

A. a fish
B. a cat
C. a lizard
D. a dog

If You Chose Mostly ...

A's

Oceanographer. You're meant for a life on the sea. Whether it's scuba diving with sharks or working on reducing ocean waste, your love for the water and life beneath the surface makes you a perfect match for a career in the marine world.

B's

Wildlife Photographer. Wild about animals? Passionate about photography? As a wildlife photographer, you can combine your passion for both. Spending hours observing animals and documenting their every move from behind the lens could be the future you should focus on.

C's

Archaeologist. History is never a mystery for you, and you love piecing together clues from the past. Collecting dinosaur bones or discovering ancient civilizations? Now that's something you'd definitely dig.

D's

Mountaineer. Your sporty lifestyle and enthusiasm for all things active make you the perfect match for a career as a mountaineer. As a true trailblazer, you'd spend time scaling the planet's highest peaks, scampering over boulders, and exploring parts of Earth few people have ever been to before.

Lions Forever!

NATIONAL GEOGRAPHIC KiDS
ALMANAC CHALLENGE 2019

Thandiwe shares details about her career—and why it's so important to protect these iconic animals.

THANDIWE MWEETWA

Can you imagine a world without lions?

Neither can we! But their numbers are dwindling. That's why this year's challenge focuses on the threats lions face in the wild and the importance of saving them.

It's not easy saving lions. They're large predators that need a lot of open space to roam and big prey to eat. It takes hard work, cooperation, and dedicated people, like National Geographic Emerging Explorer Thandiwe Mweetwa, to lead the way.

Thandiwe is a lion biologist. She spends most of her days in Zambia's Luangwa Valley, tracking and observing these big cats in the hopes of boosting their numbers in the wild. With support from National Geographic's Big Cats Initiative, Thandiwe is working with local communities to inspire the next generation of conservationists. View videos of her tracking and tagging lions at natgeokids.com/almanac.

TELL US WHAT IT WAS LIKE GROWING UP IN ZAMBIA AND HOW YOU BECAME INTERESTED IN WILDLIFE CONSERVATION.

As a kid, my village was near a national park, so I would see wildlife like monkeys, elephants, and small antelope. I became fascinated by these animals, and joined my school's conservation club to learn about the environmental issues affecting our area. This inspired me to go into the conservation field and do something to help protect wildlife.

HOW DID YOU DISCOVER YOUR PASSION FOR PROTECTING LIONS IN PARTICULAR?

The defining moment was experiencing the power of three male lions roaring about three meters (10 ft) from my car while I was in the field. I had never heard anything like that before. Then and there I decided to pursue a career working with lions and helping conserve them.

WHY IS IT SO IMPORTANT TO SAVE LIONS?

Lions are essential to maintaining healthy ecosystems. Having lions on the landscape helps maintain balance in nature, which is beneficial to all living things on the planet, including humans. The recent estimated number of lions in the wild is about 20,000, and populations are declining in many places across Africa. Lions are also cultural icons, symbolizing strength and courage across the globe. Losing this important part of our natural heritage would be a global disaster.

WHAT'S ONE OF THE MOST MEMORABLE ENCOUNTERS YOU'VE HAD WITH A LION?

When I won a staring contest with a 400-pound (181-kg) male lion. We had immobilized him to fit a radio tracking collar, but the tranquilizer dart malfunctioned and he only got a partial dose. The lion woke up early while we were still working. He spent the next minute or so looking straight at me and growling. It felt like an eternity! Luckily, I stood dead still and the lion eventually lost interest.

WHAT KIND OF IMPACT DO YOU HOPE TO MAKE WITH YOUR RESEARCH?

I hope to continue developing and expanding wildlife research in my country. Although nearly 31 percent of Zambia's surface area is set aside for conservation and wildlife management, so many people still need to be educated on endangered and threatened species. I want to help change that.

WHAT CAN KIDS DO TO HELP SAVE BIG CATS?

Take action! Support causes like the Almanac Challenge and National Geographic's Big Cats Initiative, which gives funding to scientists and conservationists working to save big cats around the world. The key is having the right knowledge and then sharing that knowledge. Protecting these species requires a global response and the more people know about it, the better.

To learn more about National Geographic's Big Cats Initiative, visit natgeo.org/bigcats.

THIS YEAR'S CHALLENGE

CELEBRATE THESE MAJESTIC CREATURES BY CREATING AN AWESOME LION POSTER!

Send it to us along with a message about why we must save lions and your entry could be featured in *National Geographic Kids* magazine and next year's Almanac! The winner will also receive a $500 cash prize to host a Lions Forever party to share what he or she discovered about lion conservation with friends, family, or classmates. Find official rules and more fun stuff at **natgeokids.com/almanac.**

JESSICA CRAMP

LAST YEAR'S CHALLENGE

Thanks to the thousands of kids who participated in the Save Our Sharks challenge led by National Geographic Explorer and marine conservationist Jessica Cramp. Keep learning about sharks and inspiring others to care about these amazing creatures.

THE GOBLIN SHARK WAS THE FAVORITE IN OUR ONLINE POLL!

Meerkat Close Encounter

Wildlife photographer Will Burrard-Lucas gives new meaning to the term "up close and personal" while photographing meerkats in the wild.

Makgadikgadi Pans, Botswana

When a family of meerkats discovered a wildlife photographer on his stomach angling for a picture outside their burrow, they didn't hide. Instead they used him as a lookout rock!

Baby meerkat pups venturing aboveground for the first time took turns playing with photographer Will Burrard-Lucas's camera. One bold adult hoisted himself onto Burrard-Lucas's head and scaled to the top of the camera lens he was holding. "They were trying to get as high as they could to have a good look around," Burrard-Lucas says.

"For meerkats, the higher you get, the safer you are, because you can hopefully spot a predator before it spots you," says Kenton Kerns, a biologist at the Smithsonian's National Zoo in Washington, D.C. "If they can find a stable spot that's higher than their normal places, they'll do anything to get there—including climbing a human."

Before packing up for the day, Burrard-Lucas waited patiently while one curious meerkat peered through the lens of his camera on the ground. Another meerkat walked right in front of it. How's that for a close-up?

FROZEN IN TIME

ERNEST SHACKLETON'S PRESERVED HUT IN CAPE ROYDS, ANTARCTICA

ANTARCTIC EXPLORERS ERNEST SHACKLETON, ROBERT FALCON SCOTT, AND EDWARD WILSON, CIRCA 1903

When British adventurers Ernest Shackleton and Robert Falcon Scott explored Antarctica in the early 1900s, they set up camp in wooden huts, which they left behind in the icy environs once the expeditions were over.

One would think that over time, the huts would completely deteriorate in the harsh conditions of the coldest continent. But the structures remained upright, albeit damaged by water, wind, and snow over the years. Now a team of conservationists have completely restored them, offering a time capsule into the explorers' lives a century ago.

So what's inside the huts? Thousands of artifacts, like clothes, scientific equipment, photographs, and even frozen butter. Here's a closer look at some of the items originally used then—and how they compare to the gear used by today's Antarctic explorers.

THE FOOD
THEN: Scott's crew mostly munched on pemmican, a mixture of dried beef and fat, plus water and plenty of biscuits.

NOW: Explorers eat a customized diet fine-tuned to give them enough calories to withstand the cold conditions and physical demands. On the menu? Porridge and cream for breakfast, energy bars, electrolyte drinks, and chicken curry for dinner.

THE SLEDS
THEN: Shackleton and Scott's teams hauled heavy loads in wooden sleds dragged by ponies and dogs.
NOW: Modern lightweight sleds are made of carbon fiber and are capable of carrying more equipment while still being sleek enough to smoothly travel over the ice.

THE CLOTHES
THEN: Early explorers wore wool, cotton, and animal fur. Gloves, boots, and sleeping bags were lined with reindeer fur.
NOW: High-tech mountaineering clothing is made from breathable fabrics that have been specially designed for the Antarctic's cold and dry environment.

Scientist at Base Orcadas in Antarctica

THE COMMUNICATION
THEN: Completely isolated in the Antarctic, explorers had no means of communicating with the outside world and could only write the details of their journey in notebooks.
NOW: Ultralight laptops connected to a mobile satellite hub help explorers stay connected, post pictures, and even watch movies.

PHOTO ARK

Joel Sartore and His Wild Project

Picture this: An elephant, set against a black backdrop, photographed at such a close angle that you can see every wrinkle and groove in its curled trunk. Then there's a stunning shot of a green tree python's eye, with scales layered around it like tiny flower petals. Or a portrait of a pair of baby fennec foxes, their beady-eyed gazes locked and giant ears perked as though they're listening to your every word.

A s a longtime National Geographic photographer, Joel Sartore has captured it all. And in an effort to put more focus on endangered species, he has photographed a growing collection of over 6,000 species of animals, from baboons to butterflies. Known as the Photo Ark, this project aims to capture every single animal living in captivity around the world (eventually, the project will include an estimated 12,000 species). Sartore, who has visited zoos, aquariums, and animal rehabilitation centers in more than 40 countries to find his subjects, hopes that the images will encourage people to be more aware of just how vulnerable these animals are.

"Every year I see more habitat loss, more species consumed for food, medicine, or simply decoration," Sartore says. "The Photo Ark was born out of desperation to halt, or at least slow, the loss of global biodiversity."

Aside from awareness, Sartore also hopes to share a unique and intimate look at the animals—especially those that no longer live in the wild. And in the event that the species disappears altogether? "The goal is to see these animals as they actually looked in life," Sartore says.

TIPS FROM A PRO
How to Take Great Photos

As far as the eye can see, there are photographs waiting to be captured or created. Life swirls around us without stopping, but as a photographer, you can put a frame around moments in time. A lot more goes into taking a good photograph than just pushing a button, though.

Learn how to use a camera, but most of all, learn how to think like a photographer. Here are some valuable tips from expert photographer Neil Johnson to help you get started on your way.

COMPOSITION
- Making your subject the focus of attention does not mean that you have to put it in the middle of the frame. Placing the subject slightly off center can help lead the viewer into the picture.

SUBJECT
- When taking pictures of animals, getting down to their eye level and moving in close will improve your photographs.
- When taking pictures of people, try to get them to forget about the camera and just go about doing what they enjoy.

LIGHT
- When lighting a subject, it is important to consider not only the direction of the light (front, side, or back), but also the color of the background.
- Light does not always have to fall on the front of your subject.
- On-camera flash is most useful for subjects that are 10 to 15 feet (3 to 4.5 m) away.

QUICK TIPS!

- **Get close.** A lot of cameras have zoom features, but nothing beats being right there next to your subject.

- **Experiment with the different modes** on your digital camera, like portrait, sports, and macro. See what works and what doesn't.

- **Don't spend too much time** looking at the pictures on your digital camera—doing this drains the batteries! Download your photos instead.

- **Stay still,** especially if you're using a camera phone. The steadier you are, the clearer your shot will be.

QUIZ WHIZ

Explore just how much you know about adventure with this quiz!

Write your answers on a piece of paper. Then check them below.

1 Where did photographer Will Burrard-Lucas encounter meerkats in the wild?
- **a.** Bahamas
- **b.** Brazil
- **c.** Botswana
- **d.** Bulgaria

2 **True or false?** Penguins swim up to 3,100 miles (5,000 km) in a year.

3 What was left behind in Ernest Shackleton's century-old preserved hut in Antarctica?
- **a.** clothes
- **b.** photographs
- **c.** frozen butter
- **d.** all of the above

4 Hippopotamuses are closely related to _____.

5 A _____ studies amphibians and reptiles.
- **a.** herpetologist
- **b.** primatologist
- **c.** marine biologist
- **d.** slime-ologist

Not **STUMPED** yet? Check out the *NATIONAL GEOGRAPHIC KIDS QUIZ WHIZ* collection for more crazy **ADVENTURE** questions!

ANSWERS: 1. c; 2. True; 3. d; 4. dolphins; 5. a

HOMEWORK HELP

How to Write a Perfect Essay

Need to write an essay? Does the assignment feel as big as climbing Mount Everest? Fear not. You're up to the challenge! The following step-by-step tips will help you with this monumental task.

1 **BRAINSTORM.** Sometimes the subject matter of your essay is assigned to you, sometimes it's not. Either way, you have to decide what you want to say. Start by brainstorming some ideas, writing down any thoughts you have about the subject. Then read over everything you've come up with and consider which idea you think is the strongest. Ask yourself what you want to write about the most. Keep in mind the goal of your essay. Can you achieve the goal of the assignment with this topic? If so, you're good to go.

2 **WRITE A TOPIC SENTENCE.** This is the main idea of your essay, a statement of your thoughts on the subject. Again, consider the goal of your essay. Think of the topic sentence as an introduction that tells your reader what the rest of your essay will be about.

3 **OUTLINE YOUR IDEAS.** Once you have a good topic sentence, you then need to support that main idea with more detailed information, facts, thoughts, and examples. These supporting points answer one question about your topic sentence—"Why?" This is where research and perhaps more brainstorming come in. Then organize these points in the way you think makes the most sense, probably in order of importance. Now you have an outline for your essay.

4 **ON YOUR MARK, GET SET, WRITE!** Follow your outline, using each of your supporting points as the topic sentence of its own paragraph. Use descriptive words to get your ideas across to the reader. Go into detail, using specific information to tell your story or make your point. Stay on track, making sure that everything you include is somehow related to the main idea of your essay. Use transitions to make your writing flow.

5 **WRAP IT UP.** Finish your essay with a conclusion that summarizes your entire essay and restates your main idea.

6 **PROOFREAD AND REVISE.** Check for errors in spelling, capitalization, punctuation, and grammar. Look for ways to make your writing clear, understandable, and interesting. Use descriptive verbs, adjectives, or adverbs when possible. It also helps to have someone else read your work to point out things you might have missed. Then make the necessary corrections and changes in a second draft. Repeat this revision process once more to make your final draft as good as you can.

The Grand Prismatic Spring at Yellowstone National Park in Wyoming, U.S.A., gets its unique coloration from heat-loving bacteria living in the spring.

Biomes

A BIOME, OFTEN CALLED A MAJOR LIFE ZONE, is one of the natural world's major communities where plants and animals adapt to their specific surroundings. Biomes are classified depending on the predominant vegetation, climate, and geography of a region. They can be divided into six major types: forest, freshwater, marine, desert, grassland, and tundra. Each biome consists of many ecosystems.

Biomes are extremely important. Balanced ecological relationships among biomes help to maintain the environment and life on Earth as we know it. For example, an increase in one species of plant, such as an invasive one, can cause a ripple effect throughout a whole biome.

FOREST

Forests occupy about one-third of Earth's land area. There are three major types of forests: tropical, temperate, and boreal (taiga). Forests are home to a diversity of plants, some of which may hold medicinal qualities for humans, as well as thousands of animal species, some still undiscovered. Forests can also absorb carbon dioxide, a greenhouse gas, and give off oxygen.

The rabbit-size royal antelope lives in West Africa's dense forests.

FRESHWATER

Most water on Earth is salty, but freshwater ecosystems—including lakes, ponds, wetlands, rivers, and streams—usually contain water with less than one percent salt concentration. The countless animal and plant species that live in a freshwater biome vary from continent to continent, but they include algae, frogs, turtles, fish, and the larvae of many insects.

The place where fresh and salt water meet is called an estuary.

MARINE

The marine biome covers almost three-fourths of Earth's surface, making it the largest habitat on our planet. Oceans make up the majority of the saltwater marine biome. Coral reefs are considered to be the most biodiverse of any of the biome habitats. The marine biome is home to more than one million plant and animal species.

> Estimated to be up to 100,000 years old, sea grass growing in the Mediterranean Sea may be the oldest living thing on Earth.

DESERT

Covering about one-fifth of Earth's surface, deserts are places where precipitation is less than 10 inches (25 cm) per year. Although most deserts are hot, there are other kinds as well. The four major kinds of deserts are hot, semiarid, coastal, and cold. Far from being barren wastelands, deserts are biologically rich habitats.

> Some sand dunes in the Sahara are tall enough to bury a 50-story building.

GRASSLAND

Biomes called grasslands are characterized by having grasses instead of large shrubs or trees. Grasslands generally have precipitation for only about half to three-fourths of the year. If it were more, they would become forests. Grasslands can be divided into two types: tropical (savannas) and temperate. Some of the world's largest land animals, such as elephants, live there.

> Grasslands in North America are called prairies; in South America, they're called pampas.

TUNDRA

The coldest of all biomes, a tundra is characterized by an extremely cold climate, simple vegetation, little precipitation, poor nutrients, and a short growing season. There are two types of tundra: arctic and alpine. A tundra is home to few kinds of vegetation. Surprisingly, though, there are quite a few animal species that can survive the tundra's extremes, such as wolves, caribou, and even mosquitoes.

> Formed 10,000 years ago, the arctic tundra is the world's youngest biome.

1 About **ONE-FIFTH** of **EARTH'S** surface is **DESERT.**

2 THE DORCAS GAZELLE LIVES IN THE SAHARA AND DOESN'T DRINK ANY WATER. IT ALSO DOESN'T EVER PEE.

3  **KELSO SAND DUNES** in the Mojave Desert, U.S.A., make a tuba-like honking or booming sound when sand slips down over the dunes.

4 The Sahara in North Africa, spanning 3.5 million square miles (9.1 million sq km), is the LARGEST HOT DESERT on Earth, with temperatures that can reach 136°F (58°C).

5 THE UYUNI DESERT IN BOLIVIA IS THE SALTIEST DESERT, CONTAINING ONE BILLION TONS (907 million t) OF SALT.

19 FACTS ABOUT

6  A **BEETLE** THAT LIVES IN THE HOT **NAMIB DESERT** USES ITS **SHELL** TO COLLECT WATER IN THE MORNING. LATER IN THE DAY THE WATER DRIPS DOWN INTO ITS **MOUTH.**

7 The world's **SMALLEST DESERT** is the Atacama Desert in Chile. It spans only 40,600 square miles (105,200 sq km).

8  The world's **LARGEST DESERT is ANTARCTICA.** It is a POLAR DESERT that covers **5.1 million square miles** (13.2 million sq km).

9 The Atacama Desert in Chile, South America, is the DRIEST DESERT on Earth. It usually gets less than .04 inch (1 mm) of rain a year.

10 AN ENDANGERED CACTUS KNOWN AS THE **BASEBALL PLANT** IS FOUND ONLY IN THE DESERTS OF SOUTH AFRICA.

11 IN 2012, SCIENTISTS FOUND **WATER RESERVES** UNDERNEATH THE DESERTS OF AFRICA—INCLUDING THE **SAHARA,** WHICH WAS THOUGHT TO BE ONE OF THE DRIEST PLACES ON EARTH.

12 **CHUCKWALLAS** ARE LIZARDS THAT LIVE IN THE DESERTS OF MEXICO AND THE UNITED STATES OF AMERICA. WHEN IN DANGER, THEY **WEDGE THEMSELVES INTO ROCK CREVICES** AND **PUFF UP FOR PROTECTION.**

13 **SAND DUNES** are a common sight in deserts. They are created by **WIND** pushing **GRAINS OF SAND** into large hills.

14 In 1979 and 2012, **SNOW FELL** on parts of the SAHARA.

15 MYSTERIOUS "FAIRY CIRCLES"—BARREN PATCHES IN GRASSY AREAS—CAN BE FOUND IN **AFRICA'S NAMIB DESERT.**

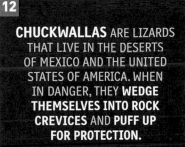

DESERTS

16 **DESERTS** are not limited to **EARTH**—they have also been discovered on **MARS.**

17 MORE THAN **ONE BILLION PEOPLE** IN THE WORLD **LIVE IN DESERTS.**

19 The **MARATHON DES SABLES** is an annual six-day **MARATHON** through 150 miles (241 km) of the **SAHARA.** Competitors have to carry everything they need except water.

18 **CAMELS** have been used for DESERT TRANSPORTATION for hundreds of years—their POOP can also be used to fuel a campfire.

THE OC

PACIFIC OCEAN

STATS

Surface area
65,436,200 sq mi (169,479,000 sq km)

Portion of Earth's water area
47 percent

Greatest depth
Challenger Deep
(in the Mariana Trench)
-36,070 ft (-10,994 m)

Surface temperatures
Summer high: 90°F (32°C)
Winter low: 28°F (-2°C)

Tides
Highest: 30 ft (9 m) near Korean peninsula
Lowest: 1 ft (0.3 m) near Midway Islands

Cool creatures: giant Pacific octopus, bottlenose whale, clownfish, great white shark

ATLANTIC OCEAN

STATS

Surface area
35,338,500 sq mi (91,526,300 sq km)

Portion of Earth's water area
25 percent

Greatest depth
Puerto Rico Trench
-28,232 ft (-8,605 m)

Surface temperatures
Summer high: 90°F (32°C)
Winter low: 28°F (-2°C)

Tides
Highest: 52 ft (16 m)
Bay of Fundy, Canada
Lowest: 1.5 ft (0.5 m)
Gulf of Mexico and Mediterranean Sea

Cool creatures: blue whale, Atlantic spotted dolphin, sea turtle

GREAT WHITE SHARK

GREEN SEA TURTLE

EANS

INDIAN OCEAN

STATS

Surface area
28,839,800 sq mi (74,694,800 sq km)

Portion of Earth's water area
21 percent

Greatest depth
Java Trench
-23,376 ft (-7,125 m)

Surface temperatures
Summer high: 93°F (34°C)
Winter low: 28°F (-2°C)

Tides
Highest: 36 ft (11 m)
Lowest: 2 ft (0.6 m)
Both along Australia's west coast

Cool creatures: humpback whale, Portuguese man-of-war, dugong (sea cow)

DUGONG

ARCTIC OCEAN

STATS

Surface area
5,390,000 sq mi (13,960,100 sq km)

Portion of Earth's water area
4 percent

Greatest depth
Molloy Deep
-18,599 ft (-5,669 m)

Surface temperatures
Summer high: 41°F (5°C)
Winter low: 28°F (-2°C)

Tides
Less than 1 ft (0.3 m) variation throughout the ocean

Cool creatures: beluga whale, orca, harp seal, narwhal

ORCA

To see the major oceans and bays in relation to landmasses, look at the map on pages 256 and 257.

PRISTINE SEAS

Explorers work to protect the last truly wild places in the ocean.

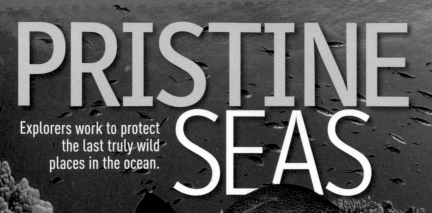

80 percent of marine pollution originates from the land.

A YELLOW-EDGED LYRETAIL PROWLS CORAL NEAR PITCAIRN ISLAND.

DR. ENRIC SALA

KEEPING OUR OCEANS PRISTINE

Oceans cover more than 70 percent of Earth's surface. Even with all of that water, only a tiny percentage is not impacted by human activity—but conservationists are working to change that. The National Geographic Pristine Seas team, led by National Geographic Explorer-in-Residence Enric Sala, travels to some of the most remote parts of the oceans to explore life underwater and create protected areas. One such location? The Pitcairn Islands in the South Pacific, where the Pristine Seas squad created the world's largest marine reserve, setting aside a swath of sea bigger than the entire state of California, U.S.A., for special protection. That means there is no fishing or seafloor mining allowed in the reserve, a move meant to keep the thousands of fish, plants, and coral living there healthy and thriving.

PITCAIRN ISLAND

A DIVER EXPLORES BOUNTY BAY NEAR PITCAIRN ISLAND.

So far, Pristine Seas has protected more than 1.69 million square miles (4.4 million sq km) of ocean territory.

GRAY REEF SHARK

The goal of Pristine Seas is to help fully protect 10 percent of the world's oceans by 2020.

SAVING THE SHARKS

The Pristine Seas expedition has also made its mark on the uninhabited Southern Line Islands, an archipelago deep in the South Pacific. Dozens of gray reef sharks swirl around these islands, feeding on the fish around the coral reefs. But they face constant danger. Sought out by humans for their fins—considered a delicacy in some parts of Asia—these sharks are vulnerable to overfishing, which is when people catch them at too fast a rate for the species to replace its numbers. But by working with the local government, Sala and his crew have established a 12-nautical-mile fishing exclusion zone around each island. It's a step in the right direction for protecting the ecology of the island and, ultimately, boosting the shark's dwindling population.

Weather and Climate

Weather is the condition of the atmosphere—temperature, wind, humidity, and precipitation—at a given place at a given time. Climate, however, is the average weather for a particular place over a long period of time. Different places on Earth have different climates, but climate is not a random occurrence. It is a pattern that is controlled by factors such as latitude, elevation, prevailing winds, the temperature of ocean currents, and location on land relative to water. Climate is generally constant, but evidence indicates that human activity is causing a change in its patterns.

WEATHER EXTREMES

RAINBOW SHOW: The longest-lasting rainbow reportedly shone for six hours over England.

LIGHTNING HOT: Temperatures in the air around a lightning bolt can hit 50,000°F (27,760°C).

RAINIEST DAY: 72 inches (183 cm) of rain was recorded in a 24-hour period in 1966 on Réunion Island, a French island in the Indian Ocean, during Tropical Cyclone Denise.

GLOBAL CLIMATE ZONES

Climatologists, people who study climate, have created different systems for classifying climates. One that is often used is called the Köppen system, which classifies climate zones according to precipitation, temperature, and vegetation. It has five major categories—Tropical, Dry, Temperate, Cold, and Polar—with a sixth category for locations where high elevations override other factors.

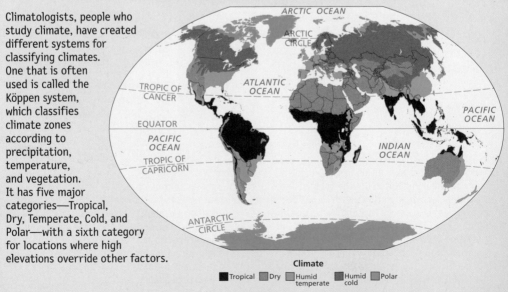

Climate

■ Tropical ■ Dry ■ Humid temperate ■ Humid cold ■ Polar

WATER CYCLE

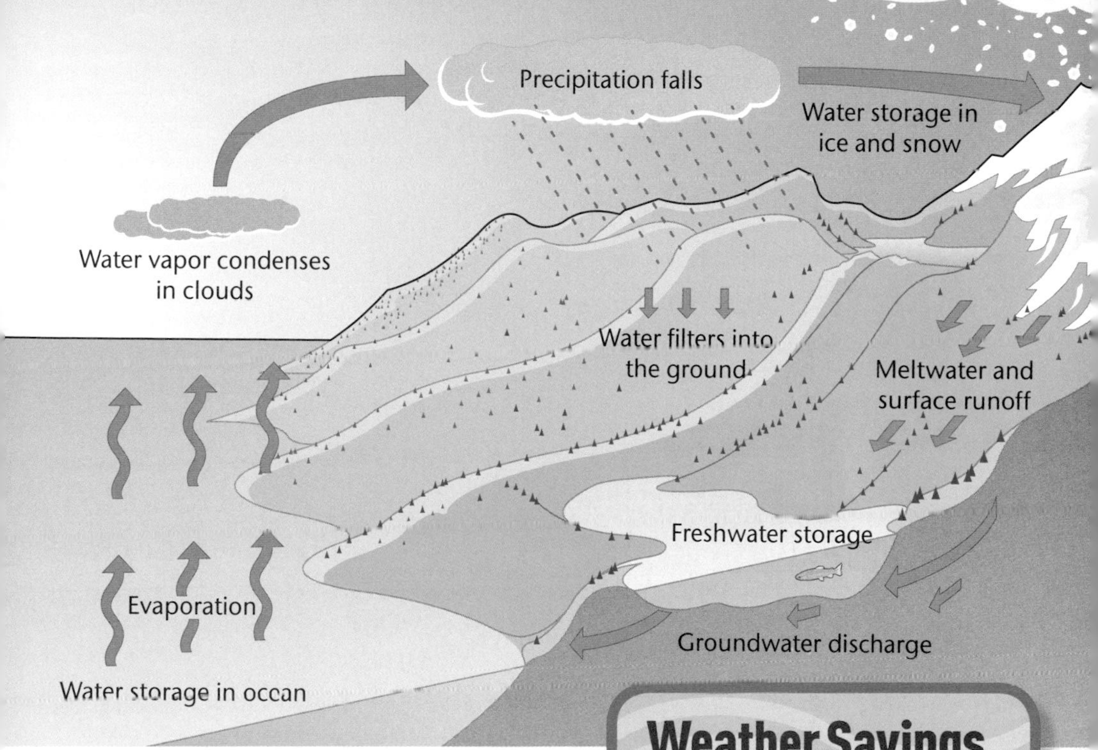

Precipitation falls

Water storage in ice and snow

Water vapor condenses in clouds

Water filters into the ground

Meltwater and surface runoff

Freshwater storage

Evaporation

Groundwater discharge

Water storage in ocean

The amount of water on Earth is more or less constant—

only the form changes. As the sun warms Earth's surface, liquid water is changed into water vapor in a process called **evaporation**. Water on the surface of plants' leaves turns into water vapor in a process called **transpiration**. As water vapor rises into the air, it cools and changes form again. This time it becomes clouds in a process called **condensation**. Water droplets fall from the clouds as **precipitation**, which then travels as groundwater or runoff back to the lakes, rivers, and oceans, where the cycle (shown above) starts all over again.

To a meteorologist— a person who studies the weather— a "light rain" is less than 1/48 of an inch (0.5 mm). A "heavy rain" is more than 1/6 of an inch (4 mm).

Weather Sayings

These words of weather wisdom have been passed down for generations. But they're not always accurate—be sure to check the forecast!

- Red sky in the morning, sailors take warning. Red sky at night, sailors' delight.

- Clear nights mean cold days.

- If a circle forms 'round the moon, then it will rain very soon.

- Rain before seven stops by eleven.

- In a green sky, the cows will fly.

Types of Clouds

If you want a clue about the weather, look up at the clouds. They'll tell a lot about the condition of the air and what weather might be on the way. Clouds are made of both air and water. On fair days, warm air currents rise up and push against the water in clouds, keeping it from falling. But as the raindrops in a cloud get bigger, it's time to set them free. The bigger raindrops become too heavy for the air currents to hold up, and they fall to the ground.

How Much Does a Cloud Weigh?

A light, fluffy cumulus cloud typically weighs about 216,000 pounds (97,975 kg). That's about the weight of 18 elephants. A rain-soaked cumulonimbus cloud typically weighs 105.8 million pounds (48 million kg), or about the same as 9,000 elephants.

1 STRATUS These clouds make the sky look like a bowl of thick gray porridge. They hang low in the sky, blanketing the day in dreary darkness. Stratus clouds form when cold, moist air close to the ground moves over a region.

2 CIRRUS These wispy tufts of clouds are thin and hang high up in the atmosphere where the air is extremely cold. Cirrus clouds are made of tiny ice crystals.

3 CUMULONIMBUS These are the monster clouds. Rising air currents force fluffy cumulus clouds to swell and shoot upward, as much as 70,000 feet (21,000 m). When these clouds bump against the top of the troposphere, or the tropopause, they flatten out on top like tabletops.

4 CUMULUS These white, fluffy clouds make people sing, "Oh, what a beautiful morning!" They form low in the atmosphere and look like marshmallows. They often mix with large patches of blue sky. Formed when hot air rises, cumulus clouds usually disappear when the air cools at night.

Make a Barometer

ARE YOU FASCINATED BY WEATHER? Then you should make your own barometer to track the weather where you live!

SUPPLY LIST

- Ruler
- Tall glass
- Drinking straw
- Bubble gum
- Tape
- Water and blue food coloring

1

STEPS

1. Tape a clear drinking straw to a ruler. The bottom of the straw should line up with the ½-inch (12–13 mm) mark on the ruler.

2. Stand the ruler up in a tall glass and tape it to the inside of the glass so it stays straight. Fill the glass ¾ full with water.

2

3. Here's the fun part: Chew on a piece of gum for a while, then stick it to the top of the straw.

4. Pour out ¼ of the water so that the water in the straw is higher than the water in the cup.

5. Keep an eye on your barometer. When atmospheric pressure increases, the water level in your straw will rise (which usually means fair weather). When atmospheric pressure decreases, the water level will fall (and can mean clouds or rain are on the way). Record your findings in your meteorologist notebook!

> Barometers were invented in Italy in the early 1600s by Evangelista Torricelli.

Time: about 10 minutes

KEEP A WEATHER JOURNAL

Recording the daily temperature, rainfall, and barometric changes will help you track patterns in the weather. Try to take a measurement every day and record it in a journal. Set up a chart for each component of your weather station. After a few weeks, you might start to see some patterns, and soon you'll be making predictions—like a regular meteorologist!

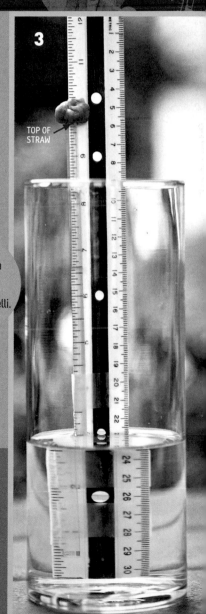

3

TOP OF STRAW

Natural Disasters

Every world region has its share of natural disasters—the mix just varies from place to place. And the names of similar storms may vary as well. Take, for example, cyclones, typhoons, and hurricanes. The only difference among these disasters is where in the world they strike. In the Atlantic and the Northeast Pacific, they're hurricanes; in the Northwest Pacific near Asia they're typhoons; and in the South Pacific and Indian Oceans, they're cyclones.

Despite their distinct titles, these natural disasters are each classified by violent winds, massive waves, torrential rain, and floods. The only obvious variation among these storms? They spin in the opposite direction if they're south of the Equator.

Hurricane Irma (center) with less severe storms Hurricane Jose (left) and Hurricane Katia (right).

HURRICANES IN 2019

HELLO, MY NAME IS ...

Hurricane names come from six official international lists. The names alternate between male and female. When a storm becomes a hurricane, a name from the list is used, in alphabetical order. Each list is reused every six years. A name "retires" if that hurricane caused a lot of damage or many deaths.

Andrea
Barry
Chantal
Dorian
Erin
Fernand
Gabrielle
Humberto
Imelda
Jerry
Karen
Lorenzo
Melissa
Nestor
Olga
Pablo
Rebekah
Sebastien
Tanya
Van
Wendy

In August 2017, **Hurricane Harvey** slammed into Houston, Texas, U.S.A. With winds whipping at speeds of up to 130 miles an hour (209 km/h) and relentless rain dumping 20 trillion gallons (76 trillion L) of water over Texas and Louisiana in just a few days, Hurricane Harvey was one of the strongest—and costliest—storms to ever make landfall in the United States.

And the hits kept coming: On the heels of Harvey, **Hurricane Irma** stormed into the Caribbean in early September 2017, flattening parts of the Florida Keys and the islands in its path, including Barbuda and St. John. A few days later, **Hurricane Maria** caused unprecedented damage in Dominica and Puerto Rico. All told, by early October 2017, some 107 lives were lost and millions more people were left homeless and without power after this trio of devastating storms.

Fortunately for the victims of these hurricanes, help poured in from many sources. Several large companies pledged money for relief efforts. Telethons featuring pop stars and famous actors pulled in millions. A concert featuring all five living former U.S. presidents donated all proceeds to recovery efforts in Texas, Florida, and the Caribbean. While rebuilding and recovering won't happen overnight, this kind of support will hopefully ensure that all of the affected areas will, one day, recover and come back stronger than ever.

Scale of Hurricane Intensity

CATEGORY	ONE	TWO	THREE	FOUR	FIVE
DAMAGE	Minimal	Moderate	Extensive	Extreme	Catastrophic
WINDS	74–95 mph (119–153 km/h)	96–110 mph (154–177 km/h)	111–129 mph (178–208 km/h)	130–156 mph (209–251 km/h)	157 mph or higher (252+ km/h)
(DAMAGE refers to wind and water damage combined.)					

FOREST FIRE!

The flames ripped through the forest fast and furiously. What began as a moderate blaze in Pedrógão Grande in central Portugal soon splintered into at least five separate and powerful fires, eventually engulfing 74,000 acres (30,000 ha) of forest. The forest fire—which killed at least 60 people and torched several houses—was one of the worst natural disasters Portugal had faced in decades.

What started the blaze? Experts aren't so sure. Likely, it was caused by lightning during a dry thunderstorm, which is when lightning strikes, but there is no rain. The area had also been experiencing a heat wave, with temperatures topping 100°F (40°C) when the initial flames sparked in June 2017. Once the fire started to spread, shifting winds, hot weather, low humidity, and an arid landscape contributed to the quick-spreading fire.

Some 900 firefighters—including those dispatched from Spain, France, and Greece—arrived to tackle the blaze. The fire was extinguished after five days, but not before causing devastation and destruction that will be felt for decades.

LANDSLIDE!

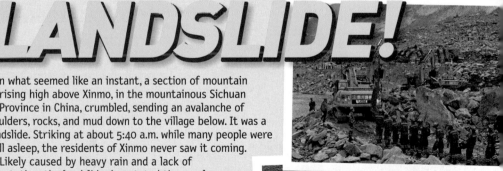

In what seemed like an instant, a section of mountain rising high above Xinmo, in the mountainous Sichuan Province in China, crumbled, sending an avalanche of boulders, rocks, and mud down to the village below. It was a landslide. Striking at about 5:40 a.m. while many people were still asleep, the residents of Xinmo never saw it coming.

Likely caused by heavy rain and a lack of vegetation, the landslide devastated the rural village that was still reeling from an 8.0 earthquake that killed tens of thousands in 2008. The 2017 landslide—which sent rock tumbling down the mountain, some of it falling from a mile (1.6 km) above—crushed dozens of houses, killing 15 instantly, and trapping some 100 others beneath piles of rocks.

Thousands of rescue workers came to Xinmo in the hours after the landslide, using heavy equipment to sort through the debris, while sniffer dogs sought out the scent of those who were trapped. Thanks to these efforts, some people managed to do the incredible and survive the devastating natural disaster.

What is a
tornado?

TORNADOES, ALSO KNOWN AS TWISTERS, are funnels of rapidly rotating air that are created during a thunderstorm. With wind speeds of up to 300 miles an hour (483 km/h), tornadoes have the power to pick up and destroy everything in their path.

Supercell

A massive rotating thunderstorm that generates the most destructive of all tornadoes. A series of supercells in the southern United States caused an outbreak of 92 tornadoes in 10 states over a 15-hour period in 2008.

Weather Alert

TORNADOES HAVE OCCURRED IN ALL 50 U.S. STATES AND ON EVERY CONTINENT EXCEPT ANTARCTICA.

Funnel cloud

This rotating funnel of air formed in a cumulus or cumulonimbus cloud becomes a tornado if it touches the ground.

Fire whirls

These tornadoes made of wind and fire occur during a wildfire. Their flaming towers can be 5 to 10 stories tall and can last for more than an hour. They are also called fire devils.

THE ENHANCED FUJITA SCALE

The Enhanced Fujita (EF) Scale, named after tornado expert T. Theodore Fujita, classifies tornadoes based on wind speed and the intensity of damage that they cause.

EF0
65–85 mph winds
(105–137 km/h)
Slight damage

EF1
86–110 mph winds
(138–177 km/h)
Moderate damage

EF2
111–135 mph winds
(178–217 km/h)
Substantial damage

EF3
136–165 mph winds
(218–266 km/h)
Severe damage

EF4
166–200 mph winds
(267–322 km/h)
Massive damage

EF5
More than
200 mph winds
(322+ km/h)
Catastrophic damage

Waterspout

This funnel-shaped column forms over water and is usually weaker than a land tornado.

QUIZ WHIZ

Quiz yourself to find out if you're a natural when it comes to nature knowledge!

Write your answers on a piece of paper. Then check them below.

1 **True or false?** Some sand dunes in the Sahara are tall enough to bury a 50-story building.

2 A fluffy cumulus cloud weighs about the same as _____ elephants.
a. 1.8
b. 18
c. 180
d. 1,800

3 A beetle that lives in the Namib Desert uses _____ to collect water to drink.
a. its mouth
b. its shell
c. leaves
d. holes it has dug

4 What's the name of the place where fresh and salt water meet?
a. creek
b. tide pool
c. estuary
d. marina

5 In June 2017, _____ faced a powerful forest fire—one of the country's worst natural disasters in decades.
a. France
b. Norway
c. Portugal
d. Slovakia

Not **STUMPED** yet? Check out the *NATIONAL GEOGRAPHIC KIDS QUIZ WHIZ* collection for more crazy **NATURE** questions!

ANSWERS:
1. True; 2. b; 3. b; 4. c; 5. c

SPEAK NATURALLY

Oral Reports Made Easy

Does the thought of public speaking start your stomach churning like a tornado? Would you rather get caught in an avalanche than give a speech?

Giving an oral report does not have to be a natural disaster. The basic format is very similar to that of a written essay. There are two main elements that make up a good oral report—the writing and the presentation. As you write your oral report, remember that your audience will be hearing the information as opposed to reading it. Follow the guidelines below, and there will be clear skies ahead.

> **TIP:**
> Make sure you practice your presentation a few times. Stand in front of a mirror or have a parent record you so you can see if you need to work on anything, such as eye contact.

Writing Your Material

Follow the steps in the "How to Write a Perfect Essay" section on p. 199, but prepare your report to be spoken rather than written.

Try to keep your sentences short and simple. Long, complex sentences are harder to follow. Limit yourself to just a few key points. You don't want to overwhelm your audience with too much information. To be most effective, hit your key points in the introduction, elaborate on them in the body, and then repeat them once again in your conclusion.

An oral report has three basic parts:

- **Introduction**—This is your chance to engage your audience and really capture their interest in the subject you are presenting. Use a funny personal experience or a dramatic story, or start with an intriguing question.

- **Body**—This is the longest part of your report. Here you elaborate on the facts and ideas you want to convey. Give information that supports your main idea, and expand on it with specific examples or details. In other words, structure your oral report in the same way you would a written essay, so that your thoughts are presented in a clear and organized manner.

- **Conclusion**—This is the time to summarize the information and emphasize your most important points to the audience one last time.

Preparing Your Delivery

1 Practice makes perfect.
Practice! Practice! Practice! Confidence, enthusiasm, and energy are key to delivering an effective oral report, and they can best be achieved through rehearsal. Ask family and friends to be your practice audience and give you feedback when you're done. Were they able to follow your ideas? Did you seem knowledgeable and confident? Did you speak too slowly or too fast, too softly or too loudly? The more times you practice giving your report, the more you'll master the material. Then you won't have to rely so heavily on your notes or papers, and you will be able to give your report in a relaxed and confident manner.

2 Present with everything you've got.
Be as creative as you can. Incorporate videos, sound clips, slide presentations, charts, diagrams, and photos. Visual aids help stimulate your audience's senses and keep them intrigued and engaged. They can also help to reinforce your key points. And remember that when you're giving an oral report, you're a performer. Take charge of the spotlight and be as animated and entertaining as you can. Have fun with it.

3 Keep your nerves under control.
Everyone gets a little nervous when speaking in front of a group. That's normal. But the more preparation you've done— meaning plenty of researching, organizing, and rehearsing—the more confident you'll be. Preparation is the key. And if you make a mistake or stumble over your words, just regroup and keep going. Nobody's perfect, and nobody expects you to be.

2019 marks the 30th anniversary of the fall of the Berlin Wall, which had blocked East Germans from traveling to West Germany. Parts of the Berlin Wall remain on display in Germany today.

History Happens

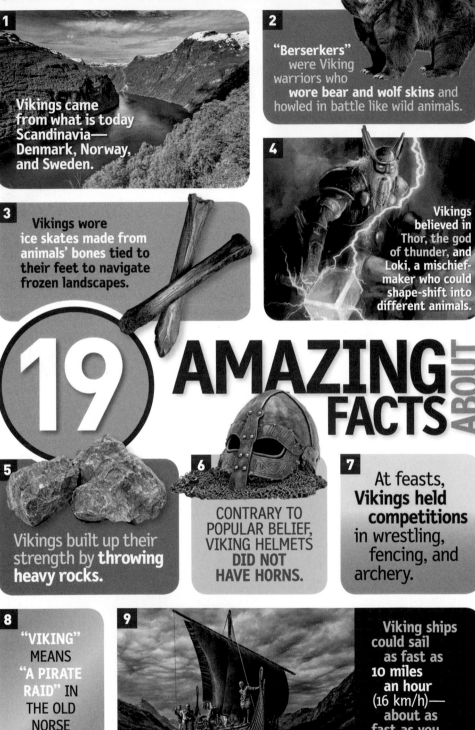

1 Vikings came from what is today Scandinavia—Denmark, Norway, and Sweden.

2 "Berserkers" were Viking warriors who **wore bear and wolf skins** and howled in battle like wild animals.

3 Vikings wore ice skates made from animals' bones **tied to their feet to navigate frozen landscapes.**

4 Vikings believed in Thor, the god of thunder, **and Loki, a mischief-maker who could shape-shift into different animals.**

19 AMAZING FACTS ABOUT

5 Vikings built up their strength by **throwing heavy rocks.**

6 CONTRARY TO POPULAR BELIEF, VIKING HELMETS **DID NOT HAVE HORNS.**

7 At feasts, **Vikings held competitions** in wrestling, fencing, and archery.

8 "VIKING" MEANS "A PIRATE RAID" IN THE OLD NORSE LANGUAGE.

9 Viking ships could sail as fast as **10 miles an hour** (16 km/h)— about as fast as you ride a bike.

10 Vikings sometimes wore protective chain mail jackets with metal rings laced together to avoid the penetration of a spear

11 Eastern Roman emperors hired Vikings as guards.

12 FENRIR GREYBACK, A WEREWOLF IN THE HARRY POTTER SERIES, WAS NAMED AFTER A GIANT WOLF FROM ANCIENT VIKING MYTHOLOGY.

13 SOME 30 TO 50 PEOPLE LIVED TOGETHER IN VIKING HOUSES.

14 AS BABIES, VIKINGS WERE GIVEN THOR HAMMERS AS CHARMS.

VIKINGS

15 Viking ships had one big sail made from wool.

16 VIKING WOMEN WORE BROOCHES MADE OF GOLD.

17 Vikings rode small horses that were the size of today's ponies.

18 Vikings made whistles from **bird bones.**

19 STARTING AROUND A.D. 900, VIKINGS RULED NORTHERN SCOTLAND FOR 500 YEARS.

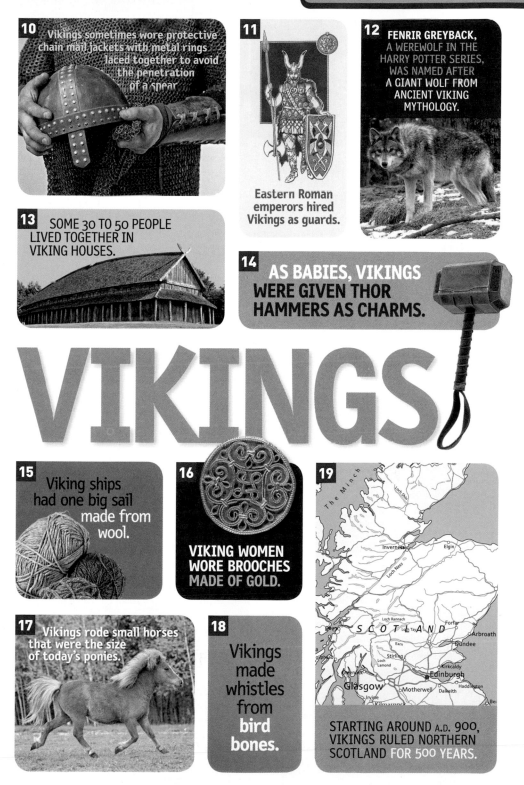

awes8me

ROYALLY AMAZING
CASTLES

2 KNIGHT LIFE

Walk the paths roamed by medieval knights and princesses at the 14th-century Bodiam Castle in East Sussex, England. The castle's splashiest feature? It's completely surrounded by a moat.

3 FIT FOR A WIZARD

Alnwick Castle, a 900-year-old building in Northumberland, England, was the site of Harry's first flying lesson in the film *Harry Potter and the Sorcerer's Stone*.

4 FIERCE FORTRESS

Perched high in the Austrian Alps, Hohenwerfen Fortress was the site of numerous sieges and attacks for 900 years. The castle was also featured in the 1965 film *The Sound of Music*.

5 DEFYING GRAVITY

The Mont-Saint-Michel abbey is a French monastery that rests on an island surrounded by the English Channel. When the tide rises around the island, the abbey seems to float.

1 TALK ABOUT A FAIRY TALE!

Germany's King Ludwig II built Neuschwanstein Castle on a cliff in Bavaria. Every year more than a million people visit the 19th-century structure, which is said to have been the inspiration for Disneyland's iconic Sleeping Beauty Castle.

7 CASTLE IN FLIGHT

Himeji Castle, the largest castle in Japan, is an 83-building complex! Its look has been likened to a white heron spreading its wings.

8 SPOOKY SPOT

The author who created Count Dracula in 1897 based the vampire's home on Bran Castle in Romania, which is why it's also known as Dracula's Castle. But no bloodthirsty monsters actually live there. This nickname has no teeth!

6 COLOSSAL CASTLE

Founded in the ninth century, Prague Castle in the Czech Republic is the largest ancient castle complex in the world, with an area of more than 750,000 square feet (69,677 sq m).

Jungle of Secrets

Scientists uncover a hidden city near the temple called ANGKOR WAT

In the midst of Cambodia's steamy jungle looms a majestic medieval temple. Called Angkor Wat, the nearly 900-year-old structure was built in the capital of the Khmer Empire, a powerful civilization in Southeast Asia. But until recently, few were aware of something tucked in the forest beyond the temple—a hidden city.

MISSING METROPOLIS

The Khmer Empire thrived between the 9th and 15th centuries. Many people worshipped at the temple of Angkor Wat in the capital city of Angkor, which was about the size (area) of New York City. Scientists believe that in the 14th and 15th centuries, droughts and other extreme natural disasters caused many people to abandon the region and move south. Eventually, thick forests grew over much of the area.

In Cambodia, it's considered an insult to touch someone's head.

Built in the 12th century to honor a god, Angkor Wat was in continual use even after the capital city was abandoned. When a French explorer came across the temple in the 1800s, he spread word of its beauty, drawing visitors and archaeologists to the area.

Scientists suspected that another, older city from the Khmer Empire, called Mahendraparvata, was hidden in the jungle around the temple. According to writings found in old texts, the city was built in A.D. 802 and served as the Khmer Empire's capital before it moved to Angkor.

AIRBORNE DETECTIVES

In 2012 a team of scientists wanted to investigate the region in search of the remains of Mahendraparvata. A thick tangle of trees

Angkor Wat appears on Cambodia's flag (left).

TREE ROOTS GROW OVER RUINS IN A JUNGLE NEAR ANGKOR WAT.

ASIA

PACIFIC OCEAN

CAMBODIA

INDIAN OCEAN

THAILAND LAOS

Angkor Wat
Tonle Sap
C A M B O D I A
Phnom Penh ★

VIETNAM

Gulf of Thailand

South China Sea

covering the land made exploring on foot difficult. So instead, the team took to the skies.

Crisscrossing over forest canopies in a helicopter, archaeologist Damian Evans used an instrument called LIDAR to scan the ground. LIDAR works by rapidly firing off pulses of laser light. A sensor on the instrument measures how long it takes for each pulse to bounce back from the ground. If a set of laser beams has a shorter return time than the previous pulses sent, it could mean the beams have hit something elevated, such as a building. A longer return time could mean that the beams are bouncing off of a low valley or deep riverbed. Using GPS technology, cartographers then combined all of the measurements to create a map of the terrain.

As the scientists analyzed the map, they noticed an area with a network of roads and canals built into a mountain. It appeared to match the

description of Mahendraparvata found in the old texts. Evans and his team knew this had to be the hidden city.

IT'S A JUNGLE OUT THERE

The archaeologists started their expedition north of Angkor Wat under the heat of a sizzling sun. They cut away tree leaves blocking their path with machetes, waded knee-deep in bogs, and dodged dangerous land mines that had been left in the jungle after a war.

Finally, they stumbled upon dozens of crumbled temples and evidence of roads and canals, all organized into city blocks. They had reached their destination, and it was indeed Mahendraparvata.

In the coming years, Evans and his team will continue to investigate the area. But the scientists will have their work cut out for them. After all, this jungle is very good at keeping secrets.

Must-See
SIGHTS

WHAT: HERCULANEUM
WHERE: Ercolano, Italy

WHY IT'S COOL: Buried by ash and lava from the eruption of Mount Vesuvius in A.D. 79, this port town is said to be better preserved than its neighbor Pompeii. Some ruins here stand up to two stories high.

WHAT: THE GREAT BUDDHA
WHERE: Kamakura, Japan

WHY IT'S COOL: More than 760 years old, this giant bronze statue has stayed standing through a lot—even surviving a giant tsunami. At 44 feet (13.35 m) tall, it's one of Japan's most famous icons.

WHAT: U.S.S. *ARIZONA* MEMORIAL
WHERE: Honolulu, Hawaii, U.S.A.

WHY IT'S COOL: This site, which can be reached by ferry from the visitor's center, marks the memory of Japan's attack on the United States on December 7, 1941.

When you visit these historical landmarks around the world, you'll step into places almost untouched by time.

WHAT: PETRA
WHERE: Jordan

WHY IT'S COOL: You have to walk in the desert to reach this more than 2,000-year-old ancient city. But the trek is worth it, as it reveals awe-inspiring buildings carved into cliffs.

WHAT: TEMPLO MAYOR
WHERE: Mexico City, Mexico

WHY IT'S COOL: With a pyramid as tall as a 15-story building as its centerpiece, this site was the heart of the Aztec community. The pyramid and temples have since been destroyed, but the artifacts and ruins that remain offer a glimpse of Aztec life over 600 years ago.

WHAT: ST. BASIL'S CATHEDRAL
WHERE: Moscow, Russia

WHY IT'S COOL: This colorful cathedral was commissioned by Ivan the Terrible in 1552 to celebrate a military victory. Today, it remains a stunning symbol of classic Russian architecture.

CURSED!

Did these objects unleash some seriously bad luck?

A mummy rumored to unleash bad luck on all who enter his tomb. A brutal emperor's final resting place surrounded by armed clay warriors. A supposedly deadly diamond that glows red. Most people would probably leave these creepy historical relics alone. And some say that those who didn't ended up paying the ultimate price. But are these stories just tall tales, or are they the real deal? Decide for yourself.

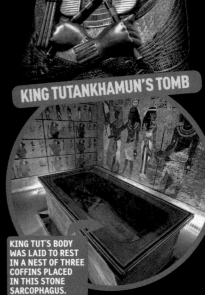

KING TUTANKHAMUN'S TOMB

WHERE Valley of the Kings, Egypt

THE STORY Don't mess with Tut! That's the lesson some researchers have discovered after handling King Tut's tomb. For starters? One man, who funded the original search for Tut's tomb, unexpectedly died of blood poisoning. Later, when Egyptologist Zahi Hawass removed the mummy to study it in 2005, he got a call that a family member passed away, and his search was slowed by a major storm. Then, when he got the mummy into his lab, the scanning machine broke. It's no wonder visitors to the tomb tread lightly so they don't disturb the long-gone pharaoh.

KING TUT'S BODY WAS LAID TO REST IN A NEST OF THREE COFFINS PLACED IN THIS STONE SARCOPHAGUS.

THE TOMB OF THE TERRA-COTTA WARRIORS

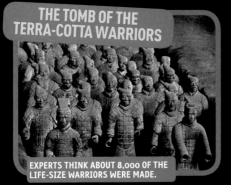

EXPERTS THINK ABOUT 8,000 OF THE LIFE-SIZE WARRIORS WERE MADE.

WHERE Xi'an, China

THE STORY When it was time for Qin Shi Huang, China's first emperor, to build his tomb 2,200 years ago, he had workers make thousands of life-size clay soldiers to protect him and a trove of treasures in the afterlife.

For years, nobody knew these guardians existed. After being discovered in 1974, some nearby farmers contracted diseases and died early deaths.

Today, no one has discovered the treasure-filled tomb. Perhaps it's because the tomb is supposedly rigged with crossbows. Or maybe because the army is still guarding its leader long after they've been removed.

WHERE Smithsonian Institution National Museum of Natural History, Washington, D.C.

THE STORY In the mid-1600s, a diamond was stolen from a temple in India, angering the gods. It's said they cursed the future owners of the jewel.

Later, the diamond ended up with France's King Louis XVI and his wife, Marie Antoinette ... until they were beheaded in 1793. When an American socialite later bought it, some of her family members met untimely deaths.

Now called the Hope Diamond, the gem was donated to the Smithsonian Institution in 1958, and the person who delivered it had his leg crushed in a car accident. Not much has happened since, except that the blue diamond glows a bloody red when exposed to ultraviolet light. Spooky.

THE HOPE DIAMOND

THE HOPE DIAMOND IS SURROUNDED BY 16 WHITE DIAMONDS AND HANGS ON A CHAIN OF 45 WHITE DIAMONDS.

CITY IN THE SKY

Scientists search for clues about why the community of Machu Picchu was built.

How do you pronounce Machu Picchu? Like this: MAH-chu PEA-chu.

Peru's Colca Canyon is nearly twice as deep as the Grand Canyon.

Perched nearly 8,000 feet (2,438 m) high is an old city made of stone. Known as Machu Picchu (or "Old Peak" in the local language of Quechua), the site has been here for centuries. But not even the descendants of the builders know for sure why it was built.

THE RISE OF MACHU PICCHU

Machu Picchu was constructed some 500 years ago during the Inca Empire. Archaeologists believe that it took hundreds of builders to construct the mountaintop city, but after the Inca Empire fell in the mid-1500s, Machu Picchu was abandoned.

Few knew about the neglected metropolis until an American explorer stumbled upon its ruins in July 1911. As news of his discovery spread, so did theories about the mysterious sky-high city. Many people thought Machu Picchu was a fortress. Some have even suggested that aliens built it to have a base on Earth. (Yeah, not likely.) Recently, scientists digging for clues about the purpose of Machu Picchu have made some interesting finds.

LOVE OF THE LAND

Anthropologist and National Geographic Explorer-in-Residence Johan Reinhard thinks answers to the Machu Picchu puzzle lie in the surrounding landscape. "The Inca believed that gods lived in landforms and bodies of water," Reinhard says. "And they worshipped these

sites." During one expedition to Machu Picchu, Reinhard found several large stones carved into the shape of the surrounding peaks. "The area was important to the Inca," Reinhard says. "And Machu Picchu may have been built to honor this cherished landscape where mighty gods were thought to dwell."

STAR POWER

It's likely that the site was also a gathering place during astronomical events such as the summer and winter solstices (the longest and shortest days of the year). Celestial events were important to the Inca, even affecting how buildings were designed. For instance, a temple in the city was built so that the sun shines into its window on the morning of the winter solstice, illuminating a stone shrine.

So are the mysteries of Machu Picchu solved? Not quite. Evidence certainly exists that the site was built to honor sacred land and used as an astronomical observatory. But without written records—or a time machine to travel back and question the Inca— we may never be absolutely sure.

NORTH AMERICA
ATLANTIC OCEAN
PERU
SOUTH AMERICA
PACIFIC OCEAN

231

CAN AN ISLAND PARADISE DISAPPEAR IN A DAY? THAT'S WHAT ONE ANCIENT LEGEND SAYS ABOUT THE EMPIRE OF ATLANTIS. TODAY, SCIENTISTS CONTINUE TO TRY TO LOCATE THE LOST ISLAND.

MYSTERY OF ATLANTIS

Plato, an ancient Greek philosopher, described Atlantis as a wealthy city with palaces, a silver-and-gold temple, abundant fruit trees, and elephants roaming the land. But the good times didn't last. Plato wrote that sudden earthquakes jolted Atlantis and whipped up waves that sank the island within a day.

Was Plato's story true? Recently, researchers in Spain used underground radar in search of buried buildings. Results showed something like a crumbled wall in the soil 40 feet (12.1 m) below, but because there was water beneath the site, a dig seemed improbable.

Other explorers think Atlantis is in the Mediterranean Sea, where images supposedly show remains of canals and walls. Others are skeptical about the story entirely. Such an advanced city, they say, couldn't have been built in the Stone Age, when Plato's story was set.

So, was Atlantis real, fake, or something in between? The search continues.

THE SECRETS OF
STONEHENGE

Could a new discovery help solve this ancient puzzle?

Dazzling rays from the sun burst through a strange ring of stones set on a grassy field. This huge monument, called Stonehenge, has towered above England's Salisbury Plain for thousands of years—but it's still one of the world's biggest mysteries.

THE UNEXPLAINED

For centuries people have tried to unlock Stonehenge's secrets.

Some theories have suggested that migrants from continental Europe built the site as an astronomical observatory or as a temple to the sun and moon gods. No theories have been proven. But a new discovery may provide more information about the builders of Stonehenge and could help explain why the monument was constructed in this region.

HUNTING FOR CLUES

While digging around a spring about a mile and a half (2.4 km) from Stonehenge, archaeologist David Jacques and his team uncovered hundreds of bones belonging to aurochs—a species of cattle twice the size of a modern-day bull that thrived in ancient times. In fact, the site held the largest collection of auroch bones ever found in Europe. This suggests that the spring was a pit stop along an auroch migration route where the animals drank water.

The team also unearthed 31,000 flints, a stone tool used for hunting. "We started to wonder if the area was also a hunting ground and feasting site for ancient people," Jacques says. "Just one auroch could've fed a hundred people, so the place would've been a big draw."

The animal bones and tools date back to 7500 B.C. The age of the artifacts caused Jacques to conclude that people moved to the region around 9,500 years ago to hunt auroch. And he thinks descendants of these settlers assembled the mysterious stone ring.

233

WAR!

Since the beginning of time, different countries, territories, and cultures have feuded with each other over land, power, and politics. Major military conflicts include the following wars:

1095–1291 THE CRUSADES
Starting late in the 11th century, these wars over religion were fought in the Middle East for nearly 200 years.

1337–1453 HUNDRED YEARS' WAR
France and England battled over rights to land for more than a century before the French eventually drove the English out in 1453.

1754–1763 FRENCH AND INDIAN WAR (part of Europe's Seven Years' War)
A nine-year war between the British and French for control of North America.

1775–1783 AMERICAN REVOLUTION
Thirteen British colonies in America united to reject the rule of the British government and to form the United States of America.

1861–1865 AMERICAN CIVIL WAR
Occurred when the northern states (the Union) went to war with the southern states, which had seceded, or withdrawn, to form the Confederate States of America. Slavery was one of the key issues in the Civil War.

1910–1920 MEXICAN REVOLUTION
The people of Mexico revolted against the rule of dictator President Porfirio Díaz, leading to his eventual defeat and to a democratic government.

1914–1918 WORLD WAR I
The assassination of Austria's Archduke Ferdinand by a Serbian nationalist sparked this wide-spreading war. The U.S. entered after Germany sunk the British ship *Lusitania*, killing more than 120 Americans.

1918–1920 RUSSIAN CIVIL WAR
Following the 1917 Russian Revolution, this conflict pitted the Communist Red Army against the foreign-backed White Army. The Red Army won, leading to the establishment of the Union of Soviet Socialist Republics (U.S.S.R.) in 1922.

1936–1939 SPANISH CIVIL WAR
Aid from Italy and Germany helped the Nationalists gain victory over the Communist-supported Republicans. The war resulted in the loss of more than 300,000 lives and increased tension in Europe leading up to World War II.

1939–1945 WORLD WAR II
This massive conflict in Europe, Asia, and North Africa involved many countries that aligned with the two sides: the Allies and the Axis. After the bombing of Pearl Harbor in Hawaii in 1941, the U.S. entered the war on the side of the Allies. More than 50 million people died during the war.

1946–1949 CHINESE CIVIL WAR
Also known as the "War of Liberation," this war pitted the Communist and Nationalist parties in China against each other. The Communists won.

1950–1953 KOREAN WAR
Kicked off when the Communist forces of North Korea, with backing from the Soviet Union, invaded their democratic neighbor to the south. A coalition of 16 countries from the United Nations stepped in to support South Korea.

75th Anniversary

D-Day

1950s–1975 VIETNAM WAR

Fought between the Communist North, supported by allies including China, and the government of South Vietnam, supported by the United States and other anticommunist nations.

1967 SIX-DAY WAR

A battle for land between Israel and the states of Egypt, Jordan, and Syria. The outcome resulted in Israel's gaining control of coveted territory, including the Gaza Strip and the West Bank.

1991–PRESENT
SOMALI CIVIL WAR

Began when Somalia's last president, a dictator named Mohamed Siad Barre, was overthrown. The war has led to years of fighting and anarchy.

2001–2014
WAR IN AFGHANISTAN

After attacks in the U.S. by the terrorist group al Qaeda, a coalition that eventually included more than 40 countries invaded Afghanistan to find Osama bin Laden and other al Qaeda members and to dismantle the Taliban. Bin Laden was killed in a U.S. covert operation in 2011. The North Atlantic Treaty Organization (NATO) took control of the coalition's combat mission in 2003. That combat mission officially ended in 2014.

2003–2011 WAR IN IRAQ

A coalition led by the U.S., and including Britain, Australia, and Spain, invaded Iraq over suspicions that Iraq had weapons of mass destruction.

O n June 6, 1944, some 160,000 American, British, Canadian, and other Allied troops stormed the shores of France's Normandy region during World War II. The forces pulled off a successful attack on Germany.

Hitler's Germany had invaded and occupied France for four years and had taken control of much of Europe. While the Soviets and other Allies fought Germany from the east, the Western Allies started planning D-Day, hoping to push the Germans out of France. (The *D* in D-Day stood for "day," as in the day the military operation began.)

In late 1943, the Allies put U.S. general Dwight D. Eisenhower in command of the planned invasion of Normandy. First, the Allies would to trick their foes into thinking they were about to attack somewhere else. They used double agents and even set up fake military bases in Great Britain to hide the fact that troops were advancing toward France.

Then the troops charged into Normandy, surprising the Germans with the largest naval, air, and land assault in history. The Germans fought back—all told, some 10,000 Allied troops were killed, wounded, or went missing in action during the Normandy invasion. But the Allies managed to gain strength and push farther into France, which gave them the advantage they needed to defeat Nazi Germany for good.

Seventy-five years later, D-Day is remembered as one of the most important moments in history. Not only did it mark successful teamwork among the Allies, but it also played a large part in ending World War II in Europe.

The Constitution & the Bill of Rights

The United States Constitution was written in 1787 by a group of political leaders from the 13 states that made up the U.S. at the time. Thirty-nine men, including Benjamin Franklin and James Madison, signed the document to create a national government. While some feared the creation of a strong federal government, all 13 states eventually ratified, or approved, the Constitution, making it the law of the land. The Constitution has three major parts: the preamble, the articles, and the amendments.

Here's a summary of what topics are covered in each part of the Constitution. Check out the Constitution online or at your local library for the full text.

THE PREAMBLE outlines the basic purposes of the government: *We the People of the United States, in order to form a more perfect Union, establish justice, insure domestic tranquility, provide for the common defense, promote the general welfare, and secure the blessings of liberty to ourselves and our posterity, do ordain and establish this Constitution for the United States of America.*

SEVEN ARTICLES outline the powers of Congress, the president, and the court system:

Article I outlines the legislative branch—the Senate and the House of Representatives—and its powers and responsibilities.

Article II outlines the executive branch—the presidency—and its powers and responsibilities.

Article III outlines the judicial branch—the court system—and its powers and responsibilities.

Article IV describes the individual states' rights and powers.

Article V outlines the amendment process.

Article VI establishes the Constitution as the law of the land.

Article VII gives the requirements for the Constitution to be approved.

THE AMENDMENTS, or additions to the Constitution, were put in later as needed. In 1791, the first 10 amendments, known as the **Bill of Rights,** were added. Since then, another 17 amendments have been added. This is the Bill of Rights:

1st Amendment: guarantees freedom of religion, speech, and the press, and the right to assemble and petition. The U.S. may not have a national religion.

2nd Amendment: discusses the militia and the right of people to bear arms

3rd Amendment: prohibits the military or troops from using private homes without consent

4th Amendment: protects people and their homes from search, arrest, or seizure without probable cause or a warrant

5th Amendment: grants people the right to have a trial and prevents punishment before prosecution; protects private property from being taken without compensation

6th Amendment: guarantees the right to a speedy and public trial

7th Amendment: guarantees a trial by jury in certain cases

8th Amendment: forbids "cruel and unusual punishments"

9th Amendment: states that the Constitution is not all-encompassing and does not deny people other, unspecified rights

10th Amendment: grants the powers not covered by the Constitution to the states and the people

Read the full text version of the United States Constitution at constitutioncenter.org/constitution/full-text

Branches of Government

The **UNITED STATES GOVERNMENT** is divided into three branches: **executive**, **legislative**, and **judicial**. The system of checks and balances is a way to control power and to make sure one branch can't take the reins of government. For example, most of the president's actions require the approval of Congress. Likewise, the laws passed in Congress must be signed by the president before they can take effect.

White House

Executive Branch

The Constitution lists the central powers of the president: to serve as commander in chief of the armed forces; make treaties with other nations; grant pardons; inform Congress on the state of the union; and appoint ambassadors, officials, and judges. The executive branch includes the president and the 15 governmental departments.

Legislative Branch

This branch is made up of Congress—the Senate and the House of Representatives. The Constitution grants Congress the power to make laws. Congress is made up of elected representatives from each state. Each state has two representatives in the Senate, while the number of representatives in the House is determined by the size of the state's population. Washington, D.C., and the territories elect nonvoting representatives to the House of Representatives. The Founding Fathers set up this system as a compromise between big states—which wanted representation based on population—and small states—which wanted all states to have equal representation rights.

The U.S. Capitol in Washington, D.C.

Judicial Branch

The judicial branch is composed of the federal court system— the U.S. Supreme Court, the courts of appeals, and the district courts. The Supreme Court is the most powerful court. Its motto is "Equal Justice Under Law." This influential court is responsible for interpreting the Constitution and applying it to the cases that it hears. The decisions of the Supreme Court are absolute—they are the final word on any legal question.

There are nine justices on the Supreme Court. They are appointed by the president of the United States and confirmed by the Senate.

The U.S. Supreme Court Building in Washington, D.C.

237

The Indian Experience

American Indians are indigenous to North and South America—they are the people who were here before Columbus and other European explorers came to these lands. They lived in nations, tribes, and bands across both continents. For decades following the arrival of Europeans in 1492, American Indians clashed with the newcomers who had ruptured the Indians' ways of living.

Tribal Land

During the 19th century, both United States legislation and military action restricted the movement of American Indians, forcing them to live on reservations and attempting to dismantle tribal structures. For centuries, Indians were displaced or killed, or became assimilated into the general U.S. population. In 1924 the Indian Citizenship Act granted citizenship to all American Indians. Unfortunately, this was not enough to end the social discrimination and mistreatment that many Indians have faced. Today, American Indians living in the U.S. still face many challenges.

Healing the Past

Many members of the 560-plus recognized tribes in the United States live primarily on reservations. Some tribes have more than one reservation, while others have none. Together these reservations make up less than 3 percent of the nation's land area. The tribal governments on reservations have the right to form their own governments and to enforce laws, similar to individual states. Many feel that this sovereignty is still not enough to right the wrongs of the past: They hope for a change in the U.S. government's relationship with American Indians.

Some American Indians used cranberry juice to dye clothing, rugs, and blankets.

Thousands of years ago, some American Indians may have kept bobcats as pets.

Top: A Navajo youth dancing at a powwow
Middle: A Salish woman in traditional dress in Montana
Bottom: Little Shell men in traditional costume

The president of the United States is the chief of the executive branch, the commander in chief of the U.S. armed forces, and head of the federal government. Elected every four years, the president is the highest policy-maker in the nation. The 22nd Amendment (1951) says that no person may be elected to the office of president more than twice. There have been 45 presidencies and 44 presidents.

JAMES MADISON
4th President of the United States ★ 1809–1817
BORN March 16, 1751, at Belle Grove, Port Conway, VA
POLITICAL PARTY Democratic-Republican
NO. OF TERMS two
VICE PRESIDENTS 1st term: George Clinton
2nd term: Elbridge Gerry
DIED June 28, 1836, at Montpelier, Orange County, VA

GEORGE WASHINGTON
1st President of the United States ★ 1789–1797
BORN Feb. 22, 1732, in Pope's Creek, Westmoreland County, VA
POLITICAL PARTY Federalist
NO. OF TERMS two
VICE PRESIDENT John Adams
DIED Dec. 14, 1799, at Mount Vernon, VA

JAMES MONROE
5th President of the United States ★ 1817–1825
BORN April 28, 1758, in Westmoreland County, VA
POLITICAL PARTY Democratic-Republican
NO. OF TERMS two
VICE PRESIDENT Daniel D. Tompkins
DIED July 4, 1831, in New York, NY

JOHN ADAMS
2nd President of the United States ★ 1797–1801
BORN Oct. 30, 1735, in Braintree (now Quincy), MA
POLITICAL PARTY Federalist
NO. OF TERMS one
VICE PRESIDENT Thomas Jefferson
DIED July 4, 1826, in Quincy, MA

JOHN QUINCY ADAMS
6th President of the United States ★ 1825–1829
BORN July 11, 1767, in Braintree (now Quincy), MA
POLITICAL PARTY Democratic-Republican
NO. OF TERMS one
VICE PRESIDENT John Caldwell Calhoun
DIED Feb. 23, 1848, at the U.S. Capitol, Washington, D.C.

THOMAS JEFFERSON
3rd President of the United States ★ 1801–1809
BORN April 13, 1743, at Shadwell, Goochland (now Albemarle) County, VA
POLITICAL PARTY Democratic-Republican
NO. OF TERMS two
VICE PRESIDENTS 1st term: Aaron Burr
2nd term: George Clinton
DIED July 4, 1826, at Monticello, Charlottesville, VA

ANDREW JACKSON
7th President of the United States ★ 1829–1837
BORN March 15, 1767, in the Waxhaw region, NC and SC
POLITICAL PARTY Democrat
NO. OF TERMS two
VICE PRESIDENTS 1st term: John Caldwell Calhoun
2nd term: Martin Van Buren
DIED June 8, 1845, in Nashville, TN

Jeffersonia diphylla **wildflowers** are named after Thomas Jefferson.

MARTIN VAN BUREN
8th President of the United States ★ 1837–1841
BORN Dec. 5, 1782, in Kinderhook, NY
POLITICAL PARTY Democrat
NO. OF TERMS one
VICE PRESIDENT Richard M. Johnson
DIED July 24, 1862, in Kinderhook, NY

WILLIAM HENRY HARRISON

9th President of the United States ★ 1841

BORN Feb. 9, 1773, in Charles City County, VA

POLITICAL PARTY Whig

NO. OF TERMS one (cut short by death)

VICE PRESIDENT John Tyler

DIED April 4, 1841, in the White House, Washington, D.C.

JOHN TYLER

10th President of the United States ★ 1841–1845

BORN March 29, 1790, in Charles City County, VA

POLITICAL PARTY Whig

NO. OF TERMS one (partial)

VICE PRESIDENT none

DIED Jan. 18, 1862, in Richmond, VA

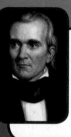

JAMES K. POLK

11th President of the United States ★ 1845–1849

BORN Nov. 2, 1795, near Pineville, Mecklenburg County, NC

POLITICAL PARTY Democrat

NO. OF TERMS one

VICE PRESIDENT George Mifflin Dallas

DIED June 15, 1849, in Nashville, TN

ZACHARY TAYLOR

12th President of the United States ★ 1849–1850

BORN Nov. 24, 1784, in Orange County, VA

POLITICAL PARTY Whig

NO. OF TERMS one (cut short by death)

VICE PRESIDENT Millard Fillmore

DIED July 9, 1850, in the White House, Washington, D.C.

MILLARD FILLMORE

13th President of the United States ★ 1850–1853

BORN Jan. 7, 1800, in Cayuga County, NY

POLITICAL PARTY Whig

NO. OF TERMS one (partial)

VICE PRESIDENT none

DIED March 8, 1874, in Buffalo, NY

FRANKLIN PIERCE

14th President of the United States ★ 1853–1857

BORN Nov. 23, 1804, in Hillsborough (now Hillsboro), NH

POLITICAL PARTY Democrat

NO. OF TERMS one

VICE PRESIDENT William Rufus De Vane King

DIED Oct. 8, 1869, in Concord, NH

> Franklin Pierce was the **FIRST PRESIDENT** to use a **FULL-TIME BODYGUARD.**

JAMES BUCHANAN

15th President of the United States ★ 1857–1861

BORN April 23, 1791, in Cove Gap, PA

POLITICAL PARTY Democrat

NO. OF TERMS one

VICE PRESIDENT John Cabell Breckinridge

DIED June 1, 1868, in Lancaster, PA

ABRAHAM LINCOLN

16th President of the United States ★ 1861–1865

BORN Feb. 12, 1809, near Hodgenville, KY

POLITICAL PARTY Republican (formerly Whig)

NO. OF TERMS two (assassinated)

VICE PRESIDENTS 1st term: Hannibal Hamlin
2nd term: Andrew Johnson

DIED April 15, 1865, in Washington, D.C.

ANDREW JOHNSON

17th President of the United States ★ 1865–1869

BORN Dec. 29, 1808, in Raleigh, NC

POLITICAL PARTY Democrat

NO. OF TERMS one (partial)

VICE PRESIDENT none

DIED July 31, 1875, in Carter's Station, TN

ULYSSES S. GRANT

18th President of the United States ★ 1869–1877

BORN April 27, 1822,
in Point Pleasant, OH

POLITICAL PARTY Republican

NO. OF TERMS two

VICE PRESIDENTS 1st term: Schuyler Colfax
2nd term: Henry Wilson

DIED July 23, 1885, in Mount
McGregor, NY

RUTHERFORD B. HAYES

19th President of the United States ★ 1877–1881

BORN Oct. 4, 1822,
in Delaware, OH

POLITICAL PARTY Republican

NO. OF TERMS one

VICE PRESIDENT William Almon Wheeler

DIED Jan. 17, 1893, in Fremont, OH

JAMES A. GARFIELD

20th President of the United States ★ 1881

BORN Nov. 19, 1831, near
Orange, OH

POLITICAL PARTY Republican

NO. OF TERMS one (assassinated)

VICE PRESIDENT Chester A. Arthur

DIED Sept. 19, 1881, in Elberon, NJ

CHESTER A. ARTHUR

21st President of the United States ★ 1881–1885

BORN Oct. 5, 1829, in Fairfield, VT

POLITICAL PARTY Republican

NO. OF TERMS one (partial)

VICE PRESIDENT none

DIED Nov. 18, 1886, in New York, NY

GROVER CLEVELAND

22nd and 24th President of the United States
1885–1889 ★ 1893–1897

BORN March 18, 1837, in Caldwell, NJ

POLITICAL PARTY Democrat

NO. OF TERMS two (nonconsecutive)

VICE PRESIDENTS 1st administration:
Thomas Andrews Hendricks
2nd administration:
Adlai Ewing Stevenson

DIED June 24, 1908, in Princeton, NJ

BENJAMIN HARRISON

23rd President of the United States ★ 1889–1893

BORN Aug. 20, 1833, in North Bend, OH

POLITICAL PARTY Republican

NO. OF TERMS one

VICE PRESIDENT Levi Parsons Morton

DIED March 13, 1901, in Indianapolis, IN

WILLIAM MCKINLEY

25th President of the United States ★ 1897–1901

BORN Jan. 29, 1843, in Niles, OH

POLITICAL PARTY Republican

NO. OF TERMS two (assassinated)

VICE PRESIDENTS 1st term:
Garret Augustus Hobart
2nd term:
Theodore Roosevelt

DIED Sept. 14, 1901, in Buffalo, NY

THEODORE ROOSEVELT

26th President of the United States ★ 1901–1909

BORN Oct. 27, 1858, in New York, NY

POLITICAL PARTY Republican

NO. OF TERMS one, plus balance of
McKinley's term

VICE PRESIDENTS 1st term: none
2nd term: Charles
Warren Fairbanks

DIED Jan. 6, 1919, in Oyster Bay, NY

WILLIAM HOWARD TAFT

27th President of the United States ★ 1909–1913

BORN Sept. 15, 1857, in Cincinnati, OH

POLITICAL PARTY Republican

NO. OF TERMS one

VICE PRESIDENT James Schoolcraft
Sherman

DIED March 8, 1930, in Washington, D.C.

William
Howard Taft
was a
**CHAMPION
WRESTLER**
in college.

WOODROW WILSON
28th President of the United States ★ *1913–1921*
BORN Dec. 29, 1856, in Staunton, VA
POLITICAL PARTY Democrat
NO. OF TERMS two
VICE PRESIDENT Thomas Riley Marshall
DIED Feb. 3, 1924, in Washington, D.C.

WARREN G. HARDING
29th President of the United States ★ *1921–1923*
BORN Nov. 2, 1865, in Caledonia
(now Blooming Grove), OH
POLITICAL PARTY Republican
NO. OF TERMS one (died while in office)
VICE PRESIDENT Calvin Coolidge
DIED Aug. 2, 1923, in San Francisco, CA

CALVIN COOLIDGE
30th President of the United States ★ *1923–1929*
BORN July 4, 1872, in Plymouth, VT
POLITICAL PARTY Republican
NO. OF TERMS one, plus balance of
Harding's term
VICE PRESIDENTS 1st term: none
2nd term:
Charles Gates Dawes
DIED Jan. 5, 1933, in Northampton, MA

Calvin Coolidge
kept an
ELECTRIC HORSE
inside the White House to
**PRACTICE TROTTING
AND GALLOPING.**

HERBERT HOOVER
31st President of the United States ★ *1929–1933*
BORN Aug. 10, 1874,
in West Branch, IA
POLITICAL PARTY Republican
NO. OF TERMS one
VICE PRESIDENT Charles Curtis
DIED Oct. 20, 1964, in New York, NY

FRANKLIN D. ROOSEVELT
32nd President of the United States ★ *1933–1945*
BORN Jan. 30, 1882, in Hyde Park, NY
POLITICAL PARTY Democrat
NO. OF TERMS four (died while in office)
VICE PRESIDENTS 1st & 2nd terms: John
Nance Garner; 3rd term:
Henry Agard Wallace;
4th term: Harry S. Truman
DIED April 12, 1945,
in Warm Springs, GA

HARRY S. TRUMAN
33rd President of the United States ★ *1945–1953*
BORN May 8, 1884, in Lamar, MO
POLITICAL PARTY Democrat
NO. OF TERMS one, plus balance of
Franklin D. Roosevelt's term
VICE PRESIDENTS 1st term: none
2nd term:
Alben William Barkley
DIED Dec. 26, 1972, in Independence, MO

DWIGHT D. EISENHOWER
34th President of the United States ★ *1953–1961*
BORN Oct. 14, 1890, in Denison, TX
POLITICAL PARTY Republican
NO. OF TERMS two
VICE PRESIDENT Richard Nixon
DIED March 28, 1969,
in Washington, D.C.

JOHN F. KENNEDY
35th President of the United States ★ *1961–1963*
BORN May 29, 1917, in Brookline, MA
POLITICAL PARTY Democrat
NO. OF TERMS one (assassinated)
VICE PRESIDENT Lyndon B. Johnson
DIED Nov. 22, 1963, in Dallas, TX

LYNDON B. JOHNSON
36th President of the United States ★ *1963–1969*
BORN Aug. 27, 1908, near Stonewall, TX
POLITICAL PARTY Democrat
NO. OF TERMS one, plus balance of
Kennedy's term
VICE PRESIDENTS 1st term: none
2nd term: Hubert
Horatio Humphrey
DIED Jan. 22, 1973, near San Antonio, TX

RICHARD NIXON

37th President of the United States ★ *1969–1974*
BORN Jan. 9, 1913, in Yorba Linda, CA
POLITICAL PARTY Republican
NO. OF TERMS two (resigned)
VICE PRESIDENTS 1st term & 2nd term (partial): Spiro Theodore Agnew; 2nd term (balance): Gerald R. Ford
DIED April 22, 1994, in New York, NY

GERALD R. FORD

38th President of the United States ★ *1974–1977*
BORN July 14, 1913, in Omaha, NE
POLITICAL PARTY Republican
NO. OF TERMS one (partial)
VICE PRESIDENT Nelson Aldrich Rockefeller
DIED Dec. 26, 2006, in Rancho Mirage, CA

JIMMY CARTER

39th President of the United States ★ *1977–1981*
BORN Oct. 1, 1924, in Plains, GA
POLITICAL PARTY Democrat
NO. OF TERMS one
VICE PRESIDENT Walter Frederick (Fritz) Mondale

RONALD REAGAN

40th President of the United States ★ *1981–1989*
BORN Feb. 6, 1911, in Tampico, IL
POLITICAL PARTY Republican
NO. OF TERMS two
VICE PRESIDENT George H. W. Bush
DIED June 5, 2004, in Los Angeles, CA

GEORGE H. W. BUSH

41st President of the United States ★ *1989–1993*
BORN June 12, 1924, in Milton, MA
POLITICAL PARTY Republican
NO. OF TERMS one
VICE PRESIDENT James Danforth (Dan) Quayle III

BILL CLINTON

42nd President of the United States ★ *1993–2001*
BORN Aug. 19, 1946, in Hope, AR
POLITICAL PARTY Democrat
NO. OF TERMS two
VICE PRESIDENT Albert Arnold Gore, Jr.

GEORGE W. BUSH

43rd President of the United States ★ *2001–2009*
BORN July 6, 1946, in New Haven, CT
POLITICAL PARTY Republican
NO. OF TERMS two
VICE PRESIDENT Richard Bruce Cheney

BARACK OBAMA

44th President of the United States ★ *2009–2017*
BORN Aug. 4, 1961, in Honolulu, HI
POLITICAL PARTY Democrat
NO. OF TERMS two
VICE PRESIDENT Joseph R. Biden, Jr.

> Donald Trump
> LIKES
> CHERRY VANILLA
> ICE CREAM.

DONALD TRUMP

45th President of the United States ★ *2017–present*
BORN June 14, 1946, in Queens, NY
POLITICAL PARTY Republican
VICE PRESIDENT Mike Pence

Cool Things About AIR FORCE ONE

The president of the United States takes a lot of work trips as part of the job. But the commander in chief doesn't fly business class on a regular plane—he or she takes a private jet, Air Force One. Here are five reasons why Air Force One is the coolest plane in the air.

President Barack Obama flew OVER ONE MILLION MILES (1.6 million km) on more than 940 FLIGHTS aboard Air Force One.

1 JUMBO JET

Most private planes are small. Air Force One is definitely *not*. The customized 747 airliner, designed to carry up to 102 passengers, has three levels, stands as tall as a six-story building, and is longer than five school buses. With a full load, Air Force One can weigh up to a whopping 416 tons (377 t), which is the equivalent of more than 80 big elephants. In the air it's nimble enough to cruise at more than 600 miles an hour (966 km/h).

2 SUPER FIRST-CLASS

The president doesn't just get a big seat on Air Force One—there's a whole apartment. Located in the nose of the plane under the cockpit, the presidential suite includes a bedroom, a private bathroom with a shower, and enough space to exercise. The first family even has its own entrance to the plane. The president also has a private office, which explains one of the plane's nicknames, "the Flying White House."

3 DOCTOR ON BOARD

Air Force One doesn't have to make an emergency landing if there's a medical issue, because a doctor is on every flight. The clinic has an office with a small pharmacy, blood supplies, and an emergency operating table.

It costs about $180,000 AN HOUR to fly Air Force One.

President Obama visited MORE THAN 45 COUNTRIES during his presidency.

4. AIRPLANE FOOD

Unlike most midair meals, food on Air Force One is fine dining. Among the 26 crew members are cooks and several flight attendants who can serve 100 meals at a time from the airplane's two kitchens. The commander in chief can place orders 24/7 for whatever he or she wants—or doesn't want. (President George H.W. Bush banned broccoli from his flights on Air Force One.)

5. LIFT TO THE AIRPORT

The president doesn't have to fight traffic on the way to the airport. He or she takes a personal helicopter from the White House. Called Marine One because it's operated by the Marine Corps, the chopper lands on the White House lawn and ferries everyone over to the plane.

CIVIL RIGHTS

The Little Rock Nine study during the weeks when they were blocked from school.

Although the Constitution protects the civil rights of American citizens, it has not always been able to protect all Americans from persecution or discrimination. During the first half of the 20th century, many Americans, particularly African Americans, were subjected to widespread discrimination and racism. By the mid-1950s, many people were eager to end the bonds of racism and bring freedom to all men and women.

The civil rights movement of the 1950s and 1960s sought to end racial discrimination against African Americans, especially in the southern states. The movement wanted to restore the fundamentals of economic and social equality to those who had been oppressed.

The Little Rock Nine

September 4, 1957, marked the first day of school at Little Rock Central High in Little Rock, Arkansas. But this was no ordinary back-to-school scene: Armed soldiers surrounded the entrance, awaiting the arrival of Central's first ever African-American students. The welcome was not warm, however, as the students—now known as the Little Rock Nine—were refused entry into the school by the soldiers and a group of protesters, angry about the potential integration. This did not deter the students, who gained the support of President Dwight D. Eisenhower to eventually earn their right to go to an integrated school. Today, the Little Rock Nine are still considered civil rights icons for challenging a racist system—and winning!

Key Events in the Civil Rights Movement

1954	The Supreme Court case *Brown* v. *Board of Education* declares school segregation illegal.
1955	Rosa Parks refuses to give up her bus seat to a white passenger and spurs a bus boycott.
1957	The Little Rock Nine help to integrate schools.
1960	Four black college students begin sit-ins at a restaurant in Greensboro, North Carolina.
1961	Freedom Rides to southern states begin as a way to protest segregation in transportation.
1963	Martin Luther King, Jr., leads the famous March on Washington.
1964	The Civil Rights Act, signed by President Lyndon B. Johnson, prohibits discrimination based on race, color, religion, sex, and national origin.
1967	Thurgood Marshall becomes the first African American to be named to the Supreme Court.
1968	President Lyndon B. Johnson signs the Civil Rights Act of 1968, which prohibits discrimination in the sale, rental, and financing of housing.

STONE OF HOPE:
THE LEGACY OF MARTIN LUTHER KING, JR.

On April 4, 1968, Dr. Martin Luther King, Jr., was shot by James Earl Ray while standing on a hotel balcony in Memphis, Tennessee. The news of his death sent shock waves throughout the world: Dr. King, a Baptist minister and founder of the Southern Christian Leadership Conference (SCLC), was the most prominent civil rights leader of his time. His nonviolent protests and marches against segregation, as well as his powerful speeches—including his famous "I Have a Dream" speech—motivated people to fight for justice for all.

More than 50 years after his death, Dr. King's dream lives on through a memorial on the National Mall in Washington, D.C. Built in 2011, the memorial features a 30-foot (9-m) statue of Dr. King carved into a granite boulder named the "Stone of Hope."

Each year, thousands of visitors pay tribute to this inspirational figure, who will forever be remembered as a leader, a peacemaker, and a man who never backed down in his stand against racism.

EQUAL in '63 RIGHTS

"The time is always right to do what is right."

Martin Luther King, Jr. Memorial in Washington, D.C.

There are about 900 streets named after Dr. King in the United States.

Martin Luther King, Jr., is the only non-president whose birthday is celebrated as a national holiday.

8 Daring Women in U.S. History!

Who: Dolley Madison
Lived: 1768–1849
Why she's daring: As the nation's first lady from 1809 to 1817, she single-handedly saved a famous—and valuable—portrait of George Washington when it faced almost certain destruction during the War of 1812. As British troops approached the White House, Madison refused to leave until the painting was taken to safety.

Who: Nellie Tayloe Ross
Lived: 1876–1977
Why she's daring: In 1925, Ross became the nation's first woman governor after boldly campaigning for the Wyoming seat left vacant when her husband suddenly passed away. She went on to run the U.S. Mint from 1933 to 1953.

Who: Bessie Coleman
Lived: 1892–1926
Why she's daring: When U.S. flight schools denied her entry, Coleman traveled to France to earn her pilot's license and became the first African-American female aviator. Later, her high-flying, daredevil stunts in air shows earned her the nickname "Queen Bess."

Who: Sacagawea
Lived: ca 1788–1812
Why she's daring: As the only woman to accompany Lewis and Clark into the American West, Sacagawea's calm presence and smarts saved the expedition many times. She served as a Shoshone interpreter for the explorers, found edible plants to feed the crew, and even saved important documents and supplies from a capsizing boat.

Who: Julia Butterfly Hill
Lived: 1974–
Why she's daring: An environmental activist, Hill spent more than two years (1997–1999) living on a platform in a thousand-year-old redwood tree named Luna. During her marathon tree-sit to protest aggressive logging practices, Hill endured extreme weather. Her efforts eventually led to a settlement with the lumber company to forever protect Luna, saving the tree and its immediate surroundings.

Who: Annie Smith Peck
Lived: 1850–1935
Why she's daring: After taking up mountain climbing in her late 30s, former professor Smith Peck became the third woman to scale the Swiss Matterhorn. Her shocking choice to climb in pants instead of a skirt brought her international attention. In 1908, she became the first person to climb Peru's Mount Huascarán. Boasting remarkable strength and endurance, Smith Peck continued to climb well into her 80s.

Who: Dolores Huerta
Lived: 1930–
Why she's daring: As a teacher who saw many of her students living in poverty, Huerta rallied to raise awareness for the poor, especially among farmworkers, immigrants, and women. Later, she encouraged Hispanic women to enter politics, helping to increase in the number of women holding offices at the local, state, and federal levels. She received the Presidential Medal of Freedom in 2012.

Who: Lucille Ball
Lived: 1911–1989
Why she's daring: Famous for playing an iconic funny girl in the hit show *I Love Lucy*, Ball worked even more magic behind the screen. A pioneer in the entertainment industry, Ball was the first woman to head a major television studio. At the same time, she made 72 movies, cementing her position as one of the most legendary actresses and comediennes in the world.

QUIZ WHIZ

Go back in time to seek the answers to this history quiz!

Write your answers on a piece of paper. Then check them below.

① Prague Castle in the Czech Republic is the _____ ancient castle complex in the world.

a. oldest
b. largest
c. smallest
d. scariest

② **True or false?** There's a pyramid as tall as a 15-story building in Mexico City, Mexico.

③ What monumental historical event occurred 30 years ago in Germany?

a. East Germans were allowed to enter West Germany.
b. The summer Olympics were held in Munich.
c. World War I began.
d. A German man set a sausage-eating world record.

④ **True or false?** Some ancient Romans wore bear and wolf skins and howled in battle like wild animals.

⑤ What happened to the Chinese farmers who discovered a trove of ancient life-size clay soldiers?

a. They sold the soldiers and made a fortune.
b. They received a lifetime of good luck.
c. They got sick and died early deaths.
d. They were haunted by the ghost of China's first emperor.

Not **STUMPED** yet? Check out the *NATIONAL GEOGRAPHIC KIDS QUIZ WHIZ* collection for more crazy **HISTORY** questions!

ANSWERS:
1. b; 2. True; 3. a; 4. False. Some Viking warriors did this, not ancient Romans; 5. c.

Brilliant Biographies

A biography is the story of a person's life. It can be a brief summary or a long book. Biographers—those who write biographies—use many different sources to learn about their subjects. You can write your own biography of a famous person you find inspiring.

How to Get Started

Choose a subject you find interesting. If you think Cleopatra is cool, you have a good chance of getting your reader interested, too. If you're bored by ancient Egypt, your reader will be snoring after your first paragraph.

Your subject can be almost anyone: an author, an inventor, a celebrity, a politician, or a member of your family. To find someone to write about, ask yourself these simple questions:

1. Whom do I want to know more about?
2. What did this person do that was special?
3. How did this person change the world?

Do Your Research

- Find out as much about your subject as possible. Read books, news articles, and encyclopedia entries. Watch video clips and movies, and search the Internet. Conduct interviews, if possible.
- Take notes, writing down important facts and interesting stories about your subject.

Write the Biography

- Come up with a title. Include the person's name.
- Write an introduction. Consider asking a probing question about your subject.
- Include information about the person's childhood. When was this person born? Where did he or she grow up? Whom did he or she admire?
- Highlight the person's talents, accomplishments, and personal attributes.
- Describe the specific events that helped to shape this person's life. Did this person ever have a problem and overcome it?
- Write a conclusion. Include your thoughts about why it is important to learn about this person.
- Once you have finished your first draft, revise and then proofread your work.

Author
Rick Riordan

**Here's a SAMPLE BIOGRAPHY of Rick Riordan, best-selling author of series such as Percy Jackson and the Olympians and Magnus Chase and the Gods of Asgard.
Of course, there is so much more for you to discover, and write about on your own!**

Rick Riordan—Author

Rick Riordan was born on June 5, 1964, in San Antonio, Texas, U.S.A. Born into a creative family—his mom was a musician and artist and his dad was a ceramicist—Riordan began writing in middle school, and he published his first short stories while attending college.

After graduating from University of Texas at Austin, Riordan went on to teach English to middle schoolers, spending his summers as a music director at a summer camp. Writing adult mysteries on the side, Riordan soon discovered his knack for writing for younger readers and published *The Lightning Thief,* the first book in the Percy Jackson series, in 2005. *The Sea of Monsters* soon followed. Before long, Riordan quit his teaching job to become a full-time writer.

Today Riordan has penned dozens of books, firmly establishing himself as one of the most accomplished and well-known authors of our time. When he's not writing, Riordan likes to read, swim, play guitar, and travel with his wife, Becky, and their sons, Haley and Patrick.

Geography
Rocks

Researchers explore massive selenite beams in Mexico's Cave of Crystals.

THE POLITICAL WORLD

Earth's land area is made up of seven continents, but people have divided much of the land into smaller political units called countries. Australia is a continent made up of a single country, and Antarctica is used for scientific research. But the other five continents include almost 200 independent countries. The political map shown here depicts boundaries—imaginary lines created by treaties—that separate countries. Some boundaries, such as the one between the United States and Canada, are very stable and have been recognized for many years.

ARCTIC

Queen Elizabeth Is.

Chukchi Sea
Beaufort Sea
RUSSIA
Alaska (U.S.)
Bering Sea
Gulf of Alaska

Great Bear Lake
Great Slave Lake

Baffin Bay

Greenland (Denmark)

Greenland Sea

ARCTIC CIRCLE
ICELAND

CANADA

Hudson Bay

Labrador Sea

60°

Lake Winnipeg

Great Lakes

UNITED KINGDOM

IRELAND (ÉIRE)

FRANCE

Great Salt Lake

UNITED STATES

PORT.   SPAIN

See Europe map for more detail.

30°

MOROCCO

TROPIC OF CANCER

Gulf of Mexico

BAHAMAS

DOMINCAN REP.
Puerto Rico (U.S.)

Western Sahara (Morocco)

Hawai'i (U.S.)

MEXICO

CUBA
HAITI
JAMAICA
BELIZE
GUATEMALA
EL SALVADOR   HONDURAS
NICARAGUA
COSTA RICA

ST. KITTS & NEVIS
ANTIGUA & BARBUDA
Guadeloupe (France)
DOMINICA
Martinique (France)
BARBADOS
ST. VINCENT & THE GRENADINES
TRINIDAD AND TOBAGO

CABO MAURITANIA
VERDE

MALI

Caribbean Sea
ST. LUCIA
GRENADA

SENEGAL
GAMBIA
GUINEA-BISSAU

BURKINA FASO

GHANA

PANAMA

VENEZUELA

GUYANA

GUINEA
SIERRA LEONE
LIBERIA

PACIFIC

COLOMBIA

French Guiana (France)

SURINAME

CÔTE D'IVOIRE (IVORY COAST)

EQUATOR   150°   120°   90°   30°   0°

KIRIBATI

Galápagos Islands (Ecuador)

ECUADOR

EQ. GUINEA

OCEAN

Marquesas Islands (France)

PERU

BRAZIL

SAO TOME AND PRINCIPE

ATLANTIC

SAMOA
American Samoa (U.S.)
French Polynesia (France)

BOLIVIA

OCEAN

TONGA

TROPIC OF CAPRICORN

PARAGUAY

0   miles   2000
0   kilometers   3000

Winkel Tripel Projection

URUGUAY

CHILE   ARGENTINA

30°

Chatham Is. (N.Z.)

Falkland Islands (U.K.)

Tierra del Fuego

Meridian of Greenwich (London)

Strait of Magellan

Drake Passage

ANTARCTIC

60°

Weddell Sea

Ross Sea

A N T

Other boundaries, such as the one between Sudan and South Sudan in northeast Africa, are relatively new and still disputed. Countries come in all shapes and sizes. Russia and Canada are giants; others, such as El Salvador and Qatar, are small. Some countries are long and skinny—look at Chile in South America! Still other countries—such as Indonesia and Japan in Asia—are made up of groups of islands. The political map is a clue to the diversity that makes Earth so fascinating.

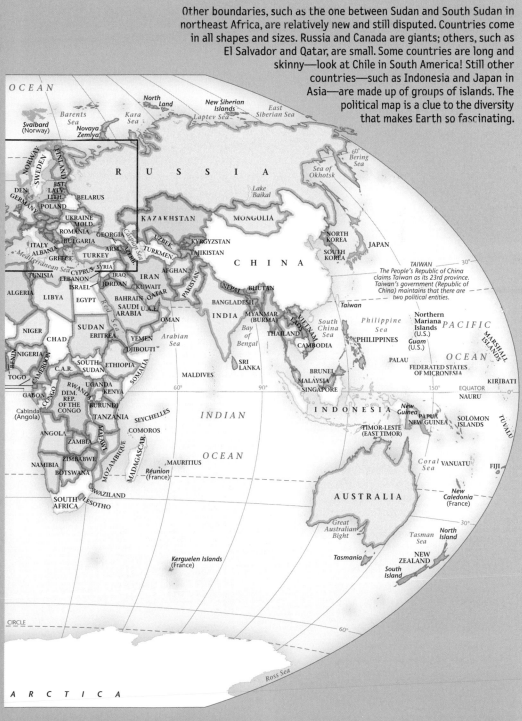

TAIWAN
The People's Republic of China claims Taiwan as its 23rd province. Taiwan's government (Republic of China) maintains that there are two political entities.

THE PHYSICAL WORLD

Earth is dominated by large landmasses called continents—seven in all—and by an interconnected global ocean that is divided into four parts by the continents. More than 70 percent of Earth's surface is covered by oceans, and the rest is made up of land areas.

   Different landforms give variety to the surface of the continents. The Rocky Mountains divide North America, the Andes mark the western edge of South America, and the Himalaya tower above South Asia. The Plateau of Tibet forms the rugged core of Asia, while

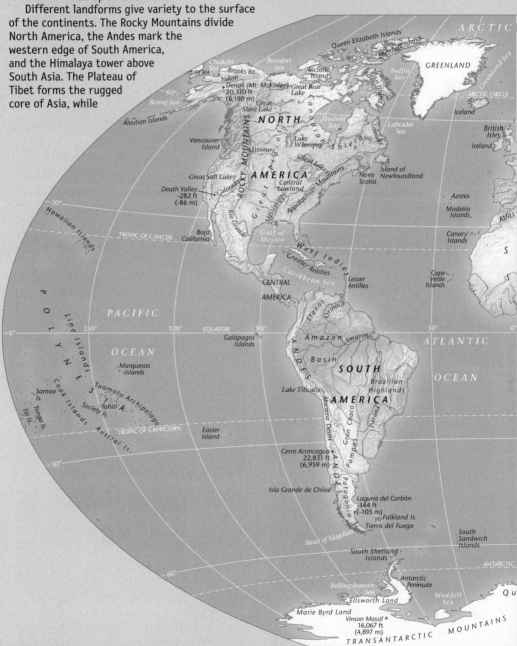

the Northern European Plain extends from the North Sea to the Ural Mountains. Much of Africa is a plateau, and dry plains cover large areas of Australia. Mountains rise more than 16,000 feet (4,877 m) above Antarctica's massive ice sheets. Mountains and trenches make the ocean floors as varied as any continent. A mountain chain called the Mid-Atlantic Ridge runs the length of the Atlantic Ocean. In the western Pacific, trenches drop deep into the ocean floor.

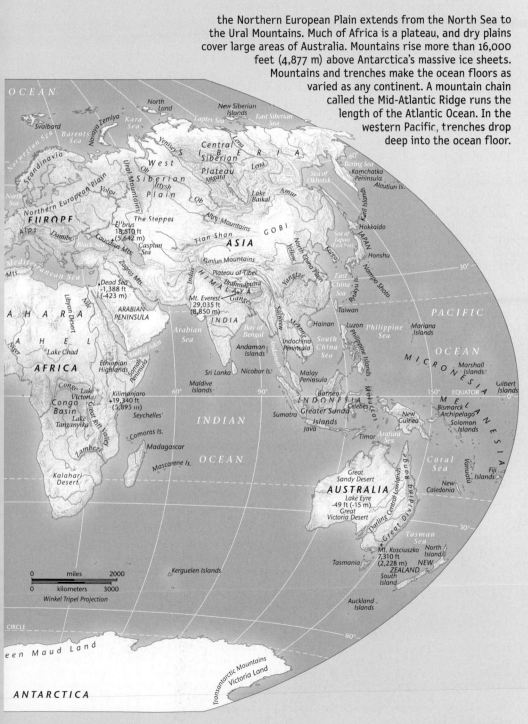

KINDS OF MAPS

Maps are special tools that geographers use to tell a story about Earth. Maps can be used to show just about anything related to places. Some maps show physical features, such as mountains or vegetation. Maps can also show climates or natural hazards and other things we cannot easily see. Other maps illustrate different features on Earth—political boundaries, urban centers, and economic systems.

AN IMPERFECT TOOL

Maps are not perfect. A globe is a scale model of Earth with accurate relative sizes and locations. Because maps are flat, they involve distortions of size, shape, and direction. Also, cartographers—people who create maps—make choices about what information to include. Because of this, it is important to study many different types of maps to learn the complete story of Earth. Three commonly found kinds of maps are shown on this page.

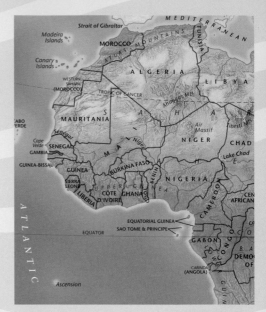

PHYSICAL MAPS. Earth's natural features—landforms, water bodies, and vegetation—are shown on physical maps. The map above uses color and shading to illustrate mountains, lakes, rivers, and deserts of western Africa. Country names and borders are added for reference, but they are not natural features.

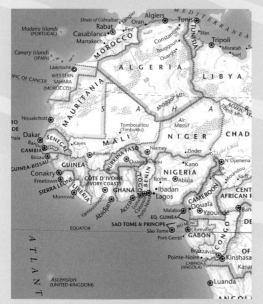

POLITICAL MAPS. These maps represent characteristics of the landscape created by humans, such as boundaries, cities, and place-names. Natural features are added only for reference. On the map above, capital cities are represented with a star inside a circle, while other cities are shown with black dots.

THEMATIC MAPS. Patterns related to a particular topic or theme, such as population distribution, appear on these maps. The map above displays the region's climate zones, which range from tropical wet (bright green) to tropical wet and dry (light green) to semiarid (dark yellow) to arid or desert (light yellow).

MAKING MAPS

Long ago, cartographers worked with pen and ink, carefully handcrafting maps based on explorers' observations and diaries. Today, mapmaking is a high-tech business. Cartographers use Earth data stored in "layers" in a Geographic Information System (GIS) and special computer programs to create maps that can be easily updated as new information becomes available.

The National Geographic staff cartographers Mike McNey and Lauren Tierney, at right, are reviewing a map of Alaska for the *National Geographic Kids United States Atlas.*

Satellites in orbit around Earth act as eyes in the sky, recording data about the planet's land and ocean areas. The data is converted to numbers that are transmitted back to computers that are specially programmed to interpret the data. They record it in a form that cartographers can use to create maps.

MAP PROJECTIONS

To create a map, cartographers transfer an image of the round Earth to a flat surface, a process called projection. All projections involve distortion. For example, an interrupted projection (bottom map) shows accurate shapes and relative sizes of land areas, but oceans have gaps. Other types of projections are cylindrical, conic, or azimuthal—each with certain advantages, but all with some distortion.

GEOGRAPHIC FEATURES

From roaring rivers to parched deserts, from underwater canyons to jagged mountains, Earth is covered with beautiful and diverse environments. Here are examples of the most common types of geographic features found around the world.

DESERT
Deserts are land features created by climate, specifically by a lack of water. Here, a camel caravan crosses the Sahara in North Africa.

VALLEY
Valleys, cut by running water or moving ice, may be broad and flat or narrow and steep, such as the Indus River Valley in Ladakh, India (above).

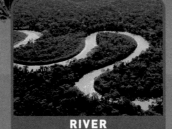

RIVER
As a river moves through flatlands, it twists and turns. Above, the Rio Los Amigos winds through a rain forest in Peru.

MOUNTAIN
Mountains are Earth's tallest landforms, and Mount Everest (above) rises highest of all, at 29,035 feet (8,850 m) above sea level.

GLACIER
Glaciers—"rivers" of ice—such as Alaska's Hubbard Glacier (above) move slowly from mountains to the sea. Global warming is shrinking them.

CANYON
Steep-sided valleys called canyons are created mainly by running water. Buckskin Gulch in Utah (above) is the deepest "slot" canyon in the American Southwest.

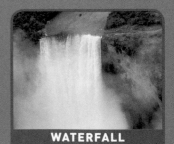

WATERFALL
Waterfalls form when a river reaches an abrupt change in elevation. Above, Kaieteur Falls, in Guyana, has a sheer drop of 741 feet (226 m).

Bet you didn't know

7 extreme facts about Earth

1 Tropical rain forests began to grow over **100 million** years ago.

2 Millions of years ago, the Earth was covered with **giant** mushrooms that grew **taller** than a **house.**

3 **97** percent of water on Earth is **undrinkable.**

4 There is **no land** underneath the ice **at the North Pole.**

5 Earth's longest mountain range is **under the sea.**

6 **The Namib** in Africa is the **oldest desert in the world,** having been dry for **55 million years.**

7 Scientists believe that millions of years ago **Earth's atmosphere** weighed less than half of what it does today.

SPOTLIGHT ON
AFRICA

Meerkats hiss when they feel threatened.

There is a town in central Ethiopia called Bike.

Meerkats

The massive continent of Africa, where humankind began millions of years ago, is second only to Asia in size. Stretching nearly as far from west to east as it does from north to south, Africa is home to both the longest river in the world (the Nile) and the largest hot desert on Earth (the Sahara).

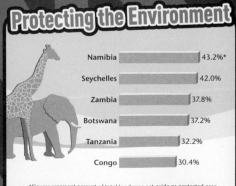

Namibian woman in traditional dress

Wildlife Wonderland

The world's largest population of African elephants can be found in Botswana's Okavango Delta. You'll also spot zebras, hippos, impalas, lions, and leopards splashing around.

Fruit Land

South Africa is one of the world's biggest producers of citrus fruit. The subtropical climate is ideal for growing oranges, grapefruits, tangerines, and lemons.

Star Struck

The force is strong in Tunisia, where parts of the original Star Wars movies were filmed. The sandy scenes were created in various desert locations in the North African nation.

Go Fish

Lake Malawi, the third largest lake in Africa, contains more species of fish than any other lake in the world, including more than 500 species of African cichlids.

Protecting the Environment

Namibia	43.2%*
Seychelles	42.0%
Zambia	37.8%
Botswana	37.2%
Tanzania	32.2%
Congo	30.4%

*Figures represent percent of total land area set aside as protected area

The Great Sphinx at Giza in Egypt

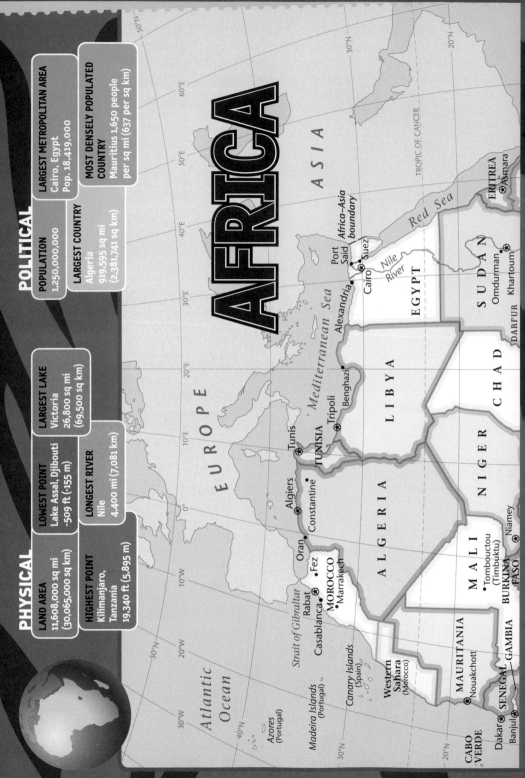

AFRICA

PHYSICAL

LAND AREA
11,608,000 sq mi
(30,065,000 sq km)

HIGHEST POINT
Kilimanjaro,
Tanzania
19,340 ft (5,895 m)

LOWEST POINT
Lake Assal, Djibouti
-509 ft (-155 m)

LONGEST RIVER
Nile
4,400 mi (7,081 km)

LARGEST LAKE
Victoria
26,800 sq mi
(69,500 sq km)

POLITICAL

POPULATION
1,250,000,000

LARGEST COUNTRY
Algeria
919,595 sq mi
(2,381,741 sq km)

LARGEST METROPOLITAN AREA
Cairo, Egypt
Pop. 18,419,000

MOST DENSELY POPULATED COUNTRY
Mauritius 1,650 people
per sq mi (637 per sq km)

EUROPE

ASIA

Atlantic Ocean

Mediterranean Sea

Red Sea

Azores
(Portugal)

Madeira Islands
(Portugal)

Canary Islands
(Spain)

Strait of Gibraltar

Rabat
Casablanca
Fez
MOROCCO
Marrakech

Oran
Algiers
Constantine
Tunis
TUNISIA
Tripoli
Benghazi

Western
Sahara
(Morocco)

MAURITANIA
Nouakchott

CABO
VERDE

Dakar
SENEGAL
Banjul
GAMBIA

BURKINA
FASO

ALGERIA

M A L I
Tombouctou
(Timbuktu)

N I G E R
Niamey

L I B Y A

C H A D

EGYPT

SUDAN
Omdurman
Khartoum
DARFUR

ERITREA
Asmara

Alexandria
Port
Said
Cairo
Suez
Nile
River
Africa–Asia
boundary

TROPIC OF CANCER

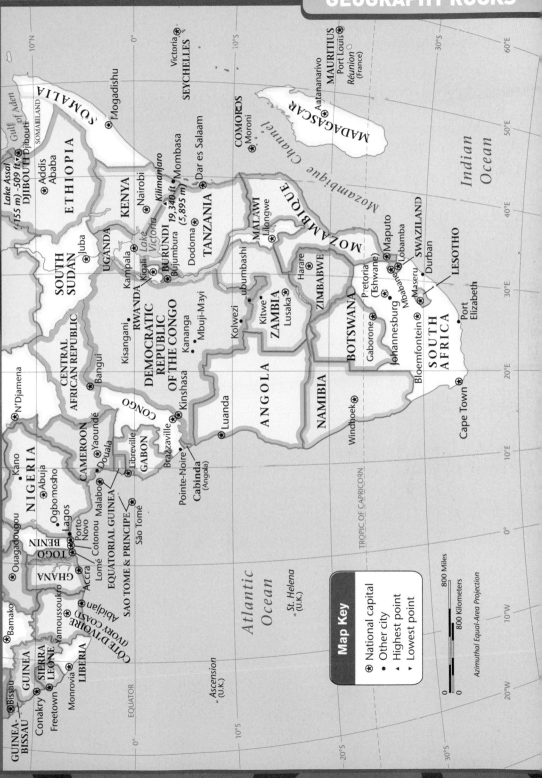

SOMALILAND

Gulf of Aden

Lake Assal (-155 m) -509 ft
DJIBOUTI Djibouti

SOMALIA

Mogadishu

Addis
Ababa

ETHIOPIA

Victoria

SEYCHELLES

MAURITIUS
Port Louis
Réunion
(France)

Antananarivo

MADAGASCAR

Indian
Ocean

Mombasa

KENYA

Nairobi

Kilimanjaro
19,340 ft
(5,895 m)

Dar es Salaam

COMOROS
Moroni

Mozambique Channel

Juba

SOUTH
SUDAN

UGANDA

Kampala

Lake
Victoria

Kigali

RWANDA

BURUNDI
Bujumbura

Dodoma

TANZANIA

MALAWI
Lilongwe

Maputo

SWAZILAND
Mbabane
Lobamba

MOZAMBIQUE

CENTRAL
AFRICAN REPUBLIC

Bangui

Kisangani

DEMOCRATIC
REPUBLIC
OF THE CONGO

Lubumbashi

Harare

ZIMBABWE

Pretoria
(Tshwane)

Maseru

LESOTHO

Durban

CONGO

Kinshasa

Kananga

Mbuji-Mayi

Kolwezi

Kitwe

ZAMBIA

Lusaka

BOTSWANA

Gaborone

Johannesburg

Bloemfontein

SOUTH
AFRICA

Port
Elizabeth

N'Djamena

CAMEROON

Yaoundé
Douala

Libreville

GABON

Brazzaville

Pointe-Noire

Cabinda
(Angola)

Luanda

ANGOLA

NAMIBIA

Windhoek

Cape Town

NIGERIA

Kano

Abuja

Ogbomosho

Lagos

Porto-
Novo

Cotonou

BENIN

TOGO

Lomé

EQUATORIAL GUINEA
Malabo

SAO TOME & PRINCIPE

São Tomé

Atlantic
Ocean

St. Helena
(U.K.)

Ouagadougou

GHANA

Accra

Yamoussoukro

Abidjan

CÔTE D'IVOIRE
(IVORY COAST)

Bamako

GUINEA

Conakry

SIERRA
LEONE
Freetown

LIBERIA

Monrovia

GUINEA-
BISSAU
Bissau

Ascension
(U.K.)

EQUATOR

TROPIC OF CAPRICORN

Azimuthal Equal-Area Projection

Map Key

⊛ National capital
• Other city
▲ Highest point
▼ Lowest point

800 Miles

800 Kilometers

SPOTLIGHT ON
ANTARCTICA

Emperor penguin
with chick

Penguins
can spend
up to 75 percent
of their lives
in the water.

No dogs are
allowed
in Antarctica.

This frozen continent may be a cool place to visit, but unless you're a penguin, you probably wouldn't want to hang out in Antarctica for long. The fact that it's the coldest, windiest, and driest continent helps explain why humans never colonized this ice-covered land surrounding the South Pole.

Russian Orthodox church, South Shetland Islands

Rock Collection

Researchers have recovered thousands of meteorites in Antarctica over the past few decades. The ice helps preserve the space rocks, some of which date back more than a billion years.

Bug Out

The midge, a wingless insect, is the largest land animal native to Antarctica. This bug is able to dehydrate itself and enter a sleepy state to survive temps close to minus 4°F (-20°C).

Old Bones

Scientists recently unearthed a trove of ancient fossils in Antarctica. The find includes dinosaur, lizard, and prehistoric bird bones that are some 70 million years old.

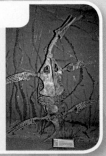

Slippery Landing

Flying into Antarctica is tricky, as many airport runways are made of blue ice. These runways need to be specially prepared to keep planes from skidding.

Earth's Largest Deserts

Largest hot desert:
Sahara, Africa
3,475,000 square miles
(9,000,000 sq km)

Largest cold desert:
Antarctica
5,100,000 square miles
(13,209,000 sq km)

Not to scale

Weddell seal

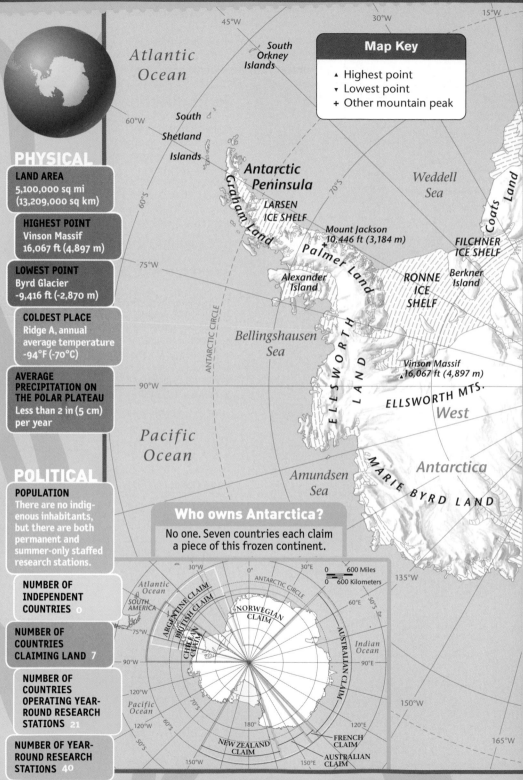

Atlantic
Ocean

South
Orkney
Islands

South
Shetland
Islands

Map Key

▲ Highest point
▼ Lowest point
+ Other mountain peak

Antarctic
Peninsula

Graham Land

LARSEN
ICE SHELF

Mount Jackson
10,446 ft (3,184 m)

Weddell
Sea

Coats Land

Palmer Land

FILCHNER
ICE SHELF

Alexander
Island

RONNE
ICE
SHELF

Berkner
Island

ANTARCTIC CIRCLE

Bellingshausen
Sea

Vinson Massif
▲16,067 ft (4,897 m)

ELLSWORTH LAND

ELLSWORTH MTS.
West

Pacific
Ocean

Amundsen
Sea

Antarctica

MARIE BYRD LAND

PHYSICAL

LAND AREA
5,100,000 sq mi
(13,209,000 sq km)

HIGHEST POINT
Vinson Massif
16,067 ft (4,897 m)

LOWEST POINT
Byrd Glacier
-9,416 ft (-2,870 m)

COLDEST PLACE
Ridge A, annual
average temperature
-94°F (-70°C)

**AVERAGE
PRECIPITATION ON
THE POLAR PLATEAU**
Less than 2 in (5 cm)
per year

POLITICAL

POPULATION
There are no indig-
enous inhabitants,
but there are both
permanent and
summer-only staffed
research stations.

**NUMBER OF
INDEPENDENT
COUNTRIES** 0

**NUMBER OF
COUNTRIES
CLAIMING LAND** 7

**NUMBER OF
COUNTRIES
OPERATING YEAR-
ROUND RESEARCH
STATIONS** 21

**NUMBER OF YEAR-
ROUND RESEARCH
STATIONS** 40

Who owns Antarctica?

No one. Seven countries each claim
a piece of this frozen continent.

Atlantic
Ocean

SOUTH
AMERICA

ARGENTINE CLAIM

BRITISH CLAIM

CHILEAN CLAIM

NORWEGIAN
CLAIM

ANTARCTIC CIRCLE

AUSTRALIAN CLAIM

Indian
Ocean

0   600 Miles
0   600 Kilometers

Pacific
Ocean

NEW ZEALAND
CLAIM

FRENCH
CLAIM

AUSTRALIAN
CLAIM

ANTARCTICA

FIMBUL
ICE SHELF

RIISER-LARSEN
ICE SHELF

Q U E E N   M A U D   L A N D

ENDERBY
LAND

*Indian
Ocean*

Valkyrie
Dome

MacKenzie Bay

75°E

Lambert
Glucier

AMERY ICE SHELF

AMERICAN

HIGHLAND

WEST
ICE SHELF

Ridge A +

POLAR PLATEAU

East

90°E

★ South Pole

SHACKLETON
ICE SHELF

Antarctica

T R A N S A N T A R C T I C   M O U N T A I N S

80°S

105°E

ROSS
ICE
SHELF

Byrd Glacier
-9,416 ft (-2,870 m)

Roosevelt
Island

Taylor
Glacier

Ross Island

Mount Erebus
12,448 ft
(3,794 m)

*Ross
Sea*

VICTORIA LAND

70°S

W I L K E S   L A N D

120°E

Talos
Dome

60°S

180°

*Indian
Ocean*

| 0 | | 600 Miles |
| 0 | | 600 Kilometers |

Azimuthal Equidistant Projection

150°E

135°E

0° 15°E 30°E 45°E 60°E

SPOTLIGHT ON
ASIA

South Koreans say "kimchi"—a pickled cabbage dish—instead of "cheese" to smile for photos.

Nearly half of the world's soccer balls are made in one city in Pakistan.

Crowds fill Myeong-Dong, one of Seoul, South Korea's main shopping districts.

Made up of 46 countries, Asia is the world's largest continent. Just how big is it? From western Turkey to the eastern tip of Russia, Asia spans nearly half the globe! Home to more than four billion citizens—that's three out of five people on the planet—Asia's population is bigger than that of all the other continents combined.

Safdarjung's Tomb, Delhi, India

Transparent Trains

An "invisible" train is set to hit tracks in Tokyo within the next couple of years. Made from a super-reflective material, the high-speed train is designed to blend into the countryside.

Sky High

Hong Kong has about 1,300 skyscrapers in its skyline—more than any other city in the world. The 118-floor International Commerce Center is Hong Kong's tallest tower.

Tiger Aid

More than half of the world's tigers—some 3,900 animals—live in India, mostly in protected nature reserves.

Flower Power

Thailand is one of the world's top orchid exporters. You can find more than 1,000 species of the flower growing wild in Thai forests.

Tallest Peaks by Continent

Everest, *Asia*

Aconcagua, *South America*

Denali, *North America*

Kilimanjaro, *Africa*

El'brus, *Europe*

Vinson Massif, *Antarctica*

Kosciusko, *Australia**

sea level   * does not include Oceania

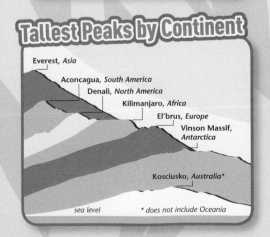

Kuala Lumpur, Malaysia

ASIA

PHYSICAL

LAND AREA
17,208,000 sq mi
(44,570,000 sq km)

HIGHEST POINT
Mount Everest,
China–Nepal
29,035 ft (8,850 m)

LOWEST POINT
Dead Sea,
Israel–Jordan
-1,388 ft (-423 m)

LONGEST RIVER
Yangtze, China
3,880 mi (6,244 km)

**LARGEST LAKE
ENTIRELY IN ASIA**
Lake Baikal, Russia
12,200 sq mi
(31,500 sq km)

POLITICAL

POPULATION
4,494,000,000

**LARGEST
METROPOLITAN AREA**
Tokyo, Japan
Pop. 37,833,000

**LARGEST COUNTRY
ENTIRELY IN ASIA**
China
3,705,406 sq mi
(9,596,960 sq km)

**MOST DENSELY
POPULATED COUNTRY**
Singapore
21,965 people
per sq mi
(8,486 per sq km)

EUROPE

Europe
Asia

Mediterranean Sea

Dardanelles
Bosporus
İzmir
TURKEY
Ankara
ARMENIA
GEORGIA
Tbilisi
Yerevan
Baku

Yekaterinburg
Nizhniy Tagil
Tyumen'
Magnitogorsk
Chelyabinsk
Omsk
Astana
Qaraghandy
KAZAKHSTAN

TURKMENISTAN

Bishkek

LEBANON
Beirut
SYRIA
Damascus
Jerusalem
Amman
ISRAEL
Dead Sea
-1,388 ft
(-423 m)
JORDAN
AZERBAIJAN
Baghdad
IRAQ
Basra
Tehran
Mashhad

UZBEKISTAN
Ashgabat
Tashkent
Almaty
Samarqand
KYRGYZSTAN
Dushanbe
TAJIKISTAN
Hotan

Medina
KUWAIT
Kuwait
City
IRAN
AFGHANISTAN
Kabul
Islamabad
Rawalpindi
Lahore

Jeddah
SAUDI ARABIA
Mecca
Riyadh
BAHRAIN
Manama
QATAR
Doha
Dubai
Abu Dhabi
Muscat
UNITED ARAB
EMIRATES

Faisalabad
PAKISTAN
Delhi
New Delhi
NEPAL
Jaipur

Sanaa
YEMEN
OMAN
Aden

Karachi

Kanpur
Indore
Bhopal
Surat

Mumbai
(Bombay)
Pune
Hyderabad
INDIA

AFRICA

Arabian
Sea

Bengaluru
(Bangalore)
Chennai
(Madras)

EQUATOR

Colombo
SRI
LANKA
Sri Jayewardenepura Kotte
Male
MALDIVES

0   800 Miles
0   800 Kilometers
Two-point Equidistant Projection

Indian Ocean

10°S
50°E
60°E
70°E
80°E

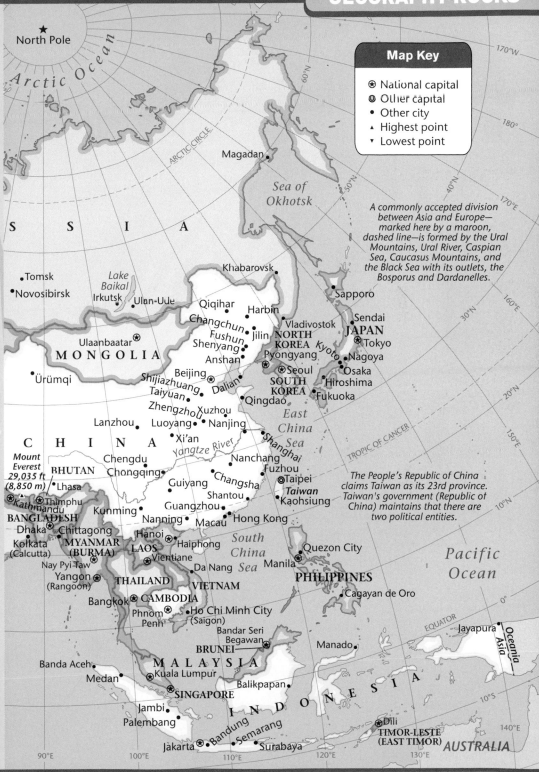

North Pole

Arctic Ocean

Map Key

⊗ National capital
◎ Other capital
• Other city
▲ Highest point
▼ Lowest point

R   S   S   I   A

Magadan

Sea of
Okhotsk

A commonly accepted division
between Asia and Europe—
marked here by a maroon,
dashed line—is formed by the Ural
Mountains, Ural River, Caspian
Sea, Caucasus Mountains, and
the Black Sea with its outlets, the
Bosporus and Dardanelles.

• Tomsk
• Novosibirsk

Lake
Baikal
Irkutsk• •Ulan-Ude

Khabarovsk

Sapporo

Qiqihar   Harbin
Changchun
Fushun   Jilin   Vladivostok   Sendai
Shenyang   JAPAN
Ulaanbaatar ⊗   NORTH   Kyoto ⊗Tokyo
M O N G O L I A   Anshan   KOREA   Nagoya
                           Pyongyang ⊙
• Ürümqi   Beijing ⊗   Seoul⊗ Osaka
          Shijiazhuang •Dalian SOUTH   Hiroshima
          Taiyuan•   KOREA   •Fukuoka
          Zhengzhou•Xuzhou   Qingdao East
C H I N A Lanzhou• Luoyang •Nanjing   China
              Xi'an   Sea
Mount   •Chengdu   Yangtze River Shanghai
Everest BHUTAN Chongqing   Nanchang TROPIC OF CANCER
29,035 ft •Lhasa   Changsha Fuzhou
(8,850 m)▲   Guiyang•   •Taipei
▲Kathmandu⊗Thimphu   Shantou Taiwan
BANGLADESH   Kunming Guangzhou• Kaohsiung The People's Republic of China
 Dhaka• •Chittagong Nanning• Macau Hong Kong claims Taiwan as its 23rd province.
Kolkata   MYANMAR   Hanoi•   Taiwan's government (Republic of
(Calcutta) (BURMA) •Haiphong   South   China) maintains that there are
Nay Pyi Taw LAOS ⊗Vientiane China   two political entities.
Yangon   THAILAND Da Nang• Sea Manila⊗ •Quezon City
(Rangoon)   VIETNAM   PHILIPPINES Pacific
Bangkok⊗ ⊗CAMBODIA   •Cagayan de Oro Ocean
Phnom ⊗ •Ho Chi Minh City
Penh   (Saigon)
Banda Aceh Bandar Seri   •Manado
       Begawan
Medan• BRUNEI   EQUATOR •Jayapura Oceania
   M A L A Y S I A   Asia
  ⊗Kuala Lumpur Balikpapan•
  ⊗SINGAPORE   I N D O N E S I A
Jambi•   •Dili
Palembang•   TIMOR-LESTE
  Bandung   (EAST TIMOR) AUSTRALIA
Jakarta⊗ •Semarang Surabaya

SPOTLIGHT ON
AUSTRALIA,
NEW ZEALAND, AND OCEANIA

A striped sweetlips swims among coral in the Great Barrier Reef.

In New Zealand, trail mix is called scroggin or schmogle.

Australia's Great Barrier Reef isn't one unbroken reef, but a system of more than 3,000 reefs.

G'day, mate! This vast region, covering almost 3.3 million square miles (8.5 million sq km), includes Australia—the world's smallest and flattest continent—and New Zealand, as well as a fleet of mostly tiny islands scattered across the Pacific Ocean. Also known as "down under," most of the countries in this region are in the Southern Hemisphere, and below the Equator.

Maori children of New Zealand in ceremonial costume

Sunny Days

If you're seeking sunshine, head to Perth, the capital of Western Australia, which averages eight hours of rays per day. It's said to be the sunniest capital city on the planet.

Pretty Money

New Zealand is known for its colorful cash. The $5 bill—showing famed New Zealand mountaineer Sir Edmund Hillary and a penguin—was named 2015's best banknote of the year.

Vote Here

Registered to vote in Australia? Make sure to show up to the polls! Voting is mandatory for all citizens, and those who don't cast their vote without a valid reason may face a fine.

Protected Waters

The South Pacific island nation of Palau made big waves in 2015 when it became home to one of the world's largest marine sanctuaries, ending most fishing and mining in the area.

Australia
Sizing Up the Great Barrier Reef

Just how big is the Great Barrier Reef Marine Park? It's approximately as large as:

Germany

Great Barrier Reef Marine Park

Vietnam

Australia

or the Republic of Congo

*Based on an area of 133,000 square miles (344,400 sq km)

Sydney Harbour Bridge in Sydney, Australia

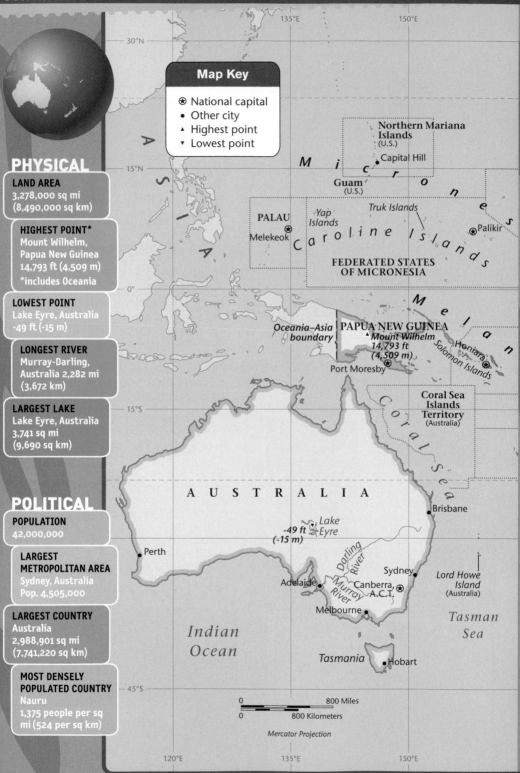

Map Key

- ⊛ National capital
- • Other city
- ▲ Highest point
- ▼ Lowest point

PHYSICAL

LAND AREA
3,278,000 sq mi
(8,490,000 sq km)

HIGHEST POINT*
Mount Wilhelm,
Papua New Guinea
14,793 ft (4,509 m)
*includes Oceania

LOWEST POINT
Lake Eyre, Australia
-49 ft (-15 m)

LONGEST RIVER
Murray-Darling,
Australia 2,282 mi
(3,672 km)

LARGEST LAKE
Lake Eyre, Australia
3,741 sq mi
(9,690 sq km)

POLITICAL

POPULATION
42,000,000

**LARGEST
METROPOLITAN AREA**
Sydney, Australia
Pop. 4,505,000

LARGEST COUNTRY
Australia
2,988,901 sq mi
(7,741,220 sq km)

**MOST DENSELY
POPULATED COUNTRY**
Nauru
1,375 people per sq
mi (524 per sq km)

ASIA

Northern Mariana
Islands
(U.S.)

Capital Hill

Guam
(U.S.)

M i c r o n e s i a

PALAU
Melekeok

Yap
Islands

Truk Islands

Palikir

Caroline Islands

FEDERATED STATES
OF MICRONESIA

M e l a n

Oceania–Asia
boundary

PAPUA NEW GUINEA

▲ Mount Wilhelm
14,793 ft
(4,509 m)

Honiara

Solomon Islands

Port Moresby

Coral Sea
Islands
Territory
(Australia)

C o r a l   S e a

AUSTRALIA

Brisbane

Lake
Eyre
-49 ft
(-15 m)

Darling
River

Murray
River

Perth

Adelaide

Sydney

Canberra
A.C.T.

Lord Howe
Island
(Australia)

Melbourne

Indian
Ocean

Tasman
Sea

Tasmania

Hobart

800 Miles

800 Kilometers

Mercator Projection

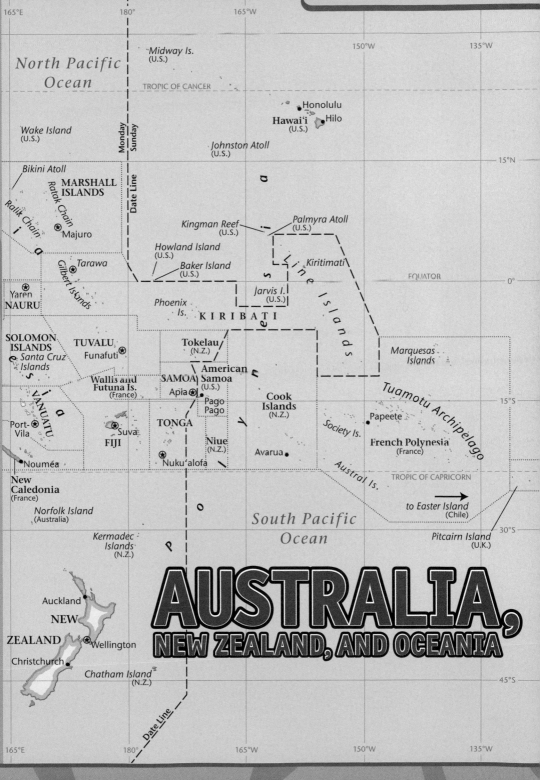

165°E · 180° · 165°W · 150°W · 135°W

North Pacific Ocean

Midway Is. (U.S.)

TROPIC OF CANCER

Honolulu
Hawai'i Hilo
(U.S.)

Wake Island (U.S.)

Monday | Sunday

Johnston Atoll (U.S.)

15°N

Bikini Atoll

MARSHALL ISLANDS

Ratak Chain

Date Line

Ralik Chain

Kingman Reef (U.S.)

Palmyra Atoll (U.S.)

Howland Island (U.S.)

Majuro

Tarawa

Gilbert Islands

Baker Island (U.S.)

Kiritimati

EQUATOR 0°

Yaren
NAURU

Line Islands

Phoenix Is.

Jarvis I. (U.S.)

KIRIBATI

SOLOMON ISLANDS

Santa Cruz Islands

TUVALU
Funafuti

Tokelau (N.Z.)

Marquesas Islands

Wallis and Futuna Is. (France)

SAMOA
Apia

American Samoa (U.S.)
Pago Pago

VANUATU

Port-Vila

TONGA

Cook Islands (N.Z.)

Society Is.

Papeete

Tuamotu Archipelago

15°S

Suva
FIJI

Niue (N.Z.)

French Polynesia (France)

Avarua

Nouméa

Nuku'alofa

Austral Is.

TROPIC OF CAPRICORN

New Caledonia (France)

Norfolk Island (Australia)

South Pacific Ocean

to Easter Island (Chile)

30°S

Kermadec Islands (N.Z.)

Pitcairn Island (U.K.)

AUSTRALIA,
NEW ZEALAND, AND OCEANIA

Auckland

NEW ZEALAND
Wellington

Christchurch

Chatham Island (N.Z.)

45°S

Date Line

165°E · 180° · 165°W · 150°W · 135°W

SPOTLIGHT ON
EUROPE

The word "robot" comes from the Czech word *robota*, meaning "work."

Roman gladiators consumed an energy drink containing ash.

Dancers in traditional costumes entertain at a festival in Prague, Czech Republic.

A cluster of islands and peninsulas jutting west from Asia, Europe is bordered by the Atlantic and Arctic Oceans and more than a dozen seas. Here you'll find a variety of scenery, from mountains to countryside to coastlines. Europe is also known for its rich culture and fascinating history, which make it one of the most visited continents on Earth.

Hedgehog

Blue Bloods

There are 12 surviving monarchies in western Europe. Denmark's royal family takes the crown for Europe's longest-running monarchy, having lasted more than 1,000 years.

Recycling Star

Sweden takes recycling very seriously. Less than one percent of the country's household garbage ends up in landfills, and an average citizen recycles 146 bottles and cans a year.

Queen's Cards

Brits who turn 100 or celebrate a 60th wedding anniversary can get a truly royal treat: a personalized card from the Queen of England. The tradition dates back to 1917.

Castle Country

Belgium has more castles per square mile than anywhere else in the world. Its 3,000 royal abodes include the 600-year-old Castle of Vêves, still occupied by the original family.

Europe's Longest Rivers

Volga	3,685 km (2,290 mi)
Danube	2,848 km (1,770 mi)
Dnieper	2,285 km (1,420 mi)
Rhine	1,230 km (765 mi)
Elbe	1,165 km (724 mi)

Oia, Greece

Map Key
⊛ National capital
• Other city
▫ Small country
▲ Highest point
▼ Lowest point

PHYSICAL

LAND AREA
3,841,000 sq mi
(9,947,000 sq km)

HIGHEST POINT
El'brus, Russia
18,510 ft (5,642 m)

LOWEST POINT
Caspian Sea
-92 ft (-28 m)

LONGEST RIVER
Volga, Russia
2,290 mi
(3,685 km)

**LARGEST LAKE
ENTIRELY IN EUROPE**
Ladoga, Russia
6,900 sq mi
(17,872 sq km)

POLITICAL

POPULATION
745,000,000

**LARGEST
METROPOLITAN AREA**
Moscow, Russia
Pop. 12,063,000

**LARGEST COUNTRY
ENTIRELY IN EUROPE**
Ukraine
233,030 sq mi
(603,550 sq km)

**MOST DENSELY
POPULATED COUNTRY**
Monaco
50,000 people per sq
mi (20,000 per sq km)

Jan Mayen
(Norway)

30°W   20°W   10°W   0°

Reykjavík
ICELAND

Norwegian
Sea

ARCTIC CIRCLE

60°N

Faroe Islands
(Denmark)

PRIME MERIDIAN

Shetland
Islands

Oslo

Orkney Islands

SCOTLAND
Glasgow   Edinburgh   Göteborg
N. IRELAND

IRELAND   Belfast   North
(ÉIRE)   UNITED KINGDOM   Sea   DENMARK
Dublin⊛   Copenhagen⊛
Liverpool Manchester   Kiel
WALES   Birmingham
Cardiff   ENGLAND   The NETH. Hamburg
London⊛   Hague Amsterdam   Berlin⊛
Brussels⊛   GERMANY
BELGIUM
⊛Paris LUX. Frankfurt Prague⊛

50°N

Atlantic
Ocean

Nantes

Munich
LIECH.
FRANCE Zürich
Bern SWITZ. AUSTRIA
Ljubljana
Bordeaux Lyon Milan Venice SLOV.
Turin
Bay of   Genoa
Biscay

Bilbao   Toulouse   SAN
Oporto Valladolid MONACO Nice MARINO
ANDORRA   Marseille ITALY
Madrid⊛ Zaragoza   VATICAN
Lisbon⊛ PORTUGAL   Corsica CITY⊛
S P A I N   (France)   Rome
Barcelona   Naples
Valencia
10°W Seville Murcia   Sardinia
Málaga   Balearic Is. (Italy)
(Spain)

40°N

Gibraltar (U.K.)   M e d i t e r r a
Messina
Palermo
Catania
n Sicily e a n
Valletta
0   400 Miles   MALTA
0   400 Kilometers
Azimuthal Equidistant Projection

A F R I C A

0°   10°E

10°E   20°E   30°E   40°E   50°E   60°E   70°E

Barents Sea

Asia
Europe

ASIA

•Murmansk

N O R W A Y

S W E D E N

F I N L A N D

R U S S I A

•Archangel

EUROPE

Lake Ladoga

60°N

Helsinki

•St. Petersburg

•Ufa

✪Stockholm   Tallinn

ESTONIA

Baltic Sea

•Yaroslavl'

Volga River Kazan'

Tver'

Nizhniy Novgorod

Samara •Orenburg

Rīga   LATVIA

✪Moscow

Ryazan'

LITHUANIA   Vitsyebsk

Smolensk

•Penza

50°N

Kaliningrad (Russia)

✪Vilnius

Kaunas

•Minsk

Bryansk

Saratov

KAZAKHSTAN

Gdańsk

BELARUS

Homyel'

•Kursk

Volgograd

POLAND   ✪Warsaw

Bydgoszcz

•Kiev

Kharkiv

Astrakhan'

Łódź

Poltava

Wrocław   •Kraków

L'viv   U K R A I N E

Donets'k

-92 ft (-28 m)

CZECHIA (CZECH REP.)

Vinnytsya

Rostov

•Dnipropetrovs'k

Vienna

SLOVAKIA

MOLDOVA

✪Chişinău

Groznyy

Caspian Sea

✪Bratislava

Budapest

Odesa

El'brus

Baku

HUNGARY

ROMANIA

Simferopol'

CRIMEA

(5,642 m) 18,510 ft

Sochi

Zagreb

Sevastopol'

GEORGIA

40°N

CROATIA

Belgrade

Bucharest

Black Sea

AZERBAIJAN ✪

BOSNIA & HERZEGOVINA

SERBIA

Sarajevo

KOSOVO

Varna

Bosporus

MONTENEGRO   Pristina

BULGARIA

Podgorica

✪Skopje

Sofia

Tirana

MACED.

Istanbul

ALBANIA

Thessaloniki

T U R K E Y

Dardanelles

GREECE

✪Athens

A commonly accepted division between Asia and Europe—marked here by a maroon, dashed line—is formed by the Ural Mountains, Ural River, Caspian Sea, Caucasus Mountains, and the Black Sea with its outlets, the Bosporus and Dardanelles.

Sea

Crete

NORTHERN CYPRUS

Nicosia ✪

CYPRUS

20°E   30°E   40°E

SPOTLIGHT ON

NORTH AMERICA

The Statue of Liberty stands in New York Harbor, U.S.A.

The Statue of Liberty has a 35-foot (10.7-m) waistline and wears a size 879 shoe.

An Aztec emperor in what is now Mexico introduced hot chocolate to Europeans.

From the Great Plains of the United States and Canada to the rain forests of Panama, North America stretches 5,500 miles (8,850 km) from north to south. The third largest continent, North America can be divided into five regions: the mountainous west (including parts of Mexico and Central America's western coast), the Great Plains, the Canadian Shield, the varied eastern region (including Central America's lowlands and coastal plains), and the Caribbean.

Steel drummers perform in Trinidad and Tobago.

Sloth Sanctuary

Orphaned, injured, and abandoned sloths roam the Sloth Sanctuary in Limon, Costa Rica. Sloths live most of their lives hanging upside down in trees in the dense rain forest canopy.

Hollywood South

Louisiana is one of the top filming locations in the United States. An abandoned Louisiana amusement park served as the setting for the blockbuster hit *Jurassic World*.

Nation's Mammal

Recently named the national mammal of the United States, the bison is North America's largest land animal. Some 500,000 of these animals roam throughout the continent.

Super Smarts

Canada is one of world's most educated countries. More than half of Canadian adults have a college degree. It is the only country other than Russia to achieve this.

World's Longest Coastlines

Canada	125,567 miles (202,080 km)
Indonesia	33,998 miles (54,716 km)
Russia	23,397 miles (37,653 km)
Philippines	22,549 miles (36,289 km)
Japan	18,486 miles (29,751 km)

Onlookers celebrate the opening of the Panama Canal expansion in 2016.

COSCO SHIPPING PAN

PHYSICAL

LAND AREA	HIGHEST POINT
9,449,000 sq mi (24,474,000 sq km)	Denali, Alaska 20,320 ft (6,194 m)

LOWEST POINT	LARGEST LAKE
Death Valley, California -282 ft (-86 m)	Lake Superior, U.S.–Canada 31,700 sq mi (82,100 sq km)

LONGEST RIVER
Mississippi–Missouri, United States 3,780 mi (6,083 km)

POLITICAL

POPULATION	LARGEST METROPOLITAN AREA
582,000,000	Mexico City, Mexico Pop. 20,843,000

LARGEST COUNTRY	MOST DENSELY POPULATED COUNTRY
Canada 3,855,103 sq mi (9,984,670 sq km)	Barbados / 1,807 people per sq mi (698 per sq km)

Map Key

⊛ National capital
• Other city
▲ Highest point
▼ Lowest point

EUROPE

ASIA

Arctic Ocean

North Pole

ARCTIC CIRCLE

Greenland (Denmark)

C A N A D A

Alaska (U.S.)

Anchorage

(Mount McKinley) Denali ▲ 20,310 ft (6,190 m)

Edmonton
Calgary

Vancouver
Victoria
Seattle

Winnipeg

Thunder Bay

Montreal

20°W
40°W
40°N
80°N
60°N
160°W
180°
40°N

800 Miles
800 Kilometers

Azimuthal Equidistant Projection

284

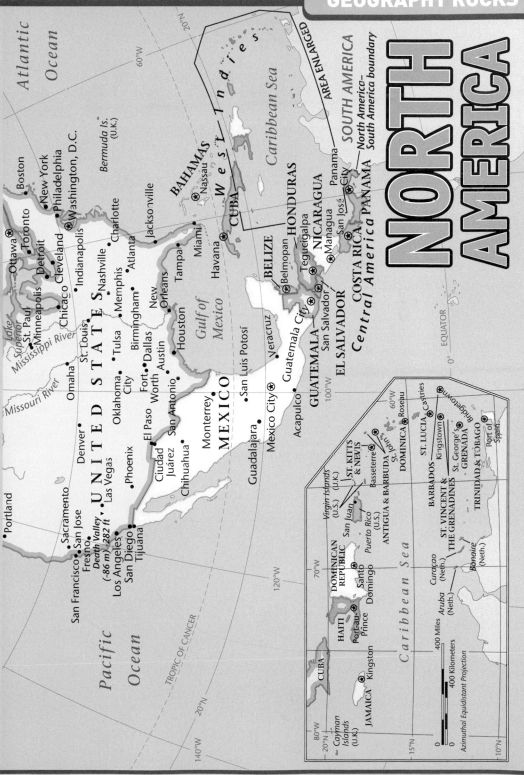

NORTH AMERICA

AREA ENLARGED

SOUTH AMERICA

North America–
South America boundary

Central America PANAMA

Atlantic Ocean

Bermuda Is.
(U.K.)

Boston
New York
Philadelphia
Washington, D.C.
Ottawa
Toronto
Detroit
Cleveland
Indianapolis
Charlotte
Nashville
Atlanta
Jacksonville
Chicago
Memphis
Birmingham
Tampa
Miami

Minneapolis
St. Paul
Lake Superior
Mississippi River
Missouri River
Omaha
St. Louis
UNITED STATES
Tulsa
Oklahoma City
Dallas
Fort Worth
Austin
San Antonio
New Orleans
Houston

Portland
San Francisco
San Jose
Fresno
Sacramento
Denver
Las Vegas
Phoenix
Death Valley
(-86 m) -282 ft ▼
Los Angeles
San Diego
Tijuana
El Paso
Ciudad Juárez
Chihuahua

Monterrey
MEXICO
San Luis Potosí
Guadalajara
Mexico City
Veracruz
Acapulco

Gulf of Mexico

West Indies

BAHAMAS
Nassau
CUBA
Havana

Caribbean Sea

BELIZE
Belmopan
GUATEMALA
Guatemala City
San Salvador
EL SALVADOR
HONDURAS
Tegucigalpa
NICARAGUA
Managua
COSTA RICA
San José
Panama City
Panama

Pacific Ocean

TROPIC OF CANCER

20°N
140°W
120°W
100°W
80°W
70°W
60°W
20°N
20°N

EQUATOR
0°

Inset map (West Indies / Caribbean)

CUBA
JAMAICA
Kingston
Cayman Islands
(U.K.)
HAITI
Port-au-Prince
DOMINICAN REPUBLIC
Santo Domingo
Puerto Rico
(U.S.)
Virgin Islands
(U.S.)
San Juan
ST. KITTS & NEVIS
Basseterre
ANTIGUA & BARBUDA
St. John's
DOMINICA
Roseau
ST. LUCIA
Castries
BARBADOS
Bridgetown
ST. VINCENT & THE GRENADINES
Kingstown
St. George's
GRENADA
TRINIDAD & TOBAGO
Port of Spain
Curaçao (Neth.)
Aruba (Neth.)
Bonaire (Neth.)

Caribbean Sea

400 Miles
400 Kilometers
0
0

Azimuthal Equidistant Projection

80°W
70°W
60°W
20°N
15°N
10°N

SPOTLIGHT ON
SOUTH AMERICA

Nearly 80 percent of Guyana is covered by rain forest.

You can find yellow, green, and red miniature bananas in Ecuador.

Common tree boa,
Iwokrama forest reserve, Guyana

South America is bordered by three major bodies of water—the Caribbean Sea, Atlantic Ocean, and Pacific Ocean. The world's fourth largest continent extends over a range of climates from tropical in the north to subarctic in the south. South America produces a rich diversity of natural resources, including nuts, fruits, sugar, grains, coffee, and chocolate.

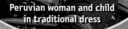
Peruvian woman and child in traditional dress

Hopping With Frogs

Despite its small size, Colombia boasts one of the biggest varieties of amphibians on the planet. The country is home to 800 species, including the tiny and highly venomous dart frog.

Cool Caves

While Chile's Easter Island is known for its giant moai statues, there's also an extensive cave system beneath the surface. Some are decorated with ancient cave paintings.

Big Horn

Known as the "unicorn bird," the horned screamer gets its name from the spiny, curved horn that juts out from its forehead. The tropical wetland bird is related to ducks and swans.

Living in Isolation

Brazil's Amazon rain forest is home to more isolated tribes than anywhere else on the planet. There are thought to be at least 77 groups with little to no contact with the outside world.

South America's Deepest Canyon

Peru's Cotahuasi Canyon is more than 11,500 feet (3,500 m) deep!

Almost twice as deep as the Grand Canyon 6,000 feet (1,111 m)

Burj Khalifa 2,717 feet (828 m)

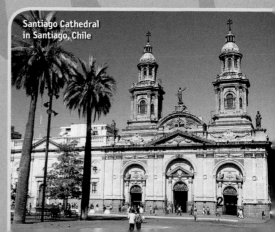
Santiago Cathedral in Santiago, Chile

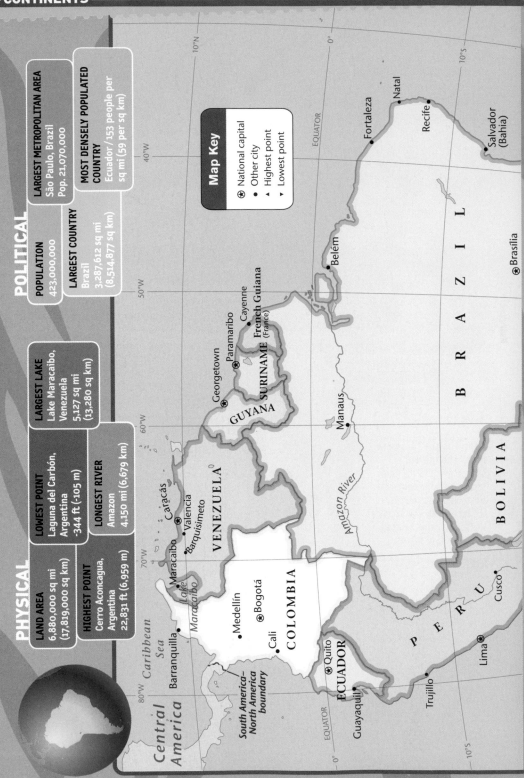

PHYSICAL

LAND AREA
6,880,000 sq mi
(17,819,000 sq km)

HIGHEST POINT
Cerro Aconcagua,
Argentina
22,831 ft (6,959 m)

LOWEST POINT
Laguna del Carbón,
Argentina
-344 ft (-105 m)

LONGEST RIVER
Amazon
4,150 mi (6,679 km)

LARGEST LAKE
Lake Maracaibo,
Venezuela
5,127 sq mi
(13,280 sq km)

POLITICAL

POPULATION
423,000,000

LARGEST COUNTRY
Brazil
3,287,612 sq mi
(8,514,877 sq km)

LARGEST METROPOLITAN AREA
São Paulo, Brazil
Pop. 21,070,000

MOST DENSELY POPULATED COUNTRY
Ecuador / 153 people per
sq mi (59 per sq km)

Map Key

⊛ National capital
• Other city
▲ Highest point
▼ Lowest point

Central
America

Caribbean
Sea

South America–
North America
boundary

Barranquilla

Maracaibo
Lake
Maracaibo

Medellín

⊛ Bogotá

Cali

COLOMBIA

⊛ Quito

ECUADOR

Guayaquil

Caracas
Valencia
Barquisimeto

VENEZUELA

Georgetown
⊛
Paramaribo
Cayenne
French Guiana
(France)

GUYANA

SURINAME

Manaus

Amazon River

B R A Z I L

Belém

⊛ Brasília

Fortaleza

Natal

Recife

Salvador
(Bahia)

PERU

Trujillo

Lima ⊛

Cusco

BOLIVIA

EQUATOR

10°N

0°

10°S

40°W

50°W

60°W

70°W

80°W

0°

EQUATOR

10°S

SOUTH AMERICA

Atlantic
Ocean

TROPIC OF CAPRICORN

Belo
Horizonte

Rio de Janeiro

Nova Iguaçu

Santos

São Paulo

Curitiba

Goiânia

Porto Alegre

Santa Cruz

PARAGUAY

Asunción

URUGUAY

Montevideo

Mar del Plata

Santa
Fe

Rosario

Sucre

San Miguel
de Tucumán

Buenos Aires

La Plata

La Paz

Córdoba

Cerro Aconcagua
22,831 ft
(6,959 m)

A R G E N T I N A

Laguna del Carbón
344 ft (-105 m)

Star ley

Falkland Islands
(U.K.)

South
Georgia
(U.K.)

Valparaíso

Santiago

C H I L E

Punta Arenas

Pacific
Ocean

600 Miles

600 Kilometers

Azimuthal Equidistant Projection

289

COUNTRIES OF THE WORLD

The following pages present a general overview of all 195 independent countries recognized by the National Geographic Society, including the newest nation, South Sudan, which gained independence in 2011.

The flags of each independent country symbolize diverse cultures and histories. The statistical data cover highlights of geography and demography and provide a brief overview of each country. They present general characteristics and are not intended to be comprehensive. For example, not every language spoken in a specific country can be listed. Thus, languages shown are the most representative of that area. This is also true of the religions mentioned.

A country is defined as a political body with its own independent government, geographical space, and, in most cases, laws, military, and taxes.

Disputed areas such as Northern Cyprus and Taiwan, and dependencies of independent nations, such as Bermuda and Puerto Rico, are not included in this listing.

Note the color key at the bottom of the pages and the locator map below, which assign a color to each country based on the continent on which it is located. All information is accurate as of press time.

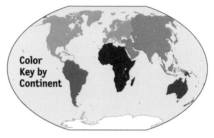

Color Key by Continent

Afghanistan

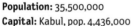

Area: 251,773 sq mi (652,090 sq km)
Population: 35,500,000
Capital: Kabul, pop. 4,436,000
Currency: afghani
Religions: Sunni Muslim, Shiite Muslim
Languages: Afghan Persian (Dari), Pashto, Turkic languages (primarily Uzbek and Turkmen), Baluchi, 30 minor languages (including Pashai)

Albania

Area: 11,100 sq mi (28,748 sq km)
Population: 2,900,000
Capital: Tirana, pop. 445,000
Currency: lek
Religions: Muslim, Albanian Orthodox, Roman Catholic
Languages: Albanian, Greek, Vlach, Romani, Slavic dialects

Algeria

Area: 919,595 sq mi (2,381,741 sq km)
Population: 42,200,000
Capital: Algiers, pop. 2,559,000
Currency: Algerian dinar
Religion: Sunni Muslim
Languages: Arabic, French, Berber dialects

Andorra

Area: 181 sq mi (469 sq km)
Population: 80,000
Capital: Andorra la Vella, pop. 23,000
Currency: euro
Religion: Roman Catholic
Languages: Catalan, French, Castilian, Portuguese

Angola

Area: 481,354 sq mi (1,246,700 sq km)
Population: 28,600,000
Capital: Luanda, pop. 5,288,000
Currency: kwanza
Religions: indigenous beliefs, Roman Catholic, Protestant
Languages: Portuguese, Bantu, other African languages

Antigua and Barbuda

Area: 171 sq mi (442 sq km)
Population: 100,000
Capital: St. John's, pop. 22,000
Currency: East Caribbean dollar
Religions: Anglican, Seventh-day Adventist, Pentecostal, Moravian, Roman Catholic, Methodist, Baptist, Church of God, other Christian
Languages: English, local dialects

Argentina

Area: 1,073,518 sq mi
(2,780,400 sq km)
Population: 44,300,000
Capital: Buenos Aires,
pop. 15,024,000
Currency: Argentine peso
Religion: Roman Catholic
Languages: Spanish, English, Italian, German, French

Armenia

Area: 11,484 sq mi
(29,743 sq km)
Population: 3,000,000
Capital: Yerevan,
pop. 1,049,000
Currency: dram
Religions: Armenian Apostolic, other Christian
Language: Armenian

Australia

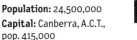

Area: 2,988,901 sq mi
(7,741,220 sq km)
Population: 24,500,000
Capital: Canberra, A.C.T.,
pop. 415,000
Currency: Australian dollar
Religions: Roman Catholic, Anglican
Language: English

Austria

Area: 32,378 sq mi (83,858 sq km)
Population: 8,800,000
Capital: Vienna, pop. 1,743,000
Currency: euro
Religions: Roman Catholic, Protestant, Muslim
Language: German

Azerbaijan

Area: 33,436 sq mi
(86,600 sq km)
Population: 9,900,000
Capital: Baku, pop. 2,317,000
Currency: Azerbaijani manat
Religion: Muslim
Language: Azerbaijani (Azeri)

Bahamas

Area: 5,382 sq mi
(13,939 sq km)
Population: 400,000
Capital: Nassau, pop. 267,000
Currency: Bahamian dollar
Religions: Baptist, Anglican, Roman Catholic,
Pentecostal, Church of God
Languages: English, Creole

5 cool things about BAHAMAS

1. Most of the 700 islands and cays in the Bahamas are uninhabited.

2. During the early 1700s, a majority of the capital city of Nassau was ruled by pirates.

3. The Bahamas is home to more than 80,000 flamingos.

4. Stretching some 190 miles (306 km), the Andros Barrier Reef off of Andros Town is the third largest living organism on the planet.

5. You can swim with pigs on the Bahamas's Big Major Cay.

Bahrain

Area: 277 sq mi (717 sq km)
Population: 1,500,000
Capital: Manama, pop. 398,000
Currency: Bahraini dinar
Religions: Shiite Muslim, Sunni Muslim, Christian
Languages: Arabic, English, Farsi, Urdu

Bangladesh

Area: 55,598 sq mi
(143,998 sq km)
Population: 164,700,000
Capital: Dhaka, pop. 16,982,000
Currency: taka
Religions: Muslim, Hindu
Languages: Bangla (Bengali), English

Barbados

Area: 166 sq mi (430 sq km)
Population: 300,000
Capital: Bridgetown, pop. 90,000
Currency: Barbadian dollar
Religions: Anglican, Pentecostal, Methodist, other Protestant, Roman Catholic
Language: English

Belarus

Area: 80,153 sq mi (207,595 sq km)
Population: 9,500,000
Capital: Minsk, pop. 1,905,000
Currency: Belarusian ruble
Religions: Eastern Orthodox, other (includes Roman Catholic, Protestant, Jewish, Muslim)
Languages: Belarusian, Russian

Belgium

Area: 11,787 sq mi (30,528 sq km)
Population: 11,300,000
Capital: Brussels, pop. 2,029,000
Currency: euro
Religions: Roman Catholic, other (includes Protestant)
Languages: Dutch, French

Belize

Area: 8,867 sq mi (22,965 sq km)
Population: 400,000
Capital: Belmopan, pop. 17,000
Currency: Belizean dollar
Religions: Roman Catholic, Protestant (includes Pentecostal, Seventh-day Adventist, Mennonite, Methodist)
Languages: Spanish, Creole, Mayan dialects, English, Garifuna (Carib), German

Benin

Area: 43,484 sq mi (112,622 sq km)
Population: 11,200,000
Capitals: Porto-Novo, pop. 268,000; Cotonou, pop. 680,000
Currency: Communauté Financière Africaine franc
Religions: Christian, Muslim, Vodoun
Languages: French, Fon, Yoruba, tribal languages

Bhutan

Area: 17,954 sq mi (46,500 sq km)
Population: 800,000
Capital: Thimphu, pop. 152,000
Currencies: ngultrum; Indian rupee
Religions: Lamaistic Buddhist, Indian- and Nepalese-influenced Hindu
Languages: Dzongkha, Tibetan dialects, Nepalese dialects

Bolivia

Area: 424,164 sq mi (1,098,581 sq km)
Population: 11,100,000
Capitals: La Paz, pop. 1,800,000; Sucre, pop. 358,000
Currency: boliviano
Religions: Roman Catholic, Protestant (includes Evangelical Methodist)
Languages: Spanish, Quechua, Aymara

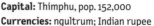

Bosnia and Herzegovina

Area: 19,741 sq mi (51,129 sq km)
Population: 3,500,000
Capital: Sarajevo, pop. 322,000
Currency: konvertibilna marka (convertible mark)
Religions: Muslim, Orthodox, Roman Catholic
Languages: Bosnian, Croatian, Serbian

Botswana

Area: 224,607 sq mi (581,730 sq km)
Population: 2,300,000
Capital: Gaborone, pop. 247,000
Currency: pula
Religions: Christian, Badimo
Languages: Setswana, Kalanga

Brazil

Area: 3,287,612 sq mi (8,514,877 sq km)
Population: 207,900,000
Capital: Brasília, pop. 4,074,000
Currency: real
Religions: Roman Catholic, Protestant
Language: Portuguese

There's a replica of the STATUE OF LIBERTY in Rio de Janeiro, Brazil.

Bulgaria

Area: 42,855 sq mi
(110,994 sq km)
Population: 7,100,000
Capital: Sofia, pop. 1,222,000
Currency: lev
Religions: Bulgarian Orthodox, Muslim
Languages: Bulgarian, Turkish, Roma

Brunei

Area: 2,226 sq mi (5,765 sq km)
Population: 400,000
Capital: Bandar Seri Begawan,
pop. 14,000
Currency: Bruneian dollar
Religions: Muslim, Buddhist, Christian, other
(includes indigenous beliefs)
Languages: Malay, English, Chinese

Burkina Faso

Area: 105,869 sq mi
(274,200 sq km)
Population: 19,600,000
Capital: Ouagadougou,
pop. 2,565,000
Currency: Communauté Financière Africaine franc
Religions: Muslim, indigenous beliefs, Christian
Languages: French, native African languages

North Yungus Road, Bolivia

Feeling brave? Hop on a bike and ride down Bolivia's North Yungus Road—if you dare. Dubbed the world's most dangerous road, this 40-mile (64-km) route attracts thousands of mountain bikers a year who make this risky ride for bragging rights and unrivaled views of the Amazon rain forest. Descending 11,000 feet (3,352 m) from the snowcapped Andes to the rain forest, cyclists navigate the dirt and gravel road, which narrows to just under 10 feet (3 m) at some points. And with no guardrails along the side of the road, there's nothing keeping travelers from tumbling down the cliffs.

Burundi

Area: 10,747 sq mi (27,834 sq km)
Population: 10,400,000
Capital: Bujumbura, pop. 707,000
Currency: Burundi franc
Religions: Roman Catholic, indigenous beliefs, Muslim, Protestant
Languages: Kirundi, French, Swahili

Cambodia

Area: 69,898 sq mi (181,035 sq km)
Population: 15,900,000
Capital: Phnom Penh, pop. 1,684,000
Currency: riel
Religion: Theravada Buddhist
Language: Khmer

Cabo Verde

Area: 1,558 sq mi (4,036 sq km)
Population: 500,000
Capital: Praia, pop. 145,000
Currency: Cape Verdean escudo
Religions: Roman Catholic (infused with indigenous beliefs), Protestant (mostly Church of the Nazarene)
Languages: Portuguese, Crioulo

Cameroon

Area: 183,569 sq mi (475,442 sq km)
Population: 25,000,000
Capital: Yaoundé, pop. 2,930,000
Currency: Communauté Financière Africaine franc
Religions: indigenous beliefs, Christian, Muslim
Languages: 24 major African language groups, English, French

You Are There!

Monteverde Cloud Forest, Costa Rica

Beneath an emerald green canopy of soaring trees, you spot a three-toed sloth lounging lazily among the branches. Far below him, on the mossy forest floor, a pair of white-faced capuchin monkeys playfully chase each other while a stream rushes over rocks. This is the Monteverde Cloud Forest Reserve, the largest cloud forest in Central America. Set some 4,662 feet (1,440 m) above sea level, this tropical evergreen forest is a haven for flora, plus 100 species of mammals, 400 species of birds, and 1,200 species of amphibians and reptiles. Here, big cats like jaguars and pumas stalk the thick forest, while colorful toucans soar in the sky and rare, exotic frogs hop in and out of freshwater ponds. Whiz through the tree canopy on a zip line or take a more leisurely tour by foot. However you travel, you're sure to take in some of the most amazing biodiversity on the planet.

COLOR KEY ● Africa ● Australia, New Zealand, and Oceania

Canada

Area: 3,855,103 sq mi (9,984,670 sq km)
Population: 36,700,000
Capital: Ottawa, pop. 1,350,000
Currency: Canadian dollar
Religions: Roman Catholic, Protestant (includes United Church, Anglican), other Christian
Languages: English, French

Central African Republic

Area: 240,535 sq mi (622,984 sq km)
Population: 4,700,000
Capital: Bangui, pop. 781,000
Currency: Communauté Financière Africaine franc
Religions: indigenous beliefs, Protestant, Roman Catholic, Muslim
Languages: French, Sangho, tribal languages

Chad

Area: 495,755 sq mi (1,284,000 sq km)
Population: 14,900,000
Capital: N'Djamena, pop. 1,212,000
Currency: Communauté Financière Africaine franc
Religions: Muslim, Catholic, Protestant, animist
Languages: French, Arabic, Sara, more than 120 languages and dialects

Chile

Area: 291,930 sq mi (756,096 sq km)
Population: 18,400,000
Capital: Santiago, pop. 6,472,000
Currency: Chilean peso
Religions: Roman Catholic, Evangelical
Language: Spanish

China

Area: 3,705,406 sq mi (9,596,960 sq km)
Population: 1,386,800,000
Capital: Beijing, pop. 19,520,000
Currency: renminbi (yuan)
Religions: Taoist, Buddhist, Christian
Languages: Standard Chinese or Mandarin, Yue, Wu, Minbei, Minnan, Xiang, Gan, Hakka dialects

Colombia

Area: 440,831 sq mi (1,141,748 sq km)
Population: 49,300,000
Capital: Bogotá, pop. 9,558,000
Currency: Colombian peso
Religion: Roman Catholic
Language: Spanish

Comoros

Area: 863 sq mi (2,235 sq km)
Population: 800,000
Capital: Moroni, pop. 56,000
Currency: Comoran franc
Religion: Sunni Muslim
Languages: Arabic, French, Shikomoro

Congo

Area: 132,047 sq mi (342,000 sq km)
Population: 5,000,000
Capital: Brazzaville, pop. 1,827,000
Currency: Communauté Financière Africaine franc
Religions: Christian, animist
Languages: French, Lingala, Monokutuba, local languages

Costa Rica

Area: 19,730 sq mi (51,100 sq km)
Population: 4,900,000
Capital: San José, pop. 1,160,000
Currency: Costa Rican colón
Religions: Roman Catholic, Evangelical
Languages: Spanish, English

Côte d'Ivoire (Ivory Coast)

Area: 124,503 sq mi (322,462 sq km)
Population: 24,400,000
Capitals: Abidjan, pop. 4,708,000; Yamoussoukro, pop. 259,000
Currency: Communauté Financière Africaine franc
Religions: Muslim, indigenous beliefs, Christian
Languages: French, Dioula, other native dialects

Croatia

Area: 21,831 sq mi
(56,542 sq km)
Population: 4,100,000
Capital: Zagreb, pop. 687,000
Currency: kuna
Religions: Roman Catholic, Orthodox
Language: Croatian

Cuba

Area: 42,803 sq mi
(110,860 sq km)
Population: 11,300,000
Capital: Havana, pop. 2,146,000
Currency: Cuban peso
Religions: Roman Catholic, Protestant, Jehovah's Witnesses, Jewish, Santería
Language: Spanish

Cyprus

Area: 3,572 sq mi (9,251 sq km)
Population: 1,200,000
Capital: Nicosia, pop. 251,000
Currencies: euro; new Turkish lira in Northern Cyprus
Religions: Greek Orthodox, Muslim, Maronite, Armenian Apostolic
Languages: Greek, Turkish, English

Czech Republic (Czechia)

Area: 30,450 sq mi (78,866 sq km)
Population: 10,600,000
Capital: Prague, pop. 1,303,000
Currency: koruny
Religion: Roman Catholic
Language: Czech

Democratic Republic of the Congo

Area: 905,365 sq mi
(2,344,885 sq km)
Population: 81,500,000
Capital: Kinshasa, pop. 11,116,000
Currency: Congolese franc
Religions: Roman Catholic, Protestant, Kimbanguist, Muslim, syncretic sects, indigenous beliefs
Languages: French, Lingala, Kingwana, Kikongo, Tshiluba

Denmark

Area: 16,640 sq mi (43,098 sq km)
Population: 5,800,000
Capital: Copenhagen, pop. 1,255,000
Currency: Danish krone
Religions: Evangelical Lutheran, other Protestant, Roman Catholic
Languages: Danish, Faroese, Greenlandic, German, English as second language

Djibouti

Area: 8,958 sq mi
(23,200 sq km)
Population: 1,000,000
Capital: Djibouti, pop. 522,000
Currency: Djiboutian franc
Religions: Muslim, Christian
Languages: French, Arabic, Somali, Afar

Dominica

Area: 290 sq mi (751 sq km)
Population: 70,000
Capital: Roseau, pop. 15,000
Currency: East Caribbean dollar
Religions: Roman Catholic, Seventh-day Adventist, Pentecostal, Baptist, Methodist, other Christian
Languages: English, French patois

The "Mountain Chicken"—one of the world's largest frogs—can be found in Dominica.

Dominican Republic

Area: 18,704 sq mi
(48,442 sq km)
Population: 10,700,000
Capital: Santo Domingo, pop. 2,873,000
Currency: Dominican peso
Religion: Roman Catholic
Language: Spanish

COLOR KEY ● Africa ● Australia, New Zealand, and Oceania

Ecuador

Area: 109,483 sq mi
(283,560 sq km)
Population: 16,800,000
Capital: Quito, pop. 1,699,000
Currency: U.S. dollar
Religion: Roman Catholic
Languages: Spanish, Quechua, other
Amerindian languages

Egypt

Area: 386,874 sq mi
(1,002,000 sq km)
Population: 93,400,000
Capital: Cairo, pop. 18,419,000
Currency: Egyptian pound
Religions: Muslim (mostly Sunni), Coptic Christian
Languages: Arabic, English, French

5 cool things about EGYPT

1. Egypt gets about an inch (2.5 cm) of rain every year, making it one of the driest places on Earth.

2. A 5,000-year-old lost city—including huts, tombs, and ancient tools—was recently discovered near present-day Luxor, Egypt.

3. The Great Pyramid of Giza weighs 6.5 million tons (5.9 million t).

4. The desert village of Bahariya Oasis, Egypt, runs on solar power—a first for the country.

5. People have played board games in Egypt for over 4,000 years.

El Salvador

Area: 8,124 sq mi
(21,041 sq km)
Population: 6,400,000
Capital: San Salvador,
pop. 1,097,000
Currency: U.S. dollar
Religions: Roman Catholic, Protestant
Languages: Spanish, Nahua

Equatorial Guinea

Area: 10,831 sq mi (28,051 sq km)
Population: 1,300,000
Capital: Malabo, pop. 145,000
Currency: Communauté
Financière Africaine franc
Religions: Christian (predominantly Roman Catholic),
pagan practices
Languages: Spanish, French, Fang, Bubi

Eritrea

Area: 45,406 sq mi
(117,600 sq km)
Population: 5,900,000
Capital: Asmara, pop. 775,000
Currency: nakfa
Religions: Muslim, Coptic Christian, Roman Catholic
Languages: Afar, Arabic, Tigre, Kunama, Tigrinya, other
Cushitic languages

Estonia

Area: 17,462 sq mi (45,227 sq km)
Population: 1,300,000
Capital: Tallinn, pop. 392,000
Currency: euro
Religions: Evangelical Lutheran, Orthodox
Languages: Estonian, Russian

MORE THAN HALF OF ESTONIA IS COVERED BY FORESTS.

Ethiopia

Area: 426,373 sq mi
(1,104,300 sq km)
Population: 105,000,000
Capital: Addis Ababa,
pop. 3,168,000
Currency: birr
Religions: Christian, Muslim, traditional
Languages: Amharic, Oromigna, Tigrinya, Guaragigna

● Asia ● Europe ● North America ● South America

Fiji

Area: 7,095 sq mi
(18,376 sq km)
Population: 900,000
Capital: Suva, pop. 176,000
Currency: Fijian dollar
Religions: Christian (Methodist, Roman Catholic, Assembly of God), Hindu (Sanatan), Muslim (Sunni)
Languages: English, Fijian, Hindustani

France

Area: 210,026 sq mi
(543,965 sq km)
Population: 65,000,000
Capital: Paris, pop. 10,764,000
Currency: euro
Religions: Roman Catholic, Muslim
Language: French

Finland

Area: 130,558 sq mi
(338,145 sq km)
Population: 5,500,000
Capital: Helsinki, pop. 1,170,000
Currency: euro
Religion: Lutheran Church of Finland
Languages: Finnish, Swedish

Gabon

Area: 103,347 sq mi (267,667 sq km)
Population: 2,000,000
Capital: Libreville, pop. 695,000
Currency: Communauté Financière Africaine franc
Religions: Christian, animist
Languages: French, Fang, Myene, Nzebi, Bapounou/Eschira, Bandjabi

You Are There!
Mole National Park, Ghana

If you're eager to see some elephants, Mole National Park is the place to be. Ghana's largest nature refuge, Mole is home to around 500 elephants. Hang out within view of a watering hole and you'll be sure to spot one, along with countless other animals that roam the grounds of Mole, including antelope, buffalo, baboons, leopards, warthogs, and 300 species of birds. A guided safari of the park's sprawling 1,869 square miles (4,840 sq km) will give you an up-close-and-personal view of the refuge's residents. But during the dry season you may not have to trek too far: Thirsty animals are known to head to the motel by the park's headquarters to sip from a nearby pond.

COLOR KEY   ● Africa   ● Australia, New Zealand, and Oceania

Gambia

Area: 4,361 sq mi (11,295 sq km)
Population: 2,100,000
Capital: Banjul, pop. 489,000
Currency: dalasi
Religions: Muslim, Christian
Languages: English, Mandinka, Wolof, Fula, other indigenous vernaculars

Georgia

Area: 26,911 sq mi (69,700 sq km)
Population: 3,900,000
Capital: Tbilisi, pop. 1,150,000
Currency: lari
Religions: Orthodox Christian, Muslim, Armenian-Gregorian
Languages: Georgian, Russian, Armenian, Azeri, Abkhaz

Germany

Area: 137,847 sq mi (357,022 sq km)
Population: 83,100,000
Capital: Berlin, pop. 3,547,000
Currency: euro
Religions: Protestant, Roman Catholic, Muslim
Language: German

Ghana

Area: 92,100 sq mi (238,537 sq km)
Population: 28,800,000
Capital: Accra, pop. 2,242,000
Currency: Ghana cedi
Religions: Christian (Pentecostal/Charismatic, Protestant, Roman Catholic, other), Muslim, traditional beliefs
Languages: Asante, Ewe, Fante, Boron (Brong), Dagomba, Dangme, Dagarte (Dagaba), Akyem, Ga, English

Greece

Area: 50,949 sq mi (131,957 sq km)
Population: 10,700,000
Capital: Athens, pop. 3,060,000
Currency: euro
Religion: Greek Orthodox
Languages: Greek, English, French

Grenada

Area: 133 sq mi (344 sq km)
Population: 100,000
Capital: St. George's, pop. 38,000
Currency: East Caribbean dollar
Religions: Roman Catholic, Anglican, other Protestant
Languages: English, French patois

Guatemala

Area: 42,042 sq mi (108,889 sq km)
Population: 16,900,000
Capital: Guatemala City, pop. 2,874,000
Currency: quetzal
Religions: Roman Catholic, Protestant, indigenous Maya beliefs
Languages: Spanish, 23 official Amerindian languages

Guinea

Area: 94,926 sq mi (245,857 sq km)
Population: 11,500,000
Capital: Conakry, pop. 1,886,000
Currency: Guinean franc
Religions: Muslim, Christian, indigenous beliefs
Languages: French, ethnic languages

Guinea-Bissau

Area: 13,948 sq mi (36,125 sq km)
Population: 1,900,000
Capital: Bissau, pop. 473,000
Currency: Communauté Financière Africaine franc
Religions: indigenous beliefs, Muslim, Christian
Languages: Portuguese, Crioulo, African languages

Guyana

Area: 83,000 sq mi (214,969 sq km)
Population: 800,000
Capital: Georgetown, pop. 124,000
Currency: Guyanese dollar
Religions: Christian, Hindu, Muslim
Languages: English, Amerindian dialects, Creole, Hindustani, Urdu

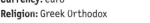

Haiti

Area: 10,714 sq mi (27,750 sq km)
Population: 10,600,000
Capital: Port-au-Prince, pop. 2,376,000
Currency: gourde
Religions: Roman Catholic, Protestant (Baptist, Pentecostal, other)
Languages: French, Creole

Honduras

Area: 43,433 sq mi (112,492 sq km)
Population: 8,900,000
Capital: Tegucigalpa, pop. 1,101,000
Currency: lempira
Religions: Roman Catholic, Protestant
Languages: Spanish, Amerindian dialects

Hungary

Area: 35,919 sq mi (93,030 sq km)
Population: 9,800,000
Capital: Budapest, pop. 1,717,000
Currency: forint
Religions: Roman Catholic, Calvinist, Lutheran
Language: Hungarian

Iceland

Area: 39,769 sq mi (103,000 sq km)
Population: 300,000
Capital: Reykjavík, pop. 184,000
Currency: Icelandic krona
Religion: Lutheran Church of Iceland
Languages: Icelandic, English, Nordic languages, German

India

Area: 1,269,221 sq mi (3,287,270 sq km)
Population: 1,352,600,000
Capital: New Delhi, pop. 24,953,000 (part of Delhi metropolitan area)
Currency: Indian rupee
Religions: Hindu, Muslim
Languages: Hindi, 21 other official languages, Hindustani (popular Hindi/Urdu variant in the north)

Indonesia

Area: 742,308 sq mi (1,922,570 sq km)
Population: 264,000,000
Capital: Jakarta, pop. 10,176,000
Currency: Indonesian rupiah
Religions: Muslim, Protestant, Roman Catholic
Languages: Bahasa Indonesia (modified form of Malay), English, Dutch, Javanese, local dialects

Iran

Area: 636,296 sq mi (1,648,000 sq km)
Population: 80,600,000
Capital: Tehran, pop. 8,353,000
Currency: Iranian rial
Religions: Shiite Muslim, Sunni Muslim
Languages: Persian, Turkic, Kurdish, Luri, Baluchi, Arabic

Iraq

Area: 168,754 sq mi (437,072 sq km)
Population: 39,200,000
Capital: Baghdad, pop. 6,483,000
Currency: Iraqi dinar
Religions: Shiite Muslim, Sunni Muslim
Languages: Arabic, Kurdish, Assyrian, Armenian

Ireland (Éire)

Area: 27,133 sq mi (70,273 sq km)
Population: 4,800,000
Capital: Dublin, pop. 1,155,000
Currency: euro
Religions: Roman Catholic, Church of Ireland
Languages: Irish (Gaelic), English

Israel

Area: 8,550 sq mi (22,145 sq km)
Population: 8,300,000
Capital: Jerusalem, pop. 829,000
Currency: new Israeli sheqel
Religions: Jewish, Muslim
Languages: Hebrew, Arabic, English

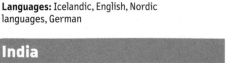

COLOR KEY ● Africa ● Australia, New Zealand, and Oceania

Italy

Area: 116,345 sq mi
(301,333 sq km)
Population: 60,500,000
Capital: Rome, pop. 3,697,000
Currency: euro
Religions: Roman Catholic, Protestant, Jewish, Muslim
Languages: Italian, German, French, Slovene

Japan

Area: 145,902 sq mi (377,887 sq km)
Population: 126,700,000
Capital: Tokyo, pop. 37,833,000
Currency: yen
Religions: Shinto, Buddhist
Language: Japanese

Jamaica

Area: 4,244 sq mi
(10,991 sq km)
Population: 2,900,000
Capital: Kingston, pop. 587,000
Currency: Jamaican dollar
Religions: Protestant (Church of God, Seventh-day Adventist, Pentecostal, Baptist, Anglican, other)
Languages: English, English patois

Jordan

Area: 34,495 sq mi
(89,342 sq km)
Population: 9,700,000
Capital: Amman, pop. 1,148,000
Currency: Jordanian dinar
Religions: Sunni Muslim, Christian
Languages: Arabic, English

You Are There!

Blue Lagoon, near Grindavík, Iceland

Tucked away in an ancient jet-black lava field you'll find the Blue Lagoon, a geothermal spa near Grindavík, Iceland. No matter the temperature outside, this sprawling, steaming spa offers warm waters hovering around 100°F (38°C) to soak in. Slide into the milky blue water and cover yourself with mineral-enriched mud, which softens and nourishes your skin. Or make your way over to the human-made waterfall and let the cascading flow massage your shoulders and back. Did someone say *ahhhh?*

● Asia ● Europe ● North America ● South America

Kazakhstan

Area: 1,049,155 sq mi
(2,717,300 sq km)
Population: 18,000,000
Capital: Astana, pop. 741,000
Currency: tenge
Religions: Muslim, Russian Orthodox
Languages: Kazakh (Qazaq), Russian

Kiribati

Area: 313 sq mi (811 sq km)
Population: 100,000
Capital: Tarawa, pop. 46,000
Currency: Australian
dollar
Religions: Roman Catholic, Protestant
(Congregational)
Languages: I-Kiribati, English

Kenya

Area: 224,081 sq mi (580,367 sq km)
Population: 49,700,000
Capital: Nairobi, pop. 3,768,000
Currency: Kenyan shilling
Religions: Protestant, Roman Catholic, Muslim,
indigenous beliefs
Languages: English, Kiswahili, many indigenous
languages

Kosovo

Area: 4,203 sq mi (10,887 sq km)
Population: 1,800,000
Capital: Prishtina, pop. 207,500
Currency: euro
Religions: Muslim, Serbian Orthodox, Roman Catholic
Languages: Albanian, Serbian, Bosnian,
Turkish, Roma

You Are There!
Trakai Island Castle, Lithuania

With its pointed turrets and thick stone walls, Trakai Castle looks as though it were plucked right out of a fairy tale. Originally built in the early 1400s and painstakingly refurbished in the 1950s, this red brick and stone palace is a throwback to the Middle Ages. Access the castle by crossing Lake Galvé on a narrow wooden footbridge, then explore its many rooms set up to offer you a glimpse of life in the 15th century. You can also tour some of the castle's corner towers, once used to imprison enemies or to house cannons. Or opt to board a sailboat and take in a lakeside view of the stunning surroundings.

COLOR KEY ● Africa ● Australia, New Zealand, and Oceania

Kuwait

Area: 6,880 sq mi
(17,818 sq km)
Population: 4,100,000
Capital: Kuwait City,
pop. 2,680,000
Currency: Kuwaiti dinar
Religions: Sunni Muslim, Shiite Muslim
Languages: Arabic, English

Kyrgyzstan

Area: 77,182 sq mi
(199,900 sq km)
Population: 6,200,000
Capital: Bishkek, pop. 858,000
Currency: som
Religions: Muslim, Russian Orthodox
Languages: Kyrgyz, Uzbek, Russian

Laos

Area: 91,429 sq mi
(236,800 sq km)
Population: 7,000,000
Capital: Vientiane, pop. 946,000
Currency: kip
Religions: Buddhist, animist
Languages: Lao, French, English, various ethnic
languages

Latvia

Area: 24,938 sq mi
(64,589 sq km)
Population: 1,900,000
Capital: Riga, pop. 629,000
Currency: Latvian lat
Religions: Lutheran, Roman Catholic,
Russian Orthodox
Languages: Latvian, Russian, Lithuanian

Lebanon

Area: 4,036 sq mi (10,452 sq km)
Population: 6,200,000
Capital: Beirut, pop. 2,179,000
Currency: Lebanese pound
Religions: Muslim, Christian
Languages: Arabic, French, English, Armenian

Lesotho

Area: 11,720 sq mi (30,355 sq km)
Population: 2,200,000
Capital: Maseru, pop. 267,000
Currencies: loti; South African rand
Religions: Christian, indigenous beliefs
Languages: Sesotho, English, Zulu, Xhosa

Liberia

Area: 43,000 sq mi
(111,370 sq km)
Population: 4,700,000
Capital: Monrovia,
pop. 1,224,000
Currency: Liberian dollar
Religions: Christian, indigenous beliefs, Muslim
Languages: English, some 20 ethnic languages

Libya

Area: 679,362 sq mi
(1,759,540 sq km)
Population: 6,400,000
Capital: Tripoli, pop. 1,126,000
Currency: Libyan dinar
Religion: Sunni Muslim
Languages: Arabic, Italian, English

Liechtenstein

Area: 62 sq mi (160 sq km)
Population: 40,000
Capital: Vaduz, pop. 5,000
Currency: Swiss franc
Religions: Roman Catholic, Protestant
Languages: German, Alemannic dialect

Lithuania

Area: 25,212 sq mi
(65,300 sq km)
Population: 2,800,000
Capital: Vilnius, pop. 519,000
Currency: litas
Religions: Roman Catholic, Russian Orthodox
Languages: Lithuanian, Russian, Polish

Luxembourg

Area: 998 sq mi (2,586 sq km)
Population: 600,000
Capital: Luxembourg, pop. 107,000
Currency: euro
Religions: Roman Catholic, Protestant, Jewish, Muslim
Languages: Luxembourgish, German, French

Maldives

Area: 115 sq mi (298 sq km)
Population: 400,000
Capital: Male, pop. 156,000
Currency: rufiyaa
Religion: Sunni Muslim
Languages: Maldivian Dhivehi, English

Macedonia
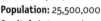
Area: 9,928 sq mi (25,713 sq km)
Population: 2,100,000
Capital: Skopje, pop. 501,000
Currency: Macedonian denar
Religions: Macedonian Orthodox, Muslim
Languages: Macedonian, Albanian, Turkish

Mali
Area: 478,841 sq mi (1,240,192 sq km)
Population: 18,900,000
Capital: Bamako, pop. 2,386,000
Currency: Communauté Financière Africaine franc
Religions: Muslim, indigenous beliefs
Languages: Bambara, French, numerous African languages

Madagascar

Area: 226,658 sq mi (587,041 sq km)
Population: 25,500,000
Capital: Antananarivo, pop. 2,487,000
Currency: Madagascar ariary
Religions: indigenous beliefs, Christian, Muslim
Languages: English, French, Malagasy

EACH YEAR, MALI PRODUCES ENOUGH GOLD TO OUTWEIGH 11 AFRICAN ELEPHANTS.

Malawi
Area: 45,747 sq mi (118,484 sq km)
Population: 18,600,000
Capital: Lilongwe, pop. 867,000
Currency: Malawian kwacha
Religions: Christian, Muslim
Languages: Chichewa, Chinyanja, Chiyao, Chitumbuka

Malta

Area: 122 sq mi (316 sq km)
Population: 400,000
Capital: Valletta, pop. 197,000
Currency: euro
Religion: Roman Catholic
Languages: Maltese, English

Malaysia

Area: 127,355 sq mi (329,847 sq km)
Population: 31,600,000
Capital: Kuala Lumpur, pop. 6,629,000
Currency: ringgit
Religions: Muslim, Buddhist, Christian, Hindu
Languages: Bahasa Malaysia, English, Chinese, Tamil, Telugu, Malayalam, Panjabi, Thai, indigenous languages

Marshall Islands

Area: 70 sq mi (181 sq km)
Population: 60,000
Capital: Majuro, pop. 31,000
Currency: U.S. dollar
Religions: Protestant, Assembly of God, Roman Catholic
Language: Marshallese

Mauritania

Area: 397,955 sq mi
(1,030,700 sq km)
Population: 4,400,000
Capital: Nouakchott, pop. 945,000
Currency: ouguiya
Religion: Muslim
Languages: Arabic, Pulaar, Soninke, French,
Hassaniya, Wolof

Mauritius

Area: 788 sq mi (2,040 sq km)
Population: 1,300,000
Capital: Port Louis, pop. 135,000
Currency: Mauritian rupee
Religions: Hindu, Roman Catholic,
Muslim, other Christian
Languages: Creole, Bhojpuri, French

Mexico

Area: 758,449 sq mi
(1,964,375 sq km)
Population: 129,200,000
Capital: Mexico City,
pop. 20,843,000
Currency: Mexican peso
Religions: Roman Catholic, Protestant
Languages: Spanish, Mayan, other indigenous languages

Micronesia

Area: 271 sq mi (702 sq km)
Population: 100,000
Capital: Palikir, pop. 7,000
Currency: U.S. dollar
Religions: Roman Catholic, Protestant
Languages: English, Trukese, Pohnpeian, Yapese,
other indigenous languages

Moldova

Area: 13,050 sq mi
(33,800 sq km)
Population: 3,600,000
Capital: Chisinau,
pop. 721,000
Currency: Moldovan leu
Religion: Eastern Orthodox
Languages: Moldovan, Russian, Gagauz

Monaco

Area: 0.8 sq mi (2.0 sq km)
Population: 40,000
Capital: Monaco, pop. 38,000
Currency: euro
Religion: Roman Catholic
Languages: French, English, Italian, Monegasque

Mongolia

Area: 603,909 sq mi
(1,564,116 sq km)
Population: 3,200,000
Capital: Ulaanbaatar,
pop. 1,334,000
Currency: togrog/tugrik
Religions: Buddhist Lamaist, Shamanist, Christian
Languages: Khalkha Mongol, Turkic, Russian

5 cool things about MONGOLIA

1. Mongolia is home to the saiga, an ancient antelope-like animal that once roamed the grasslands alongside woolly mammoths.

2. Winter temperatures in Mongolia's Gobi desert can drop below -4°F (-20°C), making it one of the coldest deserts on Earth.

3. Mongolia holds the record for the world's largest camel race, with some 1,100 jockeys competing around a track in Dalanzadgad.

4. About 30 percent of Mongolia's population are nomadic herders who live in portable tents also known as gers.

5. Mongolia and China produce 90 percent of the world's cashmere.

Montenegro

Area: 5,333 sq mi
(13,812 sq km)
Population: 600,000
Capital: Podgorica, pop. 165,000
Currency: euro
Religions: Orthodox, Muslim, Roman Catholic
Languages: Serbian (Ijekavian dialect), Bosnian,
Albanian, Croatian

● Asia ● Europe ● North America ● South America

Morocco

Area: 172,414 sq mi
(446,550 sq km)
Population: 35,100,000
Capital: Rabat, pop. 1,932,000
Currency: Moroccan dirham
Religion: Muslim
Languages: Arabic, Berber dialects, French

Myanmar (Burma)

Area: 261,218 sq mi
(676,552 sq km)
Population: 53,400,000
Capitals: Nay Pyi Taw, pop.
1,016,000; Yangon (Rangoon), pop. 4,802,000
Currency: kyat
Religions: Buddhist, Christian, Muslim
Languages: Burmese, minority ethnic languages

Mozambique

Area: 308,642 sq mi
(799,380 sq km)
Population: 29,700,000
Capital: Maputo, pop. 1,174,000
Currency: metical
Religions: Roman Catholic, Muslim, Zionist Christian
Languages: Emakhuwa, Xichangana, Portuguese,
Elomwe, Cisena, Echuwabo, other local languages

Namibia

Area: 318,261 sq mi
(824,292 sq km)
Population: 2,500,000
Capital: Windhoek, pop. 356,000
Currencies: Namibian dollar;
South African rand
Religions: Lutheran, other Christian, indigenous beliefs
Languages: Afrikaans, German, English

You Are There!
Milford Sound, New Zealand

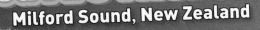

Cascading waterfalls, mountaintop glaciers, and towering cliffs: These are just some of the reasons why New Zealand's Milford Sound is often referred to as the "eighth wonder of the world." An inlet of the Tasman Sea, this 7.5-mile (12-km) body of water is not actually a sound, but a fjord carved by a glacier. The deep blue water is framed by majestic mountains, including Mitre Peak, soaring some 5,550 feet (1,690 m) into the sky. Take a hike around the trails and discover unrivaled natural beauty, or head down to an enclosed underwater observatory where you can spot 11-legged sea stars and rainbow-hued tropical fish swimming around the black coral. Really want to take it all in? Hop on a helicopter and enjoy a bird's-eye view of the entire area, from ancient forest valleys to jagged peaks, while keeping an eye out for wildlife like dolphins, seals, and penguins.

COLOR KEY   ● Africa   ● Australia, New Zealand, and Oceania

Nauru

Area: 8 sq mi (21 sq km)
Population: 10,000
Capital: Yaren, pop. 10,000
Currency: Australian dollar
Religions: Protestant, Roman Catholic
Languages: Nauruan, English

Nepal

Area: 56,827 sq mi (147,181 sq km)
Population: 29,400,000
Capital: Kathmandu, pop. 1,142,000
Currency: Nepalese rupee
Religions: Hindu, Buddhist, Muslim, Kirant
Languages: Nepali, Maithali, Bhojpuri, Tharu, Tamang, Newar, Magar

Netherlands

Area: 16,034 sq mi (41,528 sq km)
Population: 17,100,000
Capital: Amsterdam, pop. 1,084,000
Currency: euro
Religions: Roman Catholic, Dutch Reformed, Calvinist, Muslim
Languages: Dutch, Frisian

New Zealand

Area: 104,454 sq mi (270,534 sq km)
Population: 4,800,000
Capital: Wellington, pop. 380,000
Currency: New Zealand dollar
Religions: Anglican, Roman Catholic, Presbyterian, other Christian
Languages: English, Maori

Nicaragua

Area: 50,193 sq mi (130,000 sq km)
Population: 6,200,000
Capital: Managua, pop. 951,000
Currency: gold cordoba
Religions: Roman Catholic, Evangelical
Language: Spanish

Niger

Area: 489,191 sq mi (1,267,000 sq km)
Population: 20,600,000
Capital: Niamey, pop. 1,058,000
Currency: Communauté Financière Africaine franc
Religions: Muslim, other (includes indigenous beliefs and Christian)
Languages: French, Hausa, Djerma

Nigeria

Area: 356,669 sq mi (923,768 sq km)
Population: 190,900,000
Capital: Abuja, pop. 2,301,000
Currency: naira
Religions: Muslim, Christian, indigenous beliefs
Languages: English, Hausa, Yoruba, Igbo (Ibo), Fulani

North Korea

Area: 46,540 sq mi (120,538 sq km)
Population: 25,500,000
Capital: Pyongyang, pop. 2,856,000
Currency: North Korean won
Religions: Buddhist, Confucianist, some Christian and syncretic Chondogyo
Language: Korean

Norway

Area: 125,004 sq mi (323,758 sq km)
Population: 5,300,000
Capital: Oslo, pop. 970,000
Currency: Norwegian krone
Religion: Church of Norway (Lutheran)
Languages: Bokmal Norwegian, Nynorsk Norwegian, Sami

Oman

Area: 119,500 sq mi (309,500 sq km)
Population: 4,700,000
Capital: Muscat, pop. 812,000
Currency: Omani rial
Religions: Ibadhi Muslim, Sunni Muslim, Shiite Muslim, Hindu
Languages: Arabic, English, Baluchi, Urdu, Indian dialects

Pakistan

Area: 307,374 sq mi
(796,095 sq km)
Population: 199,300,000
Capital: Islamabad, pop. 1,297,000
Currency: Pakistani rupee
Religions: Sunni Muslim, Shiite Muslim
Languages: Punjabi, Sindhi, Siraiki, Pashto, Urdu, Baluchi, Hindko, English

Peru

Area: 496,224 sq mi
(1,285,216 sq km)
Population: 31,800,000
Capital: Lima, pop. 9,722,000
Currency: nuevo sol
Religion: Roman Catholic
Languages: Spanish, Quechua, Aymara, minor Amazonian languages

Palau

Area: 189 sq mi (489 sq km)
Population: 20,000
Capital: Melekeok, pop. 1,000
Currency: U.S. dollar
Religions: Roman Catholic, Protestant, Modekngei, Seventh-day Adventist
Languages: Palauan, Filipino, English, Chinese

Philippines

Area: 115,831 sq mi
(300,000 sq km)
Population: 105,000,000
Capital: Manila,
pop. 12,764,000
Currency: Philippine peso
Religions: Roman Catholic, Muslim, other Christian
Languages: Filipino (based on Tagalog), English

Panama

Area: 29,157 sq mi (75,517 sq km)
Population: 4,100,000
Capital: Panama City,
pop. 1,638,000
Currencies: balboa; U.S. dollar
Religions: Roman Catholic, Protestant
Languages: Spanish, English

Poland

Area: 120,728 sq mi
(312,685 sq km)
Population: 38,400,000
Capital: Warsaw, pop. 1,718,000
Currency: zloty
Religion: Roman Catholic
Language: Polish

Papua New Guinea

Area: 178,703 sq mi (462,840 sq km)
Population: 8,300,000
Capital: Port Moresby, pop. 338,000
Currency: kina
Religions: indigenous beliefs, Roman Catholic, Lutheran, other Protestant
Languages: Melanesian Pidgin, 820 indigenous languages

Portugal

Area: 35,655 sq mi
(92,345 sq km)
Population: 10,300,000
Capital: Lisbon, pop. 2,869,000
Currency: euro
Religion: Roman Catholic
Languages: Portuguese, Mirandese

Paraguay

Area: 157,048 sq mi
(406,752 sq km)
Population: 6,800,000
Capital: Asunción, pop. 2,307,000
Currency: guarani
Religions: Roman Catholic, Protestant
Languages: Spanish, Guarani

Qatar

Area: 4,448 sq mi
(11,521 sq km)
Population: 2,700,000
Capital: Doha, pop. 699,000
Currency: Qatari rial
Religions: Muslim, Christian
Languages: Arabic; English commonly a second language

COLOR KEY ● Africa ● Australia, New Zealand, and Oceania

Romania

Area: 92,043 sq mi
(238,391 sq km)
Population: 19,600,000
Capital: Bucharest, pop. 1,872,000
Currency: new leu
Religions: Eastern Orthodox, Protestant,
Roman Catholic
Languages: Romanian, Hungarian

Rwanda

Area: 10,169 sq mi
(26,338 sq km)
Population: 12,300,000
Capital: Kigali, pop. 1,223,000
Currency: Rwandan franc
Religions: Roman Catholic, Protestant,
Adventist, Muslim
Languages: Kinyarwanda, French, English, Kiswahili

Russia

Area: 6,592,850 sq mi
(17,075,400 sq km)
Population: 146,800,000
Capital: Moscow, pop. 12,063,000
Currency: ruble
Religions: Russian Orthodox, Muslim
Languages: Russian, many minority languages

*Note: Russia is in both Europe and Asia, but its capital is in Europe,
so it is classified here as a European country.*

Samoa

Area: 1,093 sq mi (2,831 sq km)
Population: 200,000
Capital: Apia, pop. 37,000
Currency: tala
Religions: Congregationalist, Roman Catholic,
Methodist, Church of Jesus Christ of Latter-day
Saints, Assembly of God, Seventh-day Adventist
Languages: Samoan (Polynesian), English

You Are There!

Intramuros, the Philippines

Climb into a horse-drawn cart and tour the walled old town of Intramuros, in the heart of the Philippines's capital city of Manila. Having served as the Spanish capital in Asia for more than 300 years, it is said to be one of the best-preserved Spanish colonial cities. Here, you can explore a 450-year-old cathedral that's still standing after invasions, wars, and natural disasters, or check out a museum display about life under Spanish rule. Then, stretch your legs on the green space surrounding Fort Santiago, a former fortress used during Spanish colonial times. Poke around the ruins or, on a warm day, you can splash in fountains. Wrap up your visit by catching the boldly colored sunset over Manila Bay, a perfect way to end your day.

● Asia ● Europe ● North America ● South America

San Marino

Area: 24 sq mi (61 sq km)
Population: 30,000
Capital: San Marino, pop. 4,000
Currency: euro
Religion: Roman Catholic
Language: Italian

Seychelles

Area: 176 sq mi (455 sq km)
Population: 90,000
Capital: Victoria, pop. 26,000
Currency: Seychelles rupee
Religions: Roman Catholic, Anglican, other Christian
Languages: Creole, English

Sao Tome and Principe

Area: 386 sq mi (1,001 sq km)
Population: 200,000
Capital: São Tomé, pop. 71,000
Currency: dobra
Religions: Roman Catholic, Evangelical
Language: Portuguese

Sierra Leone

Area: 27,699 sq mi (71,740 sq km)
Population: 7,600,000
Capital: Freetown, pop. 986,000
Currency: leone
Religions: Muslim, indigenous beliefs, Christian
Languages: English, Mende, Temne, Krio

Saudi Arabia

Area: 756,985 sq mi (1,960,582 sq km)
Population: 32,600,000
Capital: Riyadh, pop. 6,195,000
Currency: Saudi riyal
Religion: Muslim
Language: Arabic

Singapore

Area: 255 sq mi (660 sq km)
Population: 5,700,000
Capital: Singapore, pop. 5,517,000
Currency: Singapore dollar
Religions: Buddhist, Muslim, Taoist, Roman Catholic, Hindu, other Christian
Languages: Mandarin, English, Malay, Hokkien, Cantonese, Teochew, Tamil

Senegal

Area: 75,955 sq mi (196,722 sq km)
Population: 15,800,000
Capital: Dakar, pop. 3,393,000
Currency: Communauté Financière Africaine franc
Religions: Muslim, Christian (mostly Roman Catholic)
Languages: French, Wolof, Pulaar, Jola, Mandinka

Slovakia

Area: 18,932 sq mi (49,035 sq km)
Population: 5,400,000
Capital: Bratislava, pop. 403,000
Currency: euro
Religions: Roman Catholic, Protestant, Greek Catholic
Languages: Slovak, Hungarian

Serbia

Area: 29,913 sq mi (77,474 sq km)
Population: 7,000,000
Capital: Belgrade, pop. 1,181,000
Currency: Serbian dinar
Religions: Serbian Orthodox, Roman Catholic, Muslim
Languages: Serbian, Hungarian

Slovenia

Area: 7,827 sq mi (20,273 sq km)
Population: 2,100,000
Capital: Ljubljana, pop. 279,000
Currency: euro
Religions: Roman Catholic, Muslim, Orthodox
Languages: Slovene, Croatian, Serbian

Solomon Islands

Area: 10,954 sq mi (28,370 sq km)
Population: 700,000
Capital: Honiara, pop. 73,000
Currency: Solomon Islands dollar
Religions: Church of Melanesia, Roman Catholic, South Seas Evangelical, other Christian
Languages: Melanesian pidgin, 120 indigenous languages

Somalia

Area: 246,201 sq mi (637,657 sq km)
Population: 14,700,000
Capital: Mogadishu, pop. 2,014,000
Currency: Somali shilling
Religion: Sunni Muslim
Languages: Somali, Arabic, Italian, English

South Africa

Area: 470,693 sq mi (1,219,090 sq km)
Population: 56,500,000
Capitals: Pretoria (Tshwane), pop. 1,991,000; Bloemfontein, pop. 496,000; Cape Town, pop. 3,624,000
Currency: rand
Religions: Zion Christian, Pentecostal, Catholic, Methodist, Dutch Reformed, Anglican, other Christian
Languages: IsiZulu, IsiXhosa, Afrikaans, Sepedi, English

South Korea

Area: 38,321 sq mi (99,250 sq km)
Population: 51,400,000
Capital: Seoul, pop. 9,775,000
Currency: South Korean won
Religions: Christian, Buddhist
Languages: Korean, English

South Sudan

Area: 248,777 sq mi (644,329 sq km)
Population: 12,600,000
Capital: Juba, pop. 307,000
Currency: South Sudan pound
Religions: animist, Christian
Languages: English, Arabic, regional languages (Dinke, Nuer, Bari, Zande, Shilluk)

Spain

Area: 195,363 sq mi (505,988 sq km)
Population: 46,600,000
Capital: Madrid, pop. 6,133,000
Currency: euro
Religion: Roman Catholic
Languages: Castilian Spanish, Catalan, Galician, Basque

5 cool things about SPAIN

1. Red rain—likely the result of algae in the water—once fell on Zamora, Spain.

2. La Tomatina, the world's largest tomato fight, takes place every August in Valencia, Spain.

3. The ruins of Sant Romà de Sau—a 1,000-year-old village—are submerged beneath a reservoir in Catalonia, Spain.

4. A street in Zaragoza, Spain, is named "Avenida de Super Mario Bros" after the video game characters.

5. A restaurant in Madrid, Spain, has been open since 1725, making it the world's oldest eatery.

Sri Lanka

Area: 25,299 sq mi (65,525 sq km)
Population: 21,400,000
Capitals: Colombo, pop. 704,000; Sri Jayewardenepura Kotte, pop. 128,000
Currency: Sri Lankan rupee
Religions: Buddhist, Muslim, Hindu, Christian
Languages: Sinhala, Tamil

St. Kitts and Nevis

Area: 104 sq mi (269 sq km)
Population: 50,000
Capital: Basseterre, pop. 14,000
Currency: East Caribbean dollar
Religions: Anglican, other Protestant, Roman Catholic
Language: English

St. Lucia

Area: 238 sq mi (616 sq km)
Population: 200,000
Capital: Castries, pop. 22,000
Currency: East Caribbean dollar
Religions: Roman Catholic, Seventh-day Adventist, Pentecostal
Languages: English, French patois

St. Vincent and the Grenadines

Area: 150 sq mi (389 sq km)
Population: 100,000
Capital: Kingstown, pop. 27,000
Currency: East Caribbean dollar
Religions: Anglican, Methodist, Roman Catholic
Languages: English, French patois

Sudan

Area: 718,722 sq mi (1,861,484 sq km)
Population: 40,600,000
Capital: Khartoum, pop. 5,000,000
Currency: Sudanese pound
Religions: Sunni Muslim, indigenous beliefs, Christian
Languages: Arabic, Nubian, Ta Bedawie, many diverse dialects of Nilotic, Nilo-Hamitic, Sudanic languages

Suriname

Area: 63,037 sq mi (163,265 sq km)
Population: 600,000
Capital: Paramaribo, pop. 234,000
Currency: Suriname dollar
Religions: Hindu, Protestant (predominantly Moravian), Roman Catholic, Muslim, indigenous beliefs
Languages: Dutch, English, Sranang Tongo, Hindustani, Javanese

Swaziland

Area: 6,704 sq mi (17,363 sq km)
Population: 1,400,000
Capitals: Mbabane, pop. 66,000; Lobamba, pop. 4,600
Currency: lilangeni
Religions: Zionist, Roman Catholic, Muslim
Languages: English, siSwati

Sweden

Area: 173,732 sq mi (449,964 sq km)
Population: 10,100,000
Capital: Stockholm, pop. 1,464,000
Currency: Swedish krona
Religion: Lutheran
Languages: Swedish, Sami, Finnish

Switzerland

Area: 15,940 sq mi (41,284 sq km)
Population: 8,500,000
Capital: Bern, pop. 358,000
Currency: Swiss franc
Religions: Roman Catholic, Protestant, Muslim
Languages: German, French, Italian, Romansh

Syria

Area: 71,498 sq mi (185,180 sq km)
Population: 18,300,000
Capital: Damascus, pop. 2,574,000
Currency: Syrian pound
Religions: Sunni, other Muslim (includes Alawite, Druze), Christian
Languages: Arabic, Kurdish, Armenian, Aramaic, Circassian

Tajikistan

Area: 55,251 sq mi (143,100 sq km)
Population: 8,800,000
Capital: Dushanbe, pop. 801,000
Currency: somoni
Religions: Sunni Muslim, Shiite Muslim
Languages: Tajik, Russian

Tanzania

Area: 364,900 sq mi (945,087 sq km)
Population: 57,500,000
Capitals: Dar es Salaam, pop. 5,116,000; Dodoma, pop. 228,000
Currency: Tanzanian shilling
Religions: Muslim, indigenous beliefs, Christian
Languages: Kiswahili, Kiunguja, English, Arabic, local languages

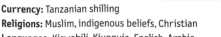

Thailand

Area: 198,115 sq mi
(513,115 sq km)
Population: 66,100,000
Capital: Bangkok, pop. 9,098,000
Currency: baht
Religions: Buddhist, Muslim
Languages: Thai, English, ethnic dialects

Timor-Leste (East Timor)

Area: 5,640 sq mi
(14,609 sq km)
Population: 1,300,000
Capital: Dili, pop. 228,000
Currency: U.S. dollar
Religion: Roman Catholic
Languages: Tetum, Portuguese, Indonesian, English, indigenous languages

Togo

Area: 21,925 sq mi (56,785 sq km)
Population: 7,800,000
Capital: Lomé, pop. 930,000
Currency: Communauté
Financière Africaine franc
Religions: indigenous beliefs, Christian, Muslim
Languages: French, Ewe, Mina, Kabye, Dagomb

Tonga

Area: 289 sq mi (748 sq km)
Population: 100,000
Capital: Nuku'alofa,
pop. 25,000
Currency: pa'anga
Religion: Christian
Languages: Tongan, English

An active underwater VOLCANO recently formed a NEW ISLAND off the coast of Tonga.

Trinidad and Tobago

Area: 1,980 sq mi (5,128 sq km)
Population: 1,400,000
Capital: Port of Spain, pop. 34,000
Currency: Trinidad and
Tobago dollar
Religions: Roman Catholic, Hindu, Anglican, Baptist
Languages: English, Caribbean Hindustani, French, Spanish, Chinese

Tunisia

Area: 63,170 sq mi
(163,610 sq km)
Population: 11,500,000
Capital: Tunis, pop. 1,978,000
Currency: Tunisian dinar
Religion: Muslim
Languages: Arabic, French

Turkey

Area: 300,948 sq mi
(779,452 sq km)
Population: 80,900,000
Capital: Ankara, pop. 4,644,000
Currency: new Turkish lira
Religion: Muslim (mostly Sunni)
Languages: Turkish, Kurdish, Dimli (Zaza), Azeri, Kabardian, Gagauz

Turkmenistan

Area: 188,456 sq mi
(488,100 sq km)
Population: 5,800,000
Capital: Ashgabat, pop. 735,000
Currency: Turkmen manat
Religions: Muslim, Eastern Orthodox
Languages: Turkmen, Russian, Uzbek

Tuvalu

Area: 10 sq mi (26 sq km)
Population: 10,000
Capital: Funafuti, pop. 6,000
Currencies: Australian dollar;
Tuvaluan dollar
Religion: Church of Tuvalu (Congregationalist)
Languages: Tuvaluan, English, Samoan, Kiribati

● Asia ● Europe ● North America ● South America

Uganda

Area: 93,104 sq mi
(241,139 sq km)
Population: 42,800,000
Capital: Kampala, pop. 1,863,000
Currency: Ugandan shilling
Religions: Protestant, Roman Catholic, Muslim
Languages: English, Ganda, other local languages, Kiswahili, Arabic

United Arab Emirates

Area: 30,000 sq mi
(77,700 sq km)
Population: 9,400,000
Capital: Abu Dhabi,
pop. 1,114,000
Currency: Emirati dirham
Religion: Muslim
Languages: Arabic, Persian, English, Hindi, Urdu

Ukraine

Area: 233,030 sq mi
(603,550 sq km)
Population: 42,300,000
Capital: Kiev, pop. 2,917,000
Currency: hryvnia
Religions: Ukrainian Orthodox, Orthodox, Ukrainian Greek Catholic
Languages: Ukrainian, Russian

United Kingdom

Area: 93,788 sq mi
(242,910 sq km)
Population: 66,200,000
Capital: London, pop. 10,189,000
Currency: British pound
Religions: Anglican, Roman Catholic, Presbyterian, Methodist
Languages: English, Welsh, Scottish form of Gaelic

You Are There!

Dubai, United Arab Emirates

Can you say dream destination? There's tons to do in Dubai, a city sitting on the coast of the Persian Gulf in the United Arab Emirates. Need a quick itinerary? First, take a lightning-quick elevator ride up to the top of Burj Khalifa, the tallest building in the world. From 148 stories up, watch the cars and people, as tiny as ants, mill below you. Once you're back on the ground, head on over to Ski Dubai, the Middle East's first indoor ski resort. No matter the weather, you can schuss down the slopes on human-made snow at this giant arena, complete with a black diamond run and a chairlift. While you're there, check out the resident king and gentoo penguins—you can even feed and hug one if you'd like. End your day with a fountain and light show on Burj Khalifa Lake in downtown Dubai. With the spray synched up to music and lights, it's literally a can't-miss sight: The water sprays as high as a 50-story building, making it the world's largest dancing fountain.

COLOR KEY ● Africa ● Australia, New Zealand, and Oceania

United States

Area: 3,794,083 sq mi (9,826,630 sq km)
Population: 325,400,000
Capital: Washington, D.C., pop. 681,170
Currency: U.S. dollar
Religions: Protestant, Roman Catholic
Languages: English, Spanish

Uruguay

Area: 68,037 sq mi (176,215 sq km)
Population: 3,500,000
Capital: Montevideo, pop. 1,698,000
Currency: Uruguayan peso
Religion: Roman Catholic
Language: Spanish

Uzbekistan

Area: 172,742 sq mi (447,400 sq km)
Population: 32,400,000
Capital: Tashkent, pop. 2,241,000
Currency: Uzbekistani sum
Religions: Muslim (mostly Sunni), Eastern Orthodox
Languages: Uzbek, Russian, Tajik

Vanuatu

Area: 4,707 sq mi (12,190 sq km)
Population: 300,000
Capital: Port Vila, pop. 53,000
Currency: vatu
Religions: Presbyterian, Anglican, Roman Catholic, other Christian, indigenous beliefs
Languages: more than 100 local languages, pidgin (known as Bislama or Bichelama)

Vatican City

Area: 0.2 sq mi (0.4 sq km)
Population: 800
Capital: Vatican City, pop. 800
Currency: euro
Religion: Roman Catholic
Languages: Italian, Latin, French

Venezuela

Area: 352,144 sq mi (912,050 sq km)
Population: 31,400,000
Capital: Caracas, pop. 2,912,000
Currency: bolivar
Religion: Roman Catholic
Languages: Spanish, numerous indigenous dialects

Vietnam

Area: 127,844 sq mi (331,114 sq km)
Population: 93,700,000
Capital: Hanoi, pop. 3,470,000
Currency: dong
Religions: Buddhist, Roman Catholic
Languages: Vietnamese, English, French, Chinese, Khmer

Yemen

Area: 207,286 sq mi (536,869 sq km)
Population: 28,300,000
Capital: Sanaa, pop. 2,833,000
Currency: Yemeni rial
Religions: Muslim, including Shaf'i (Sunni) and Zaydi (Shiite)
Language: Arabic

Zambia

Area: 290,586 sq mi (752,614 sq km)
Population: 16,400,000
Capital: Lusaka, pop. 2,078,000
Currency: Zambian kwacha
Religions: Christian, Muslim, Hindu
Languages: English, Bemba, Kaonda, Lozi, Lunda, Luvale, Nyanja, Tonga, about 70 other indigenous languages

Zimbabwe

Area: 150,872 sq mi (390,757 sq km)
Population: 16,600,000
Capital: Harare, pop. 1,495,000
Currency: Zimbabwean dollar
Religions: Syncretic (part Christian, part indigenous beliefs), Christian, indigenous beliefs
Languages: English, Shona, Sindebele, tribal dialects

THE POLITICAL UNITED STATES

9:00AM **PACIFIC TIME**

Cape Flattery
Seattle
Olympia • Tacoma
WASHINGTON
Spokane
Portland
Yakima
Salem
Columbia
Eugene
OREGON
Medford
Klamath Falls
Eureka
Boise
Redding
IDAHO
Idaho Falls
Snake
Pocatello

10:00AM
MOUNTAIN TIME

Great Falls
Missouri
MONTANA
Butte • Helena
Billings
GREAT
Cody
Yellowstone L.
WYOMING
Casper
N. Platte
Cheyenne
Laramie
Fort Collins
Boulder
S. Platte
Denver
COLORADO
Grand Junction
Colorado Springs
Pueblo
Arkansas

Minot
NORTH DAKOTA
Bismarck
Aberdeen
SOUTH DAKOTA
Pierre
Rapid City
Missouri
NEBRASKA
Grand Island
Platte
KANSAS
Dodge City
Wichita

Reno
Carson City
Lake Tahoe
Great Salt Lake
Ogden
Salt Lake City
Provo
Sacramento
Oakland
NEVADA
UTAH
San Francisco
San Jose
Salinas
Fresno
Mojave
Lake Powell
Colorado
St. George
Las Vegas
Lake Mead
Grand Canyon
Desert
Bakersfield
Point Conception
Flagstaff
Santa Fe
Los Angeles
Long Beach
Riverside
ARIZONA
Albuquerque
Salton Sea
Phoenix • Mesa
Yuma
NEW MEXICO
San Diego
Tucson
Las Cruces
Roswell
El Paso
Rio Grande

Great Basin
Sierra Nevada
CALIFORNIA

OKLAH
Oklahoma City
Lawton
Amarillo
Wichita Falls
Lubbock
Fort Worth
Midland • Abilene
Odessa
Waco
TEXAS
Austin
San Antonio
Rio Grande
Corpus Christi
Laredo
Brownsville
Red

7:00AM
HAWAI'I-ALEUTIAN TIME

North Slope
Brooks Range
Yukon
Alaska Range
Juneau
Anchorage
ALASKA
0   400 miles
0   400 kilometers
ALEUTIAN ISLANDS
Alaska Peninsula

8:00AM
ALASKA TIME

Kaua'i
Ni'ihau
O'ahu
Honolulu
Moloka'i
Lana'i • Maui
Kaho'olawe
HAWAI'I
Hilo
Hawai'i
0   150 mi
0   150 km

7:00AM
HAWAI'I-ALEUTIAN TIME

The United States is made up of 50 states joined like a giant quilt. Each is unique, but together they make a national fabric held together by a constitution and a federal government. State boundaries, outlined in dotted lines on the map, set apart internal political units within the country. The national capital—Washington, D.C.—is marked by a star in a double circle. The capital of each state is marked by a star in a single circle.

11:00 AM

CENTRAL TIME

12:00 NOON

EASTERN TIME

TIME ZONES: Earth is divided into 24 time zones, each about 15 degrees of longitude wide, reflecting the distance Earth turns from west to east each hour. The U.S. is divided into six time zones, indicated by red dotted lines on the map.

THE PHYSICAL
UNITED STATES

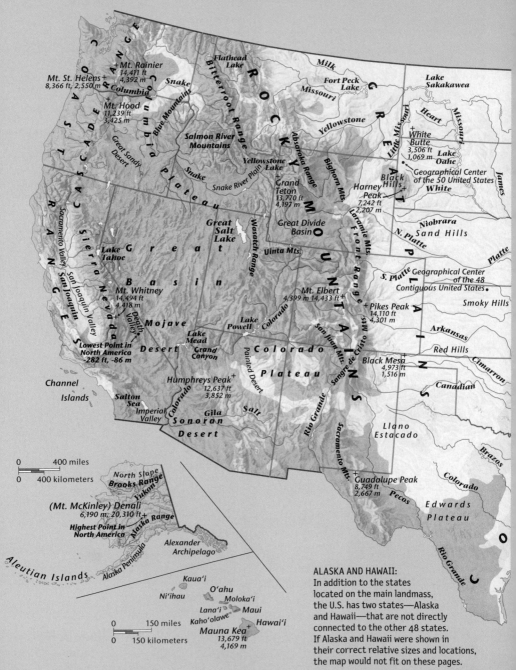

Mt. St. Helens+
8,366 ft, 2,550 m

CASCADE RANGE

COAST RANGE

+Mt. Rainier
14,411 ft
4,392 m

Snake

Columbia

Mt. Hood+
11,239 ft
3,425 m

Great Sandy
Desert

Columbia Plateau

Snake

Blue Mountains

Bitterroot Range

Flathead
Lake

ROCKY

Salmon River
Mountains

Yellowstone
Lake

Snake River Plain

Grand
Teton
13,770 ft
4,197 m

Absaroka Range

Yellowstone

Bighorn Mts.

Milk

GREAT

Fort Peck
Lake

Missouri

Little Missouri

Missouri

Lake
Sakakawea

Heart

Missouri

+White
Butte
3,506 ft
1,069 m

James

Lake
Oahe

Geographical Center
of the 50 United States
White

Sierra Nevada

Sacramento Valley

San Joaquin

San Joaquin Valley

Lake
Tahoe

Great

Basin

Mt. Whitney
14,494 ft
4,418 m

Death
Valley+

Mojave

Lowest Point in
North America
-282 ft, -86 m

Desert

Great
Salt
Lake

Wasatch Range

Uinta Mts.

Great Divide
Basin

MOUNTAINS

Front Range

Laramie Mts.

Black
Hills

Harney
Peak
7,242 ft
2,207 m

N. Platte

Niobrara

Sand Hills

Platte

S. Platte

Geographical Center
of the 48
Contiguous United States.

Smoky Hills

PLAINS

Channel

Islands

Salton
Sea

Imperial
Valley

Lake
Powell

Lake
Mead

Colorado

Grand
Canyon

Colorado

Painted Desert

Mt. Elbert
4,399 m 14,433 ft+

Plateau

San Juan Mts.

+Pikes Peak
14,110 ft
4,301 m

Sangre de Cristo Mts.

Arkansas

Red Hills

Black Mesa
4,973 ft
1,516 m

Canadian

Humphreys Peak+
12,637 ft
3,852 m

Colorado

Gila

Sonoran

Desert

Salt

Rio Grande

Sacramento Mts.

Llano
Estacado

Cimarron

Brazos

Colorado

0   400 miles
0   400 kilometers

North Slope
Brooks Range

Yukon

(Mt. McKinley) Denali
6,190 m, 20,310 ft+

Highest Point in
North America

Alaska Range

Aleutian Islands

Alaska Peninsula

Alexander
Archipelago

Guadalupe Peak+
8,749 ft
2,667 m

Pecos

Edwards
Plateau

Rio Grande

Kaua'i

Ni'ihau

O'ahu

Moloka'i

Lana'i   Maui
Kaho'olawe

Mauna Kea+
13,679 ft
4,169 m

Hawai'i

0   150 miles
0   150 kilometers

ALASKA AND HAWAII:
In addition to the states
located on the main landmass,
the U.S. has two states—Alaska
and Hawaii—that are not directly
connected to the other 48 states.
If Alaska and Hawaii were shown in
their correct relative sizes and locations,
the map would not fit on these pages.

Stretching from the Atlantic Ocean in the east to the Pacific Ocean in the west, the United States is the third largest country (by area) in the world. Its physical diversity ranges from mountains to fertile plains and dry deserts. Shading on the map indicates changes in elevation, while colors show different vegetation patterns.

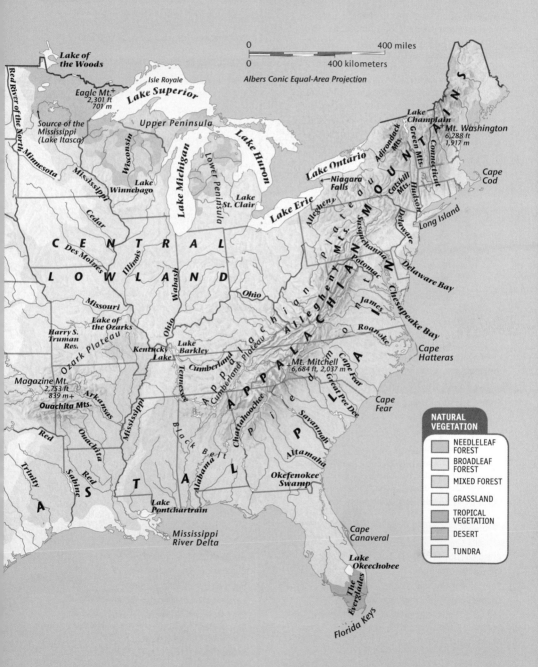

0   400 miles
0   400 kilometers
Albers Conic Equal-Area Projection

Lake of the Woods

Red River of the North

Eagle Mt.+
2,301 ft
701 m

Isle Royale

Lake Superior

Upper Peninsula

Source of the Mississippi (Lake Itasca)

Minnesota

Mississippi

Wisconsin

Lake Michigan

Lower Peninsula

Lake Huron

Lake Winnebago

Lake St. Clair

Lake Ontario

Niagara Falls

Lake Erie

Lake Champlain

Adirondack Mts.

Green Mts.

Connecticut

Mt. Washington
6,288 ft
1,917 m

Cape Cod

Catskill Mts.

Hudson

Long Island

Allegheny

Susquehanna

Delaware

Delaware Bay

Cedar

Des Moines

Illinois

Wabash

Ohio

Allegheny Plateau

Potomac

Chesapeake Bay

CENTRAL

LOWLAND

Missouri

Lake of the Ozarks

Harry S. Truman Res.

Ozark Plateau

Kentucky Lake

Lake Barkley

Ohio

Tennessee

Cumberland Plateau

Cumberland

James

Roanoke

Cape Hatteras

Magazine Mt.
2,753 ft
839 m+

Ouachita Mts.

Arkansas

Mississippi

Black Belt

APPALACHIAN

Mt. Mitchell
6,684 ft, 2,037 m

Cape Fear

Great Pee Dee

P I E D M O N T

Cape Fear

Red

Ouachita

Chattahoochee

Alabama

Savannah

Altamaha

Red

Sabine

Trinity

C O A S T A L

Lake Pontchartrain

Okefenokee Swamp

Cape Canaveral

Mississippi River Delta

Lake Okeechobee

The Everglades

Florida Keys

MOUNTAINS

NATURAL VEGETATION

- NEEDLELEAF FOREST
- BROADLEAF FOREST
- MIXED FOREST
- GRASSLAND
- TROPICAL VEGETATION
- DESERT
- TUNDRA

THE STATES

From sea to shining sea, the United States of America is a nation of diversity. In the 241 years since its creation, the nation has grown to become home to a wide range of peoples, industries, and cultures. The following pages present a general overview of all 50 states in the U.S.

The country is generally divided into five large regions: the Northeast, the Southeast, the Midwest, the Southwest, and the West. Though loosely defined, these zones tend to share important similarities, including climate, history, and geography. The color key below provides a guide to which states are in each region.

The flags of each state and highlights of demography and industry are also included. These details offer a brief overview of each state.

In addition, each state's official flower and bird are identified.

Color Key by Region

Arizona

Area: 113,998 sq mi (295,256 sq km)
Population: 6,931,071
Capital: Phoenix, pop. 1,615,017
Largest city: Phoenix, pop. 1,615,017
Industry: Real estate, manufactured goods, retail, state and local government, transportation and public utilities, wholesale trade, health services
State flower/bird: Saguaro/cactus wren

Arkansas

Area: 53,179 sq mi (137,732 sq km)
Population: 2,988,248
Capital: Little Rock, pop. 198,541
Largest city: Little Rock, pop. 198,541
Industry: Services, food processing, paper products, transportation, metal products, machinery, electronics
State flower/bird: Apple blossom/mockingbird

California

Area: 163,696 sq mi (423,972 sq km)
Population: 39,250,017
Capital: Sacramento, pop. 495,234
Largest city: Los Angeles, pop. 3,976,322
Industry: Electronic components and equipment, computers and computer software, tourism, food processing, entertainment, clothing
State flower/bird: Golden poppy/California quail

Alabama

Area: 52,419 sq mi (135,765 sq km)
Population: 4,863,300
Capital: Montgomery, pop. 200,022
Largest city: Birmingham, pop. 212,157
Industry: Retail and wholesale trade, services, government, finance, insurance, real estate, transportation, construction, communication
State flower/bird: Camellia/northern flicker

The **Californian flying fish** can glide in the air **for the** length of a bowling alley lane.

Alaska

Area: 663,267 sq mi (1,717,862 sq km)
Population: 741,894
Capital: Juneau, pop. 32,468
Largest city: Anchorage, pop. 298,192
Industry: Petroleum products, government, services, trade
State flower/bird: Forget-me-not/willow ptarmigan

Colorado

Area: 104,094 sq mi (269,602 sq km)
Population: 5,540,545
Capital: Denver, pop. 693,060
Largest city: Denver, pop. 693,060
Industry: Real estate, government, durable goods, communications, health and other services, nondurable goods, transportation
State flower/bird: Columbine/lark bunting

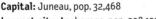

COLOR KEY ● Northeast ● Southeast

Connecticut

Area: 5,543 sq mi (14,357 sq km)
Population: 3,576,452
Capital: Hartford, pop. 123,243
Largest city: Bridgeport, pop. 145,936
Industry: Transportation equipment, metal products, machinery, electrical equipment, printing and publishing, scientific instruments, insurance
State flower/bird: Mountain laurel/robin

Delaware

Area: 2,489 sq mi (6,447 sq km)
Population: 952,065
Capital: Dover, pop. 37,786
Largest city: Wilmington, pop. 71,442
Industry: Food processing, chemicals, rubber and plastic products, scientific instruments, printing and publishing, financial services
State flower/bird: Peach blossom/blue hen chicken

CHICKENS outnumber people IN DELAWARE.

Florida

Area: 65,755 sq mi (170,304 sq km)
Population: 20,612,439
Capital: Tallahassee, pop. 190,894
Largest city: Jacksonville, pop. 880,619
Industry: Tourism, health services, business services, communications, banking, electronic equipment, insurance
State flower/bird: Orange blossom/mockingbird

Georgia

Area: 59,425 sq mi (153,910 sq km)
Population: 10,310,371
Capital: Atlanta, pop. 472,522
Largest city: Atlanta, pop. 472,522
Industry: Textiles and clothing, transportation equipment, food processing, paper products, chemicals, electrical equipment, tourism
State flower/bird: Cherokee rose/brown thrasher

Hawaii

Area: 10,931 sq mi (28,311 sq km)
Population: 1,428,557
Capital: Honolulu, pop. 351,792
Largest city: Honolulu, pop. 351,792
Industry: Tourism, trade, finance, food processing, petroleum refining, stone, clay, glass products
State flower/bird: Hibiscus/Hawaiian goose (nene)

Idaho

Area: 83,570 sq mi (216,447 sq km)
Population: 1,683,140
Capital: Boise, pop. 223,154
Largest city: Boise, pop. 223,154
Industry: Electronics and computer equipment, tourism, food processing, forest products, mining
State flower/bird: Syringa (Lewis's mock orange)/mountain bluebird

Illinois

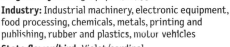

Area: 57,914 sq mi (149,998 sq km)
Population: 12,801,539
Capital: Springfield, pop. 115,715
Largest city: Chicago, pop. 2,704,958
Industry: Industrial machinery, electronic equipment, food processing, chemicals, metals, printing and publishing, rubber and plastics, motor vehicles
State flower/bird: Violet/cardinal

Indiana

Area: 36,418 sq mi (94,322 sq km)
Population: 6,633,053
Capital: Indianapolis, pop. 855,164
Largest city: Indianapolis, pop. 855,164
Industry: Transportation equipment, steel, pharmaceutical and chemical products, machinery, petroleum, coal
State flower/bird: Peony/cardinal

Iowa

Area: 56,272 sq mi (145,743 sq km)
Population: 3,134,693
Capital: Des Moines, pop. 215,472
Largest city: Des Moines, pop. 215,472
Industry: Real estate, health services, industrial machinery, food processing, construction
State flower/bird: Wild rose/American goldfinch

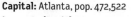

● Midwest ● Southwest ● West

Kansas

Area: 82,277 sq mi (213,097 sq km)
Population: 2,907,289
Capital: Topeka, pop. 126,808
Largest city: Wichita, pop. 389,902
Industry: Aircraft manufacturing, transportation equipment, construction, food processing, printing and publishing, health care
State flower/bird: Sunflower/western meadowlark

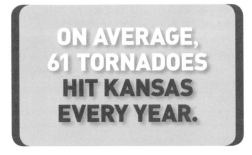

ON AVERAGE, 61 TORNADOES HIT KANSAS EVERY YEAR.

Kentucky

Area: 40,409 sq mi (104,659 sq km)
Population: 4,436,974
Capital: Frankfort, pop. 27,885
Largest city: Louisville, pop. 616,261
Industry: Manufacturing, services, government, finance, insurance, real estate, retail trade, transportation, wholesale trade, construction, mining
State flower/bird: Goldenrod/cardinal

Louisiana

Area: 51,840 sq mi (134,265 sq km)
Population: 4,681,666
Capital: Baton Rouge, pop. 227,715
Largest city: New Orleans, pop. 391,495
Industry: Chemicals, petroleum products, food processing, health services, tourism, oil and natural gas extraction, paper products
State flower/bird: Magnolia/brown pelican

Maine

Area: 35,385 sq mi (91,646 sq km)
Population: 1,331,479
Capital: Augusta, pop. 18,494
Largest city: Portland, pop. 66,937
Industry: Health services, tourism, forest products, leather products, electrical equipment
State flower/bird: White pine cone and tassel/chickadee

Maryland

Area: 12,407 sq mi (32,133 sq km)
Population: 6,016,447
Capital: Annapolis, pop. 39,418
Largest city: Baltimore, pop. 614,664
Industry: Real estate, federal government, health services, business services, engineering services
State flower/bird: Black-eyed Susan/northern (Baltimore) oriole

Massachusetts

Area: 10,555 sq mi (27,336 sq km)
Population: 6,811,779
Capital: Boston, pop. 673,184
Largest city: Boston, pop. 673,184
Industry: Electrical equipment, machinery, metal products, scientific instruments, printing and publishing, tourism
State flower/bird: Mayflower/chickadee

Michigan

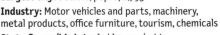

Area: 96,716 sq mi (250,495 sq km)
Population: 9,928,300
Capital: Lansing, pop. 116,020
Largest city: Detroit, pop. 672,795
Industry: Motor vehicles and parts, machinery, metal products, office furniture, tourism, chemicals
State flower/bird: Apple blossom/robin

Minnesota

Area: 86,939 sq mi (225,172 sq km)
Population: 5,519,952
Capital: St. Paul, pop. 302,398
Largest city: Minneapolis, pop. 413,651
Industry: Real estate, banking and insurance, industrial machinery, printing and publishing, food processing, scientific equipment
State flower/bird: Showy lady's slipper/common loon

Mississippi

Area: 48,430 sq mi (125,434 sq km)
Population: 2,988,726
Capital: Jackson, pop. 169,148
Largest city: Jackson, pop. 169,148
Industry: Petroleum products, health services, electronic equipment, transportation, banking, forest products, communications
State flower/bird: Magnolia/mockingbird

COLOR KEY ● Northeast ● Southeast

Missouri

Area: 69,704 sq mi (180,534 sq km)
Population: 6,093,000
Capital: Jefferson City, pop. 43,013
Largest city: Kansas City, pop. 481,420
Industry: Transportation equipment, food processing, chemicals, electrical equipment, metal products
State flower/bird: Hawthorn/eastern bluebird

Montana

Area: 147,042 sq mi (380,840 sq km)
Population: 1,042,520
Capital: Helena, pop. 31,169
Largest city: Billings, pop. 110,323
Industry: Forest products, food processing, mining, construction, tourism
State flower/bird: Bitterroot/western meadowlark

Nebraska

Area: 77,354 sq mi (200,346 sq km)
Population: 1,907,116
Capital: Lincoln, pop. 280,364
Largest city: Omaha, pop. 446,970
Industry: Food processing, machinery, electrical equipment, printing and publishing
State flower/bird: Goldenrod/western meadowlark

Nevada

Area: 110,561 sq mi (286,352 sq km)
Population: 2,940,058
Capital: Carson City, pop. 54,742
Largest city: Las Vegas, pop. 632,912
Industry: Tourism and gaming, mining, printing and publishing, food processing, electrical equipment
State flower/bird: Sagebrush/mountain bluebird

New Hampshire

Area: 9,350 sq mi (24,216 sq km)
Population: 1,334,795
Capital: Concord, pop. 42,904
Largest city: Manchester, pop. 110,506
Industry: Machinery, electronics, metal products
State flower/bird: Purple lilac/purple finch

New Jersey

Area: 8,721 sq mi (22,588 sq km)
Population: 8,944,469
Capital: Trenton, pop. 84,056
Largest city: Newark, pop. 281,764
Industry: Machinery, electronics, metal products, chemicals
State flower/bird: Violet/American goldfinch

New Mexico

Area: 121,590 sq mi (314,917 sq km)
Population: 2,081,015
Capital: Santa Fe, pop. 83,875
Largest city: Albuquerque, pop. 559,277
Industry: Electronic equipment, state and local government, real estate, business services, federal government, oil and gas extraction, health services
State flower/bird: Yucca/roadrunner

The GREATER ROADRUNNER is the STATE BIRD of NEW MEXICO.

New York

Area: 54,556 sq mi (141,300 sq km)
Population: 19,745,289
Capital: Albany, pop. 98,111
Largest city: New York City, pop. 8,537,673
Industry: Printing and publishing, machinery, computer products, finance, tourism
State flower/bird: Rose/eastern bluebird

North Carolina

Area: 53,819 sq mi (139,390 sq km)
Population: 10,146,788
Capital: Raleigh, pop. 458,880
Largest city: Charlotte, pop. 842,051
Industry: Real estate, health services, chemicals, tobacco products, finance, textiles
State flower/bird: Flowering dogwood/cardinal

● Midwest ● Southwest ● West

North Dakota

Area: 70,700 sq mi (183,113 sq km)
Population: 757,952
Capital: Bismarck, pop. 72,417
Largest city: Fargo, pop. 120,762
Industry: Services, government, finance, construction, transportation, oil and gas
State flower/bird: Wild prairie rose/ western meadowlark

Ohio

Area: 44,825 sq mi (116,097 sq km)
Population: 11,614,373
Capital: Columbus, pop. 860,090
Largest city: Columbus, pop. 860,090
Industry: Transportation equipment, metal products, machinery, food processing, electrical equipment
State flower/bird: Scarlet carnation/cardinal

Oklahoma

Area: 69,898 sq mi (181,036 sq km)
Population: 3,923,561
Capital: Oklahoma City, pop. 638,367
Largest city: Oklahoma City, pop. 638,367
Industry: Manufacturing, services, government, finance, insurance, real estate
State flower/bird: Mistletoe/scissor-tailed flycatcher

Oregon

Area: 98,381 sq mi (254,806 sq km)
Population: 4,093,465
Capital: Salem, pop. 167,419
Largest city: Portland, pop. 639,863
Industry: Real estate, retail and wholesale trade, electronic equipment, health services, construction, forest products, business services
State flower/bird: Oregon grape/western meadowlark

Pennsylvania

Area: 46,055 sq mi (119,283 sq km)
Population: 12,784,227
Capital: Harrisburg, pop. 48,904
Largest city: Philadelphia, pop. 1,567,872
Industry: Machinery, printing and publishing, forest products, metal products
State flower/bird: Mountain laurel/ruffed grouse

Rhode Island

Area: 1,545 sq mi (4,002 sq km)
Population: 1,056,426
Capital: Providence, pop. 179,219
Largest city: Providence, pop. 179,219
Industry: Health services, business services, silver and jewelry products, metal products
State flower/bird: Violet/Rhode Island red

South Carolina

Area: 32,020 sq mi (82,932 sq km)
Population: 4,961,119
Capital: Columbia, pop. 134,309
Largest city: Charleston, pop. 134,385
Industry: Service industries, tourism, chemicals, textiles, machinery, forest products
State flower/bird: Yellow jessamine/Carolina wren

5 cool things about SOUTH CAROLINA

1. South Carolina's Morgan Island is inhabited by some 3,000 Rhesus monkeys

2. Wide Awake and Due West are both names of South Carolina towns.

3. Some of the trees in Congaree National Park in Hopkins, South Carolina, stand as tall as a 14-story building.

4. A theater in Charleston, South Carolina, hosted the United States's first ever performance of an opera in 1735.

5. Only about 45 people live in Smyrna, South Carolina, the state's smallest town.

South Dakota

Area: 77,117 sq mi (199,732 sq km)
Population: 865,454
Capital: Pierre, pop. 14,008
Largest city: Sioux Falls, pop. 174,360
Indus try: Finance, services, manufacturing, government, retail trade, transportation and utilities, wholesale trade, construction, mining
State flower/bird: Pasqueflower/ring-necked pheasant

COLOR KEY ● Northeast ● Southeast

Tennessee

Area: 42,143 sq mi (109,151 sq km)
Population: 6,651,194
Capital: Nashville, pop. 660,388
Largest city: Nashville, pop. 660,388
Industry: Service industries, chemicals, transportation equipment, processed foods, machinery
State flower/bird: Iris/mockingbird

Texas

Area: 268,581 sq mi (695,624 sq km)
Population: 27,862,596
Capital: Austin, pop. 947,890
Largest city: Houston, pop. 2,303,482
Industry: Chemicals, machinery, electronics and computers, food products, petroleum and natural gas, transportation equipment
State flower/bird: Bluebonnet/mockingbird

Utah

Area: 84,899 sq mi (219,888 sq km)
Population: 3,051,217
Capital: Salt Lake City, pop. 193,744
Largest city: Salt Lake City, pop. 193,744
Industry: Government, manufacturing, real estate, construction, health services, business services, banking
State flower/bird: Sego lily/California gull

Vermont

Area: 9,614 sq mi (24,901 sq km)
Population: 624,594
Capital: Montpelier, pop. 7,535
Largest city: Burlington, pop. 42,260
Industry: Health services, tourism, finance, real estate, computer components, electrical parts, printing and publishing, machine tools
State flower/bird: Red clover/hermit thrush

Virginia

Area: 42,774 sq mi (110,785 sq km)
Population: 8,411,808
Capital: Richmond, pop. 223,170
Largest city: Virginia Beach, pop. 452,602
Industry: Food processing, communication and electronic equipment, transportation equipment, printing, shipbuilding, textiles
State flower/bird: Flowering dogwood/cardinal

Washington

Area: 71,300 sq mi (184,666 sq km)
Population: 7,288,000
Capital: Olympia, pop. 51,202
Largest city: Seattle, pop. 704,352
Industry: Aerospace, tourism, food processing, forest products, paper products, industrial machinery, printing and publishing, metals, computer software
State flower/bird: Coast rhododendron/Amer. goldfinch

West Virginia

Area: 24,230 sq mi (62,755 sq km)
Population: 1,831,102
Capital: Charleston, pop. 49,138
Largest city: Charleston, pop. 49,138
Industry: Tourism, coal mining, chemicals, metal manufacturing, forest products, stone, clay, oil, glass products
State flower/bird: Rhododendron/cardinal

Wisconsin

Area: 65,498 sq mi (169,639 sq km)
Population: 5,778,708
Capital: Madison, pop. 252,551
Largest city: Milwaukee, pop. 595,047
Industry: Industrial machinery, paper products, food processing, metal products, electronic equipment, transportation
State flower/bird: Wood violet/robin

Wyoming

Area: 97,814 sq mi (253,337 sq km)
Population: 585,501
Capital: Cheyenne, pop. 64,019
Largest city: Cheyenne, pop. 64,019
Industry: Oil and natural gas, mining, generation of electricity, chemicals, tourism
State flower/bird: Indian paintbrush/western meadowlark

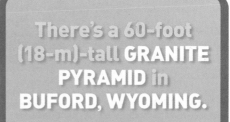

There's a 60-foot (18-m)-tall **GRANITE PYRAMID** in **BUFORD, WYOMING.**

● Midwest ● Southwest ● West

THE TERRITORIES

The United States has 14 territories— political divisions that are not states. Three of these are in the Caribbean Sea, and the other 11 are in the Pacific Ocean.

St. John, U.S. Virgin Islands

Convention Center, San Juan, Puerto Rico

Talofofo Falls, Guam

U.S. CARIBBEAN TERRITORIES

Puerto Rico

Area: 3,508 sq mi (9,086 sq km)
Population: 3,411,307
Capital: San Juan,
         pop. 357,627
Languages: Spanish, English

U.S. Virgin Islands

Area: 149 sq mi (386 sq km)
Population: 107,000
Capital: Charlotte Amalie, pop. 52,000
Languages: English, Spanish or Spanish Creole, French or French Creole

U.S. PACIFIC TERRITORIES

American Samoa

Area: 77 sq mi (199 sq km)
Population: 52,000
Capital: Pago Pago, pop. 48,000
Language: Samoan

Guam

Area: 217 sq mi (561 sq km)
Population: 167,000
Capital: Hagåtña (Agana),
         pop. 143,000
Languages: English, Chamorro, Philippine languages

Northern Mariana Islands

Area: 184 sq mi (477 sq km)
Population: 52,000
Capital: Saipan, pop. 49,000
Languages: Philippine languages, Chinese, Chamorro, English

Other U.S. Territories

Baker Island, Howland Island, Jarvis Island, Johnston Atoll, Kingman Reef, Midway Islands, Palmyra Atoll, Wake Island, Navassa Island (in the Caribbean)

Figures for capital cities vary widely between sources because of differences in the way the area is defined and other projection methods.

THE U.S. CAPITAL

District of Columbia

Area: 68 sq mi (177 sq km)
Population: 681,170

Abraham Lincoln, who was president during the Civil War and a strong opponent of slavery, is remembered in the Lincoln Memorial, located at the opposite end of the National Mall from the U.S. Capitol Building.

COLOR KEY ● Territories ● Northeast

DESTINATION GUIDE

Grand Canyon

Grand Canyon, aerial view

Happy 100th Birthday, Grand Canyon! In 2019, this national park celebrates a century of captivating visitors with its stunning natural beauly. These days, some six million people head to the Grand Canyon every year to check out the mile (1.6-km)-deep, 18-mile (29-km)-wide, 277-mile (446-km)-long canyon, plus cool evergreen forests, a winding river, gurgling streams, cascading waterfalls, and phenomenal views. Whether you're up for an epic hike or a chill camping trip, there's so much to see and do during your visit to the Grand Canyon.

WHAT TO DO:

IN THE SADDLE: One of the most popular ways to get to the bottom of the Grand Canyon is on the back of a mule. Opt for a one-day trip or stay overnight in a cabin in Phantom Ranch at the bottom of the canyon.

TAKE A HIKE: Up for an epic adventure? Try Rim Trail, which goes along the canyon's edge for about 13 miles (21 km). Or opt for some more family-friendly trails, like Bright Angel Point or Cliff Springs Trails, both of which offer sensational views of the canyons.

SKY WALK: Walk off the edge of a cliff—and onto the Grand Canyon Skywalk, a horseshoe-shaped bridge hanging over the canyon west of the park. The bridge, owned by the Hualapai Indian tribe, sits some 4,000 feet (1,291 m) above the Colorado River.

RIDE THE RAILS: Board the Grand Canyon Railroad and take a trip into the Old West. Performers keep you entertained along the 2.5-hour ride with songs, skits, and a reenactment of a cowboy shootout.

Riding mules

Grand Canyon Skywalk

Grand Canyon Railroad

The Grand Canyon is one of the Seven Natural Wonders of the World.

The Grand Canyon began forming six million years ago.

88 species of mammals and 56 kinds of reptiles and amphibians live in the Grand Canyon.

1 In 1919 a pilot flew a plane under the Arc de Triomphe in Paris, France, to mark the end of World War I.

2 CHINA'S SPRING TEMPLE BUDDHA statue is made with 13,300 copper plates.

3 KIZHI POGOST, a set of 18th-century churches in northwest Russia, WAS BUILT WITHOUT A SINGLE NAIL.

4 IN ROME, ITALY, SOME $3,000 WORTH OF COINS ARE THROWN IN THE TREVI FOUNTAIN EACH DAY.

5 England's PALACE OF WESTMINSTER has over 1,100 rooms.

19 Cool THINGS ABOUT

7 The LIBERTY BELL in Philadelphia, Pennsylvania, U.S.A., was once called the STATE HOUSE BELL.

6 It took about 20,000 workers to construct India's Taj Mahal, a 17th-century tomb.

8 CONSTRUCTION ON SPAIN'S SAGRADA FAMÍLIA— A CHURCH STARTED IN 1882— PROBABLY WON'T BE DONE UNTIL AT LEAST 2026.

9 In 1806 the French army took the statue atop Germany's Brandenburg Gate and kept it for eight years.

10 The face of the GREAT SPHINX OF GIZA in Egypt may have once been painted dark red.

11 The **Pha That Luang monument** in Laos was **once topped with** sheets of **pure gold.**

12 The Prague orloj, a SPECIAL CLOCK on display in the Czech Republic, has been operating SINCE 1410.

13 DINOSAUR FOOTPRINT

Australia's Dinosaur Stampede National Monument was built in a spot with 4,000 dinosaur footprints.

NATIONAL MONUMENTS

14 The Independence Arch in Accra, Ghana, is located in the world's second largest city square.

15 Before the 2014 World Cup, Brazil's 12-story Christ the Redeemer statue was STRUCK by LIGHTNING and needed QUICK REPAIRS in advance of the crowds.

16 The walls of Ireland's Blarney Castle are 18 feet (5.5 m) thick in some parts.

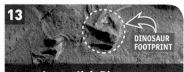

17 Japan's Itsukushima Shrine seems to float on water when the tide floods the ground on which it stands.

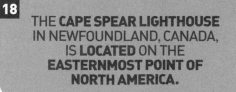

19 A CARVING OF A RHINO STICKS OUT FROM ONE WALL OF BELÉM TOWER, A 16TH-CENTURY FORT IN LISBON, PORTUGAL.

18 THE **CAPE SPEAR LIGHTHOUSE** IN NEWFOUNDLAND, CANADA, IS **LOCATED** ON THE **EASTERNMOST POINT OF NORTH AMERICA.**

Wild Vacation

SLEEP HERE!

Cave Hotel

YUNAK EVLERI HOTEL

WHERE Cappadocia region, Turkey

WHY IT'S COOL Here's a hotel that really rocks. The Yunak Evleri is built into caves left by volcanic activity 10 million years ago. Follow narrow passageways and stone stairs to rooms that are a cool 57°F (14°C). Spend the day hiking rocky terrain, exploring caverns, or hot-air ballooning over "fairy chimneys"—tall rock formations that dot the skyline. At night you won't have to worry about being awakened by eruptions, since the Cappadocia volcanoes are now dormant. So they're "sleeping," too!

COOL THINGS ABOUT TURKEY

Dating from A.D. 537, the famous Hagia Sophia was built as a church, then turned into a mosque, and is now a museum.

Early Turkish settlers once lived in the caves of the Cappadocia region.

Yogurt was invented in Turkey and is a main ingredient in local food—from soups to desserts.

King Midas may not have really turned all he touched into gold. But he did rule over the kingdom of Phrygia, in what is now Turkey, in the eighth century B.C.

THINGS TO DO IN TURKEY

Ride a camel to tour the bizarre rock formations around Cappadocia.

Take a boat ride up the Bosporus strait to get from Asia to Europe in 15 minutes.

Haggle with shopkeepers in the bustling market of Istanbul's Grand Bazaar.

EXTREME WEIRDNESS

From AROUND the WORLD

AT EASE, GORILLAS!

GORILLA FOOLS HUMANS

WHAT Ape robot

WHERE Bristol, England

DETAILS Call it *Planet of the Fake Apes.* The Bristol Zoo Gardens' "Wow! Gorillas" exhibit featured an animatronic ape and several five-foot (1.5-m)-tall fiberglass gorilla sculptures. The sculptures were later painted and decorated by local artists. What's next—papier-mâché penguins?

STRAW MAN

WHAT Straw bears

WHERE Heldra, Germany

DETAILS Somebody went overboard with their winter coat. In colder months, some Germans have a tradition of wearing outfits made of straw while attending seasonal festivals. These "straw bears" date back to an old belief that the outfits would scare winter away. All this guy needs is a straw scarf.

MEET STRAW MAN, TIN MAN'S LONG-LOST COUSIN.

BIIIGGG BINOCULARS

WHAT Binocular-shaped entrance

WHERE Venice, California, U.S.A.

DETAILS Did somebody ask for a better view? Sculptors Claes Oldenburg and Coosje van Bruggen designed this 45-foot (14-m)-tall set of binoculars that now serves as an office entrance for Google. So *that's* what they mean by "Internet search."

NOT SURE HOW TO WATCH BIRDS WITH THESE.

A WORKER REPAINTS A SECTION OF THE BRIDGE.

COLOR CONFUSION

The Golden Gate Bridge was almost given the same colors as a bumblebee! The U.S. Navy originally wanted to coat the structure with black and yellow stripes to make it extra visible to sailors. Designers ultimately chose to paint the bridge a bold orange to complement the landscape.

GOLDEN GATE BRIDGE TOWER

TOWER TIME

When the bridge was completed, it had the world's tallest bridge towers. Both columns are about 746 feet (227 m) high—over twice the height of the Statue of Liberty. Divers helped build the base of the column that sits in the open ocean. First, they swam up to 110 feet (34 m) below the water's surface. Using explosives, they then blasted a hole in the seafloor's bedrock where concrete would be poured to create a foundation for the tower. Since the waters were so murky, the divers did all of this in almost total darkness. Sounds like a towering task.

IT TOOK EIGHT YEARS FOR WORKERS TO BUILD FORT POINT.

FORT

HIDDEN FORT

Built during California's gold rush in the mid-1800s, Fort Point is tucked into the bridge's south side. It was designed to protect the region and its gold fields from foreign invaders, although it never saw battle.

SECRETS OF THE
GOLDEN GATE BRIDGE

THIS GROUNDBREAKING STRUCTURE HAS JAW-DROPPING FEATURES.

The Golden Gate Bridge in San Francisco, California, U.S.A., is a real trailblazer! Finished 82 years ago in 1937, it was the world's largest suspension bridge at the time. Get the inside scoop on this groundbreaking bridge.

HIGHS AND LOWS

Travelers crossing the Golden Gate Bridge aren't the only ones on the move. The overpass is often in motion, too! It was designed to sway up to 27 feet (8.2 m) in each direction in high winds. And its length expands and contracts by as much as 3 feet (0.9 m) as the temperature goes from warm to cool and back again. None of this damages the structure or puts people at risk, because the bridge was built to be flexible.

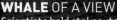

WHALE OF A VIEW

Scientists hold stakeouts on the bridge's overpass, observing and photographing marine life like gray and humpback whales and dolphin-like mammals called harbor porpoises, which munch on anchovies that thrive in San Francisco Bay.

PACIFIC OCEAN
UNITED STATES
CALIFORNIA
ATLANTIC OCEAN

★ Sacramento
NEVADA
• San Francisco
CALIFORNIA
PACIFIC OCEAN
• Los Angeles

TOWER POWER

Behind the scenes of this amazing landmark

Completed in March 1889, the Eiffel Tower in Paris, France, is one of most recognizable monuments in the world. But despite its fame, the tower has some monumental secrets. Get the lowdown on this Parisian highlight.

True Colors

The Eiffel Tower has a colorful history—literally. The tower has been painted dark red, yellow, and bronze. Today, the structure gets a paint job every seven years, and is covered in almost 16,000 gallons (60,566 L) of paint.

PAINTER

120 ANTENNAS

NEARLY **50** MILES (80 KM) OF ELECTRIC CABLES COVER THE STRUCTURE.

1,665 STAIRS

Hidden Apartment

Gustave Eiffel, who designed the landmark, built himself a small apartment on the top level of the tower. The sky-high hideaway had plush rugs, oil paintings, and even a grand piano. Unused since the 1920s after Eiffel's death, the 950-foot (290-m)-high pad is now open for public viewing.

Sky Lab

Atop the Eiffel tower you'll find two small laboratories where Eiffel conducted experiments. To learn about how objects move against air, he dropped items attached to cords from the second level of the tower (about 380 feet/116 m aboveground).

THE TOWER IS MADE OF **18,000** IRON PIECES BOLTED TOGETHER BY OVER 2.5 MILLION RIVETS.

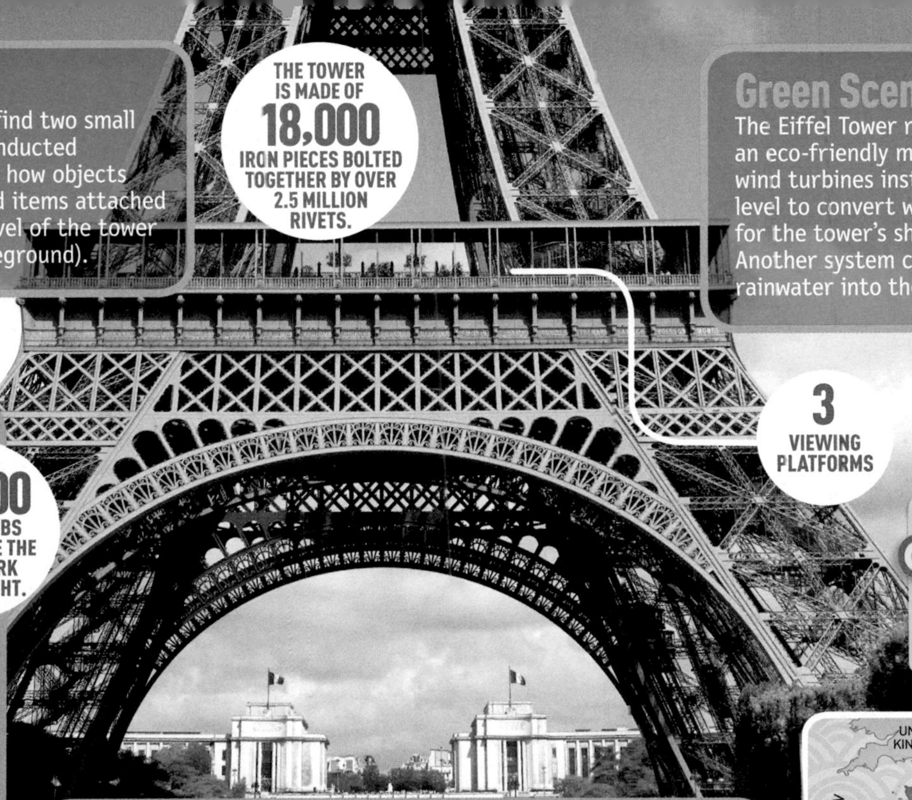

Green Scene

The Eiffel Tower recently underwent an eco-friendly makeover, with two wind turbines installed on the second level to convert wind into electricity for the tower's shops and restaurants. Another system collects and funnels rainwater into the tower's toilets.

3 VIEWING PLATFORMS

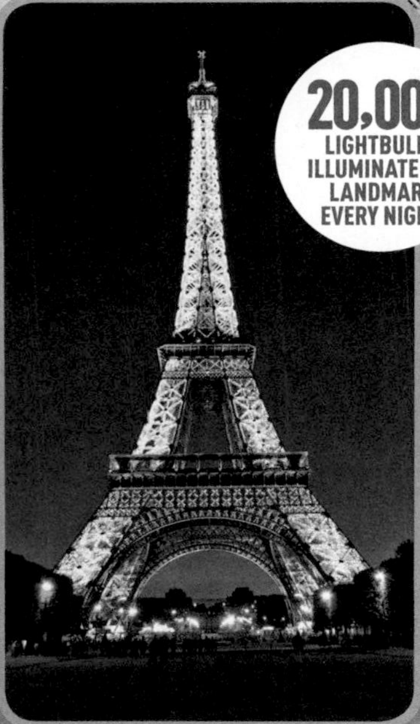

20,000 LIGHTBULBS ILLUMINATE THE LANDMARK EVERY NIGHT.

COUNTRY CONNECTION: *FRANCE!*

natgeokids.com/france

UNITED KINGDOM
BELGIUM
GERMANY
Paris
Eiffel Tower
ATLANTIC OCEAN
FRANCE
SWITZERLAND
ITALY
SPAIN
Mediterranean Sea

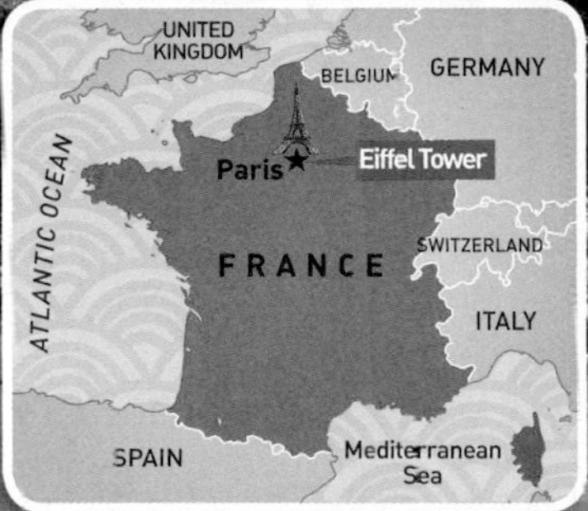

FAIR FRENZY

The Eiffel Tower was officially opened at the 1889 world's fair. First held in London, England, in 1851, world's fairs showcase cutting-edge inventions, architecture, and art from around the globe. The events have revealed many "futuristic" inventions, including the Ferris wheel, the television, x-ray machines, and ice-cream cones. The next world's fair, which is now called an expo, is in 2020 in Dubai, U.A.E., in Asia.

QUIZ WHIZ

Is your geography knowledge off the map? Quiz yourself to find out!

Write your answers on a piece of paper. Then check them below.

1 The Liberty Bell in Philadelphia, Pennsylvania, U.S.A., was once called the ____.

a. Christ Church Bell
b. State House Bell
c. Franklin Bell
d. Uncrackable Bell

2 In colder months, some Germans have a tradition of wearing outfits made of ____ while attending festivals.

a. wool
b. paper
c. straw
d. plastic

3 Which color has the Eiffel Tower been painted?

a. yellow
b. bronze
c. dark red
d. all of the above

4 Dalanzadgad, Mongolia, is home to the world's largest ____ race.

a. camel
b. chicken
c. horse
d. rabbit

5 **True or false?** Earth was once covered with giant mushrooms that grew taller than a house.

Not **STUMPED** yet? Check out the *NATIONAL GEOGRAPHIC KIDS QUIZ WHIZ* collection for more crazy **GEOGRAPHY** questions!

ANSWERS:
1. b; 2. c; 3. d; 4. a; 5. True

Finding Your Way Around

Every map has a story to tell, but first you have to know how to read one. Maps represent information by using a language of symbols. Knowing how to read these symbols provides access to a wide range of information. Look at the scale and compass rose or arrow to understand distance and direction (see box below).

To find out what each symbol on a map means, you must use the key. It's your secret decoder—identifying information by each symbol on the map.

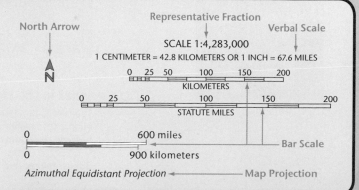

Latitude

Longitude

90°N (North Pole)
75°N
60°N
45°N
30°N
15°N
0° (Equator)
15°S
30°S
45°S

LATITUDE AND LONGITUDE

Latitude and longitude lines (above) help us determine locations on Earth. Every place on Earth has a special address called absolute location. Imaginary lines called lines of latitude run west to east, parallel to the Equator. These lines measure distance in degrees north or south from the Equator (0° latitude) to the North Pole (90°N) or to the South Pole (90°S). One degree of latitude is approximately 70 miles (113 km).

Lines of longitude run north to south, meeting at the poles. These lines measure distance in degrees east or west from 0° longitude (prime meridian) to 180° longitude. The prime meridian runs through Greenwich, England.

SCALE AND DIRECTION

The scale on a map can be shown as a fraction, as words, or as a line or bar. It relates distance on the map to distance in the real world. Sometimes the scale identifies the type of map projection. Maps may include an arrow or compass rose to indicate north on the map.

North Arrow

Representative Fraction

Verbal Scale

SCALE 1:4,283,000
1 CENTIMETER = 42.8 KILOMETERS OR 1 INCH = 67.6 MILES

0 25 50   100   150   200
KILOMETERS

0   25   50   100   150   200
STATUTE MILES

0   600 miles
0   900 kilometers

Bar Scale

Azimuthal Equidistant Projection ← Map Projection

GAME ANSWERS

Find the Hidden Animals, page 164
1. **F**, 2. **E**, 3. **C**, 4. **B**, 5. **A**, 6. **D**

What in the World? page 165
Top row: **die, deck of cards, trunk**
Middle row: **dove, lock and key, top hat**
Bottom row: **handkerchief, coins, rabbit**
Bonus: **Hoo-dini**

Lucky Break, page 166

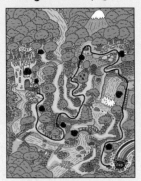

Color Coded, page 168

Brain Bogglers, page 169
Out of the Box: 1. **The friend is playing Monopoly.** 2. **They are at a playground, and the kids want to play on the seesaw.** 3. **They're building a city out of building blocks.** Beastly Phrases: 1. **bird brain,** 2. **horse sense,** 3. **A leopard can't change its spots.** 4. **black sheep of the family.** Flip Out: **ultrasonic hearing**

What in the World? page 170
Top row: **kites, lighthouse, wafer cookies**
Middle row: **noisemaker, earrings, baseball diamond**
Bottom row: **stained glass, argyle sweater, fence**
Bonus: **carats**

Signs of the Times, page 172
Signs **1** and **7** are fake.

Splash Down! page 175

What in the World? page 176
Top row: **tiger, Asian elephant, dog**
Middle row: **mandrill, sea lion, two-toed sloth**
Bottom row: **caiman, poison dart frog, sika deer**
Bonus: **sneeze and thank you**

Want to Learn More?

Find more information about topics in this book in these National Geographic Kids resources.

5,000 Awesome Facts (About Everything!) series

Awesome 8 series

By the Numbers series

Funny Fill-In series

Weird But True series

Everything Big Cats
Elizabeth Carney
April 2011

Dino Records
June 2017

Chomp!
Brady Barr
June 2017

Penguins vs. Puffins
Julie Beer
September 2017

Ultimate Space Atlas
Carolyn DeCristofano
June 2017

Don't Read This Book Before Bed
Anna Claybourne
August 2017

Weird But True Know-It-All: U.S. Presidents
Brianna DuMont
July 2017

Try This! Extreme
Karen Romano Young
September 2017

History's Mysteries
Kitson Jazynka
October 2017

1,000 Facts About Insects
Nancy Honovich
February 2018

Astronaut-Aquanaut
Jennifer Swanson
January 2018

Abbreviations:
AL: Alamy
DRMS: Dreamstime
GI: Getty Images
IS: iStockphoto
MP: Minden Pictures
NGC: National Geographic Creative
SS: Shutterstock
WHHA: White House Historical Association

All Maps
By National Geographic unless otherwise noted

All Illustrations & Charts
By Stuart Armstrong unless otherwise noted

Front Cover
(lion), Daniel J. Cox/GI; (watch), imac27/SS; (emoji), ober-art/SS; (lemur), Kamonrutm/DRMS; (diver), Dudarev Mikhail/SS

Spine
(lion), Daniel J. Cox/GI; (emoji), ober-art/SS; (stars), NASA Images/SS; (dinosaur), Rodrigo Reyes Marin/AFLO/Newscom

Back Cover
(Earth), Alex Staroseltsev/SS, (orangutan), Isselee/DRMS; (zebra phone), IS; (dinosaur), Rodrigo Reyes Marin/AFLO/Newscom; (ladybug), Serg64/SS; (stars), NASA Images/SS; (roller coaster), Mathew Imaging;

Inside Front Cover
(dolphin), ArchMan/SS; (lion), Eric Isselee/SS

Front Matter (2–7)
2-3, Bence Mate/NPL/MP; 5 (UP RT), Mark Kostich/Vetta/GI; 5 (UP LE), Joel Sartore, National Geographic Photo Ark/NGC; 5 (UP CTR LE), Brian J. Skerry/NGC; 5 (CTR RT), SS; 5 (LO CTR LE), Erik Tham/Corbis Documentary/GI; 5, martan/SS; 5 (LO LE), Sean Gallup/GI; 5 (LO RT), outdoorsman/SS; 6 (UP LE), IS/GI; 6 (UP RT), Nataliya Evmenenko/DRMS; 6 (UP CTR LE), NASA; 6 (UP CTR RT), Alexander Kharchenko/DRMS; 6 (LO CIR LE), Gary Vestal/GI; 6 (LO CTR RT), Dan Sipple; 6 (LO LE), Lonely Planet Images/GI; 6 (LO RT), Julia Kuznetsova/SS; 7 (UP LE), Ronald Phillips/Design Pics/GI; 7 (UP RT), XEG/SS; 7 (UP CTR), travelstock44/AL; 7 (LO CTR), Carsten Peter/SPELEORESEARCH & FILMS/NGC; 7 (LO), Attila Jandi/DRMS

Your World 2019 (8–17)
8-9, Joel Sartore, National Geographic Photo Ark/NGC; 10 (UP), Paul Martinka; 10 (CTR), Paul Martinka; 10 (LO LE), Asia Wire; 10 (LO RT), Asia Wire; 11 (UP LE), courtesy Waterfront Partnership of Baltimore; 11 (UP RT), Nicholas Kamm/AFP/GI; 11 (CTR), courtesy Devil Ark Australia; 11 (LO), courtesy of Devil Ark Australia; 12 (UP), 2017 Bloomberg Finance LP/GI; 12 (CTR LE), 2017 Bloomberg Finance LP/GI; 12 (CTR RT), 2017 Bloomberg Finance LP/GI; 12 (LO), 2017 Bloomberg Finance LP/GI; 13 (UP CTR), courtesy of Fleet Farming; 13 (LO CTR), courtesy of Fleet Farming; 13 (LO), courtesy of Fleet Farming; 13 (UP), Chris Balcombe/REX USA; 14 (UP LE), National Zoo/Smithsonian Institute; 14 (UP RT), courtesy Zoo Atlanta; 14 (CTR LE), courtesy of the Virginia Aquarium; 14 (CTR RT), courtesy of the Tennessee Aquarium; 14 (LO LE), National Zoo/Smithsonian Institute; 14 (LO RT), Los Angeles Zoo; 14-15 (background), Thomas Barrat/SS; 15 (UP), John Lund/GI; 15 (UP LE), Axiom RM/GI; 15 (LO LE), EyeEm/GI; 15 (LO CTR RT),

Axiom RM/GI; 15 (LO RT), De Agostini Editorial/GI; 16 (LO CIR LE), Lesya Gapchuk/GI; 16 (UP RT), Christoffer Soederqvist/SS; 16 (UP CTR LE), Lebedev Roman Olegovich/SS; 16 (UP LE), photka/SS; 16 (UP CTR RT), ChameleonsEye/SS; 16 (CTR RT), Paolo Bona/SS; 16 (LO LE), NASA/SS; 16 (LO CTR RT), Eric Isselee/SS; 16 (LO RT), DR Travel Photo and Video/SS; 17 (UP), Bartz Snow Sculptures; 17 (UP CTR), Bartz Snow Sculptures; 17 (LO CTR), Bartz Snow Sculptures; 17 (LO), Aaron Mason

Amazing Animals (18–75)
18-19, Brian J. Skerry/NGC; 20 (UP), Pete Oxford/NPL/MP; 20 (LO), Darwin Wiggett/GI; 21 (UP RT), Richard Whitcombe/Offset/SS; 21 (LO), Roger Powell/NPL/MP; 21 (UP LE), Donald M. Jones/MP; 22 (UP LE), Thomas Marant/MP; 22 (UP RT), Molly Moore; 22 (LO), Picture Alliance/Photoshot; 23 (UP LE), Alex zheezs/SS; 23 (LO LE), Andreas H/SS; 23 (UP RT), Zoological Society of London; 23 (LO RT), Tony Heald/MP; 24 (UP RT), BlueOrange Studio/SS; 24 (LO LE), RooM RF/GI; 24 (UP LE), Pete Oxford/MP; 24 (LO RT), Martin Harvey/Biosphoto; 25 (UP LE), patjo/SS; 25 (LO), Moment RF/GI; 25 (UP RT), BiosPhoto/Michael Weber/ImageBroker; 26 (UP), Thomas Marent/MP; 26 (CTR), Suzi Eszterhas/MP; 26 (LO LE), Ingo Arndt/MP; 26 (LO RT), Thomas Marent/MP; 27 (LO RT), Andy Rouse/NPL/MP; 27 (CTR), Steven Kazlowski/Naturepl.com; 27 (UP), Steven Kazlowski/NPL/MP; 28, Gil Wizen; 29 (UP), age fotostock/AL; 29 (LO), Mark Kostich/Vetta/GI; 29 (CTR), Paul D Lemke; 30 (LE CTR), Eric Isselee/SS; 30 (LO RT), Joel Sartore/NGC; 30 (UP RT), Diane McAllister/Nature Picture Library; 31 (UP LE), FloridaStock/SS; 31 (LO RT), Karen Massier/IS; 31 (UP RT), cbpix/SS; 31 (LE CTR), mashe/SS; 31 (LO), Eric Isselee/SS; 32, Staffan Widstrand/Nature Picture Library; 33 (UP LE), worldswildlifewonders/SS; 33 (UP CTR LE), Kesu/SS; 33 (UP CTR RT), WitR/SS; 33 (UPRT), Eric Isselee/SS; 33 (LE CTR), DLILLC/Corbis/GI; 33 (RT CTR), Eric Isselee/SS; 33 (LO LE), Eric Isselee/SS; 33 (LO RT), Eric Isselee/SS; 34 (1), Bruno Pambour/Biosphoto/MP; 34 (9), Michel & Christine Denis-Huot/Biosphoto/MP; 34 (6), Ellen van Bodegom/GI; 34 (7), Matthew Hawkins; 34 (2), tanuha2001/SS; 35 (4), Dave Watts/NPL/MP; 35 (16), Four Oaks/SS; 35 (18), Daniel J. Cox/GI; 35 (13), mofles/GI; 35 (5), Eric Isselee/SS; 35 (12), Andy Rouse/Nature Picture Library; 35 (10), Deon De Villiers - SafaGraphics; 35 (14), Anup Shah/NPL/MP; 35 (15), Michelangelus/SS; 35 (19), Rudolf Vlcek/GI; 36 (LE), Mark Newman/FLPA/MP; 36 (RT), Frans Lanting; 37 (UP), Suzi Eszterhas/MP; 37 (LO), Nick Gordon/Ardea; 38 (UP LE), Klein & Hubert/Nature Picture Library; 38 (LO), Frans Lanting/NGC; 38 (UP RT), Tom Murphy/NGC; 39 (CTR), Michelle Valberg/AGE Fotostock; 39 (LO LE), Paul Nicklen/NGC; 39 (LO RT), Flip Nicklin/MP; 39 (LO CTR), Russ Kinne/AGE Fotostock; 40 (UP), Brian Skerry/NGC; 40 (LO), Brian Skerry/NGC; 41 (LO), Brian Skerry/NGC; 41 (UP), Brian Skerry/NGC; 44-45, Brian J. Skerry/NGC; 44 (LO), New England Aquarium Rescue; 45 (UP RT), Terry Dickson/Florida Times-Union; 45 (LO LE), Connie Merigo/New England Aquarium; 45 (LO RT), Jekyll Island Authority; 46 (LE), Claus Meyer/MP; 46 (UP RT), Luciano Candisani/MP; 46 (LO RT), Christian Ziegler/MP; 46 (CTR RT), Pete Oxford/MP; 46 (CTR LE), Mark Taylor/Nature Picture Library; 47 (UP LE), Richard du Toit; 47 (CTR LE), Mitsuaki Iwago/MP; 47 (UP RT), Richard du Toit/MP; 47 (LO LE), Will Burrard-Lucas/NPL/MP; 47 (LO RT), Richard du Toit/MP; 48 (UP), Heidi & Hans-Juergen Koch/MP; 48 (LO), M. Watson/Ardea; 48 (LO CTR),

imageBROKER/AL; 49 (UP LE), Bianca Lavies/NGC; 49, Mark Payne-Gill/Nature Picture Library; 49 (LO LE), Bianca Lavies/NGC; 49 (CTR RT), Claus Meyer/MP; 49 (LO RT), Jason Tharp; 50 (background), Sergey Gorshkov/MP; 50 (LO), Daniel J Cox/Oxford Scientific/GI; 50 (RI), A. & J. Visage/Peter Arnold/AL; 50 (LO LE), Igor Shpilenok/Nature Picture Library; 51 (UP), Joe McDonald/Corbis/GI; 51 (LO RT), Roland Seitre/MP; 51 (LO LE), Jean Paul Ferrero/Ardea; 52-53, Eric Baccega/Nature Picture Library; 52 (LO), Eric Baccega/Nature Picture Library; 53 (UP LE), Eric Baccega/Nature Picture Library; 53 (UP RT), Eric Baccega/Nature Picture Library; 53 (UP RT), Eric Baccega/Nature Picture Library; 54 (CTR), Stephen Dalton/MP; 54 (LO), Elio Della Ferrera/MP; 54 (UP RT), Gregory Hoover; 55 (LO LE), Studio Times Ltd/MP; 55 (UP RT), Mitsuhiko Imamori/MP; 55 (LO RT), Bruce Davidson/MP; 55 (UP LE), Stephen Dalton/Nature Picture Library; 56 (UP), ImagoStock/Newscom; 56 (LO), Juniors Bildarchiv GmbH/AL; 57 (UP RT), Tetsuro Matsuzawa/PRI/Kyoto University; 57 (CTR RT), Tetsuro Matsuzawa/PRI/Kyoto University; 57 (LO LE), Ben Beaden/Australia Zoo; 57 (LO RT), Ben Beaden/Australia Zoo; 58 (CTR), REX USA/Richard Bowler/Rex; 58 (LO), REX USA/Richard Bowler/Rex; 58 (UP), REX USA/Richard Bowler/Rex; 59 (LO), Nathan Edwards/Newspix/Rex/Rex USA; 59 (UP), Nathan Edwards/Newspix/Rex/Rex USA; 60 (RT), Meredith Parmelee/Stone/GI; 60 (LE), Yoshitsugu Kimura/Fifi & Romeo; 61 (UP), Courtesy of La Petite Maison; 61 (CTR LE), Britt Erlanson/The Image Bank/GI; 61 (CTR), James Kegley; 61 (CTR RT), James Kegley; 61 (LO LE), Augustus Butera/Taxi/GI; 61 (LO RT), Courtesy of Three Dog Bakery LLC; 62 (UP LE), Jean Michel Labat/Ardea; 62 (UP RT), Johan de Meester/Ardea; 62 (LO LE), John Daniels/Ardea; 62 (LO RT), Jaromir Chalabala/SS; 63, Arco Images GmbH/AL; 64 (UP), Krissi Lundgren/SS; 64 (CTR), Jagodka/SS; 64 (LO), World History Archive/Newscom; 65 (LO), The White House/Pete Souza/GI; 65 (UP), iStock/fotgjagodka; 65 (UP CTR RT), David Douglas Duncan/Photography Collection/Harry Ransom Center; 65 (UP), Juniors Bildarchiv GmbH/AL; 65 (LO CTR), Sir Edwin Landseer/Royal Collection Trust/© Her Majesty Queen Elizabeth II 2015; 66 (UP), Chris Butler/Science Photo Library/Photo Researchers, Inc.; 66 (CTR), Publiphoto/Photo Researchers, Inc.; 66 (LO), Pixeldust Studios/NGC; 67 (B), Laurie O'Keefe/Photo Researchers, Inc.; 67 (C), Chris Butler/Photo Researchers, Inc.; 67 (D), Publiphoto/Photo Researchers, Inc.; 67 (A), Publiphoto/Photo Researchers, Inc.; 67 (E), image courtesy of Project Exploration; 68, Joe Rocco; 68-69 (CTR), Pixeldust Studios/NGC; 69, Mark Witton; 70 (LO), Andrea Meyer/SS; 71 (LO), Danielle Dufault; 71 (UP LE), Todd Marshall; 71 (UP RT), Australian Age of Dinosaurs, Travis Tischler; 72 (UP RT), Franco Tempesta; 72 (LO CTR RT), Franco Tempesta; 72 (LO RT), Franco Tempesta; 72 (UP CTR), Franco Tempesta; 72 (LO CTR RT), Franco Tempesta; 72 (UP LE), Franco Tempesta; 72 (CTR LE), Franco Tempesta; 72 (LO LE), Franco Tempesta; 73 (UP), Franco Tempesta; 73 (UP CTR), Franco Tempesta; 73 (CTR RT), Franco Tempesta; 73 (LO UP CTR), Franco Tempesta; 73 (LO LE), Franco Tempesta; 73 (LO CTR LE), Franco Tempesta; 73 (LO CTR), Franco Tempesta; 73 (LO RT), Franco Tempesta; 73 (LO), Franco Tempesta; 74 (UP RT), Eric Isselee/SS; 74 (CTR), Klein & Hubert/Nature Picture Library; 74 (LO), Steven Kazlowski/NPL/MP; 75, CampCrazy Photography/SS

Science and Technology (76–101)

76-77, Eric Tham/Corbis Documentary/GI; 78 (UP CTR), Mindsailors; 78 (UP), Mindsailors; 78 (LO), Ducere Technologies; 78 (UP CTR), Diverse Images/GI; 79 (UP LE), Courtesy Court Rye/Electric Bike Review; 79 (CTR LE), FlyKly; 79 (UP RT), Starpool; 79 (LO LE), Sébastien Darrasse/Realis/Monaco/Rex Features; 79 (LO RT), Sébastien Darrasse/Realis/Monaco/ Rex Features; 80 (UP), Richard Newstead/GI; 80 (LO LE), Paul Souders/GI; 80 (LO RT), GI; 81 (UP LE), BENEBOT Remote Sales Robot Ecovacs Robotics, Inc.; 81 (UP RT), AP Photo/Keith Srakocic; 81 (CTR), Patrick Tehan/MCT/News- com; 81 (LO LE), Patrick Tehan/MCT/Newscom; 81 (LO RT), Michael Bahlo/EPA/Newscom; 82 (9), Dimaberkut/DRMS; 82 (6), Kim Kulish/Corbis/ GI; 82 (3), Courtesy/GI; 82 (7), Nikkytok/DRMS; 82 (10), Salih Külcü/DRMS; 82 (2), Ford Prefect/SS; 83 (17), Bruce Chambers/ZUMA Press; 83 (13), NASA; 83 (12), Vladimirnenezic/DRMS; 83 (15), Wrangler/DRMS; 83 (19), Tatiana Belova/DRMS; 83 (18), mrfiza/SS; 84, Art by Joe Rocco; 85 (RT), Joe Rocco; 85 (LE), Joe Rocco; 86 (LO), David Aguilar; 87 (E), Marie C. Fields/SS; 87 (D), Fedor A. Sidorov/SS; 87 (F), sgame/SS; 87 (A), Sebastian Kaulitzki/SS; 87 (B), Steve Gschmeissner/ Photo Researchers, Inc.; 87 (C), Volker Steger/ Christian Bardele/Photo Researchers, Inc.; 87 (G), Benjamin Jessop/IS; 88 (UP), FotograFFF/ SS; 88 (LO), Craig Tuttle/Corbis/GI; 89 (LO RT), Andrey_Kuzmin/SS; 89 (UP LE), NASA/Goddard Space Flight Center; 89 (LO LE), Image Source/SuperStock; 90, Matthew Rakola; 91 (3), Matthew Rakola; 91 (4), Matthew Rakola; 91 (5), Matthew Rakola; 91 (6), Matthew Rakola; 91 (7), Matthew Rakola; 92 (UP), Brand X/GI; 92 (LO), SSPL/Science Museum/GI; 93 (LO), martan/SS; 93 (UP), Mike Agliolo/Science Source; 94 (UP), Cynthia Turner; 94 (LO), Jason Lugo/GI; 95 (LO RT), Alexia Khruscheva/SS; 95 (UP LE), Vaclav Volrab/SS; 95 (LO LE), iStock/delihayat; 95 (UP CTR), iStock/Arkhipov; 95 (UP RT), Vitalii Hulai/ SS; 95 (UP CTR LE), AnetaPics/SS; 95 (CTR RT), HughStoneIan/SS; 95 (LO CTR LE), Eric Isselee/ SS; 96, Cynthia Turner; 97 (UP), DRMS; 98, 4X-image/IS; 99 (LO), Digital Beach Media/Rex/ REX USA; 99 (UP), Jose Luis Magana/Reuters; 100 (UP), GI; 100 (CTR), Dimaberkut/DRMS; 100 (LO), 4X-image/IS; 101, Klaus Vedfelt/GI

Going Green (102–115)

102-103, Sean Gallup/GI; 104 (UP), outdoorsman/SS; 104 (LO), Richard McManus/GI; 105 (UP), Perry de Graaf/NiS/MP; 105 (CTR), Joel Sartore/NGC; 105 (LO), Tim Flach/GI; 106 (LO), Mujka Design Inc./IS; 107 (UP), Steve Smith/ SS; 108 (background), Mujka Design Inc./IS; 108 (CTR), Giorgio Cosulich/GI; 108 (LO), Featureflash/SS; 109 (UP), Rich Carey/SS; 109 (LO), Nick Garbutt/Nature Picture Library; 110 (UP LE), BRAND X; 110 (UP RT), National Geographic KIDS Magazine; 110 (CTR RT), GrigoryL/SS; 110 (CTR LE), Mariyana M/SS; 110 (LO LE), Design56/ DRMS; 110 (LO CTR), Richard Peterson/SS; 110 (LO RT), Brand X; 111 (UP LE), Jan Martin Will/ SS; 111 (UP RT), Julie Clopper/SS; 111 (UP CTR LE), AFP/GI; 111 (UP CTR RT), Stephan Wanger/Bead Town; 111 (LO CTR LE), photoDISC; 111 (LO CTR RT), Iulius Costache/SS; 111 (LO LE), Ingram/SS; 111 (LO RT), Evikka/SS; 112 (background), Walter Zerla/GI; 112 (UP LE), Jiang Hongyan/SS; 112 (UP RT), lucielang/IS; 112 (UP CTR LE), PeJo29/ IS; 112 (UP CTR RT), Imagesbybarbara/IS; 112 (UP CTR RT), toddtaulman/IS; 112 (LO CTR RT), nilsz/IS; 112 (LO CTR LE), talevr/IS; 112 (LO LE), PhotosbyAbby/IS; 112 (LO RT), kedsanee/IS; 112 (background), Walter Zerla/GI; 113 (LO), Lilkar/ DRMS; 113 (UP), Martina_L/GI; 113 (UP CTR),

tBoyan/GI; 113 (LO CTR), Jimejume/GI; 113 (background), mangiurea/SS; 113 (14), Bloomberg/ Contributor/GI; 114 (UP), GrigoryL/SS; 114 (CTR), Tim Flach/GI/GI; 114 (LO), Martina_L/GI

Culture Connection (116–139)

116-117, IS/GI; 118 (UP RT), zulufoto/SS; 118 (LO CTR LE), Maks Narodenko/SS; 118 (LO CTR RT), Maxxyustas/DRMS; 118 (3), Michiko Ishida/ DRMS; 118 (9), Matthew Benoit/SS; 118 (8), Pamela Mcadams/DRMS; 118 (1), Ksena2009/ DRMS; 119 (UP RT), photoDISC; 119 (UP CTR RT), Elnur/DRMS; 119 (LO CTR RT), Gallinagomedia/ DRMS; 119 (LO LE), Volosina/SS; 119 (LO RT), mama_mia/SS; 119 (LO RT), Celig/SS; 119 (13), Photodeti/DRMS; 119 (15), Isselee/DRMS; 120 (CTR RT), Zoonar GmbH/AL; 120 (LO RT), Ninette Maumus/AL; 120 (UP LE), Ivan Vdovin/ AL; 120 (CTR LE), iStock/Mlenny; 120 (UP RT back), iStock/apomare; 120 (UP RT), B.A.E. Inc./AL; 120 (UP RT CTR), B.A.E. Inc./AL; 120 (LO LE), Courtesy of The Banknote Book; 121 (LO CTR), D. Hurst/AL; 121 (LO LE), Nataliya Evmenenko/DRMS; 121 (UP RT), Comstock/GI; 121 (LO CTR LE), Splash News/Newscom; 121 (LO RT), Kelley Miller/NG Staff; 121 (UP LE), Kiev. Victor/SS; 121 (UP CTR LE), ALEAIMAGE/IS; 122 (RT), Tim Hill/AL; 122 (UP LE), Margo555/DRMS; 122 (UP CTR), Danny Smythe/DRMS; 122 (LO CTR), Natika/DRMS; 122 (LO), Angelo Gilardelli/ DRMS; 123 (CTR), OlgaMiltsova/GI; 123 (UP LE), Joe_Potato/GI; 123 (LO RT), Laszlo Selly/GI; 123 (UP RT), Education Images/UIG via GI; 123 (UP CTR RT), bergamont/SS; 123 (LO CTR), John Kelly/GI; 124-125, Renee Comet/Food Styling by Lisa Cherkasky; 124 (LO LE), Renee Comet/ Food Styling by Lisa Cherkasky; 124 (LO CTR), Renee Comet/Food Styling by Lisa Cherkasky; 124 (LO RT), Renee Comet/Food Styling by Lisa Cherkasky; 124 (UP CTR), Mark Thiessen/NG Staff; 124 (UP CTR), Mark Thiessen/NG Staff; 124 (UP), Mark Thiessen/NG Staff; 125 (UP RT), Mark Thiessen/NG Staff; 125 (UP CTR), Mark Thiessen/NG Staff; 125 (LO LE), Mark Thiessen/ NG Staff; 125 (UP LE), Mark Thiessen/NG Staff; 125 (LO RT), Mark Thiessen/NG Staff; 126 (UP), Junko Kimura/Jana Press/ZUMAPRESS.com; 126 (LO), AP Photo/Fresno Bee, Tomas Ovalle; 127 (LO LE), Evan Agostini/Invision/AP; 127 (CTR RT), Alex Milan Tracy/Sipa USA/Newscom; 127 (UP CTR LE), Jussi Nukari/REX SS; 127 (UP LE), Mulholland/REX SS; 127 (LO RT), Danny Martindale/GI; 127 (UP RT), Helene Wiesenhaan/GI; 128 (4), Tubol Evgeniya/SS; 128 (1), fotohunter/ SS; 128 (9), Supachita Ae/SS; 128 (6), Maarten Wouters/GI; 128 (3), Ar2r/SS; 129 (12), Dinodia/ age fotostock; 129 (14), Zee/AL; 129 (15), wacpan/SS; 131 (LO LE), Rebecca Hale/NG Staff; 131 (UP), Rebecca Hale/NG Staff; 131 (LO RT), Cathy Crawford/Nonstock/Jupiterimages; 131 (RT), Rebecca Hale/NG Staff; 132, Sergey Novikov/ SS; 133 (background), Subbotina Anna/SS; 134 (UP), Dean Macadam; 134 (LO), Dean Macadam; 135 (UP RT), Dean Macadam; 135 (LO RT), Dean Macadam; 135 (LO LE), Dean Macadam; 136 (UP), Randy Olson; 136 (LO LE), Martin Gray/NGC; 136 (LO RT), Sam Panthaky/AFP/GI; 136 (LO RT), Richard Nowitz/NGC; 137 (LO LE), Reza/NGC; 137 (UP), Filippo Monteforte/GI; 138 (UP), Isselee/ DRMS; 138 (CTR), Sergey Novikov/SS; 138 (LO), Dean Macadam; 139 (UP LE), catwalker/SS; 139 (UP RT), dimitris_k/SS; 139 (UP CTR), oconnell// SS; 139 (LO), Steve Allen/SS

Space and Earth (140–161)

140-141: JSC/NASA; 142-143 (background), Take 27 Ltd/Photo Researchers, Inc.; 143 (A), David Aguilar; 143 (B), David Aguilar; 143 (C), David Aguilar; 143 (D), David Aguilar; 143 (E), David Aguilar; 144 (5), Olga Popova/DRMS; 144 (2),

Alexander Kharchenko/DRMS; 144 (7), Corey Ford/Stocktrek Images/Corbis/GI; 144 (3), Dave Yoder/NGC; 144 (1), Roger Ressmeyer/Corbis/ GI; 145 (15), Ghadel/DRMS; 145 (13), Aaron Kohr/ DRMS; 145 (19), Steve Nagy/Design Pics/Corbis/ GI; 145 (18), STScI/NASA; 145 (10), NASA; 145 (12), Dr. Seth Shostak/Science Photo Library; 145 (17), Fatmanphotography/DRMS; 146-147 (UP), David Aguilar; 148 (UP), David Aguilar; 148 (LO RT), NASA/JHUAPL/SwRI; 149 (LO LE), Andy Rouse/GI; 149 (UP LE), Brand X Pictures/GI; 149, Mondolithic Studios Inc.; 150 (CTR RT), Tony & Daphne Hallas/Photo Researchers, Inc.; 150 (background UP), Alexxandar/GI; 150 (UP RT), Walter Myers/Stocktrek Images/Corbis/GI; 150 (LO RT), NASA; 151 (UP RT), Chris Ware; 151 (UP LE), Chris Ware; 151 (CTR RT), Karen Sneider; 151 (LO), Jean Galvão; 151, Moment RM/GI; 152 (UP), Ralph Lee Hopkins/NGC; 152 (UP CTR LE), Visuals Unlimited/GI; 152 (UP CTR RT), Visuals Unlimited/GI; 152 (LO CTR LE), Doug Martin/ Photo Researchers, Inc.; 152 (LO CTR RT), DEA/C. Dani/GI; 152 (UP RT), Jeff Goulden/IS; 152 (RT), Terry Davis/SS; 153 (LO), Joe Rocco; 154 (background), Bychkov Kirill Alexandrovich/SS; 154 (UP RT), Robert Crow/SS; 154 (LO LE), Carsten Peter/NGC; 155 (UP LE), Mark Thiessen NG Staff; 155 (UP (1)), M. Unal Ozmen/SS; 155 (UP (2)), design56/SS; 155 (UP (3)), 4kodiak/IS; 155 (UP (4)), Scott Bolster/ SS; 155 (UP (5)), Picsfive/SS; 155 (LO), NASA; 156 (CTR), by Chakarin Wattanamongkol/Getty Imasge; 156-157 (main), shinnji/GI; 157 (RT), Chris Philpot; 157 (CTR), Theo Allofs/GI; 157 (LE), Westend61/GI; 158-159, Prisma/Superstock; 160 (UP), Alexander Kharchenko/DRMS; 160 (CTR), Theo Allofs/GI; 160 (LO), Robert Crow/ SS; 161 (UP), SS

Fun and Games (162–181)

162-163, Gary Vestal/Photographer's Choice/ GI; 164 (LO LE), David Fleetham/Nature Picture Library; 164 (UP LE), Brandon Cole; 164 (CTR RT), Chris Mattison/FLPA/MP; 164 (UP RT), Kevin Schafer/GI; 164 (LO RT), Thomas Marent/MP; 164 (CTR LE), Andy Mann/GI; 165 (6), Nora Good/ Masterfile; 165 (CTR), Randy Faris/GI; 165 (UP LE), photoDISC; 165 (UP CTR), Sam72/SS; 165 (LO CTR), Vlue/SS; 165 (CTR RT), Gemenacom/SS; 165 (LO RT), Richard Peterson/SS; 165 (UP RT), Chris Brignell/AL; 165 (CTR LE), Irochka/DRMS; 165 (LO LE), gmutlu/GI; 166, CTON; 167, Dan Sipple; 168, James Yamasaki; 169 (LO), Michael Durham/MP; 169 (RT 7), Spauln/IS; 169 (RT 2), arlindo71/IS; 169 (RT 6), GlobalP/IS; 169 (RT 5), Eldad Carin/IS; 169 (RT 9), Jan_Neville/IS; 169 (RT 8), Eldad Carin/IS; 169 (RT 4), mari_art/IS; 169 (RT 3), Vizerskaya/IS; 169 (RT 1), Antagain/ IS; 169 (RT 10), laflor/IS; 169 (LE), Ron Chapple Stock/AL; 169 (UP), DNY59/GI; 170 (UP LE), Cristina Pedrazzini/Botanica/Jupiterimages/ GI; 170 (CTR RT), David Madison/Photographer's Choice/GI; 170 (LO CTR), Richard Kolker/GI; 170 (LO LE), Elena Rostunova/SS; 170 (CTR LE), Mike Flippo/SS; 170 (CTR), Preobrajenskiy/SS; 170 (UP RT), val lawless/SS; 170 (LO RT), LesPalenik/SS; 170 (UP CTR), Cultura RM Exclusive/Russ Rohde/ GI; 171 (UP), mauritius images GmbH/AL; 171 (CTR), querbeet/GI; 171 (CTR LE), Maurice van der Velden/GI; 171 (CTR RT), Hintau Aliaksei/ SS; 171 (LO), Little Perfect Stock/SS; 172 (LO LE), Annie Griffiths Belt/Corbis/GI; 172 (LO CTR RT), Rick Strange/Index Stock Imagery/GI; 172 (CTR), Royalty-Free/Corbis/GI; 172 (UP), Matthias Clamer/GI; 172 (LO RT), J.D.S/SS; 172 (UP CTR RT), Frank DiMarco/AL; 172 (CTR LE), DA Photo/ AL; 173 (ALL), Gary Fields; 174, Dan Sipple; 175, James Yamasaki; 176 (CTR RT), Pltphotography/ DRMS; 176 (CTR LE), Lloyd Luecke/DRMS; 176 (CTR LE), Eric Isselee/SS; 176 (UP RT), Mikhail

Kolesnikov/SS; 176 (UP RT), Lars Christensen/DRMS; 176 (LO CTR), Martin Harvey/GI; 176 (LO RT), Bradley Dymond/AL; 176 (LO LE), Panoramic Images/GI; 176 (UP LE), Edwin Giesbers/GI; 177, Dan Sipple; 178 (ALL), Chris Ware; 179 (prairie dog), Gerry Ellis/Globio/MP; 179 (coyote profile), NaturesDisplay/GI; 179 (snake), Rolf Nussbaumer/GI; 179 (burrowing owl), Rob Tilley/Nature Picture Library; 179 (prairie dog burrow), Ingo Arndt/MP; 179 (owl and burrow), Jurgen and Christine Sohns/FLPA/MP; 179 (snake tail), Jasper Doest/MP; 179 (coyote love), Roland Seitre/MP; 180-181, Strika Entertainment

Awesome Exploration (182-199)
182-183, Steven Greaves/Lonely Planet Images/GI; 184 (1), Rebecca Hale/NG Staff; 184 (2), INGRAM; 184 (4), L Mirror/SS; 184 (5), Jacek/SS; 184 (7), STUDIO DREAM/SS; 184 (8), Ho Yeow Hui/SS; 185 (10), Maxxyustas/DRMS; 185 (11), pinstock/IS; 185 (12), Ksander/SS; 185 (13), Nataliya Hora/DRMS; 185 (15), baibaz/SS; 185 (16), IrinaK/SS; 185 (16), Ruslan Semichev/SS; 185 (17), FeelIFree/SS; 185 (19), ANKorr/SS; 186 (CTR), Sue Moore/NGC; 186 (UP), Godfrey Merlen/NGC; 186 (LO), Pete Oxford/MP; 187 (UP RT), Cory Richards/NGC; 187 (LE), Cory Richards/NGC; 187 (CTR LE), Cory Richards/NGC; 187 (CTR RT), Cory Richards/NGC; 188 (UP RT), Sura Devore/NGC; 188 (LE), James Kydd; 188 (UP CTR RT), Tony Heald/Nature Picture Library; 188 (LO CTR RT), Richard Du Toit/MP; 188 (LO RT), Klein-Hubert/KimballStock; 189 (UP), Jenny Daltry and Andrea Otto; 189 (LO CTR), Jenny Daltry; 189 (LO RT), Jenny Daltry; 190 (CTR), Vasin Lee/SS; 190 (LO RT), Stephen Bonk/SS; 190 (UP), NadyaEugene/SS; 190 (LO LE), Duplass/SS; 191 (LO), Julia Kuznetsova/SS; 191 (UP LE), Kuttelvaserova Stuchelova/SS; 191 (UP RT), Marques/SS; 192 (UP), Federico Veronesi/NiS/MP; 192 (LO), Frans Schepers/NGC; 193 (LO LE), Dave McAloney/National Geographic Pristine Seas; 193 (UP), Anup Shah/MP; 193 (LO RT), Photo Collection/Kelvin Aitken/Biosphoto; 194 (UP LE), Will Burrard-Lucas; 194 (UP RT), Will Burrard-Lucas; 194 (CTR), Will Burrard-Lucas; 194 (LO), Will Burrard-Lucas; 195 (UP), Alasdair Turner/Aurora Photos; 195 (LO LE), Popperfoto/GI; 195 (LO RT), Ashley Cooper pics/AL; 196 (UP), NGC; 196 (CTR), courtesy Columbus Zoo and Aquarium; 196 (LO), NGC; 197 (LE), IS; 197 (CTR), IS; 197 (RT), IS, 198 (UP), Will Burrard-Lucas; 198 (CTR), Alasdair Turner/Aurora Photos; 198 (LO), Kuttelvaserova Stuchelova/SS; 199 (UP RT), Grady Reese/IS

Wonders of Nature (200-219)
200-201, Ronald Phillips/Design Pics/GI; 202 (UP), AVTG/IS; 202 (LO), Brad Wynnyk/SS; 203 (A), Rich Carey/SS; 203 (B), Richard Walters/IS; 203 (C), Karen Graham/IS; 203 (D), Michio Hoshino/MP/NGC; 204 (UP CTR LE), Wrangel/DRMS; 204 (LO CTR LE), Rafael Ben-ari/DRMS; 204 (UP CTR RT), Susana Machicao/DRMS; 204 (LO RT), Natalija Berg/DRMS; 204 (UP LE), Eduardo Gonzalez Diaz/DRMS; 205 (CTR RT), Attila Jandi/DRMS; 205 (UP CTR LE), Demerzel21/DRMS; 205 (LO CTR LE), Photojogtom/DRMS; 205 (UP LE), Daniel Raustadt/DRMS; 205 (UP RT), Mgkuijpers/DRMS; 205 (LO LE), Kevin Dunleavy/DRMS; 205 (LO RT), Christophe Dupont Elise/Icon SMI/Corbis/GI; 206-207 (UP), Jason Edwards/NGC; 206 (LO LE), Brandon Cole; 206 (LO RT), Reinhard Dirscherl/Visuals Unlimited, Inc.; 207 (LO LE), Dray van Beeck/SS; 207 (LO RT), Brandon Cole; 208-209, Enric Sala/NGC; 208 (LO LE), Rebecca Hale/NGC; 209 (UP), Danita Delimont/AL; 209 (CTR RT), Dan Burton/Nature Picture Library; 209 (LO), Brian

J. Skerry/NGC; 210 (CTR), Humming Bird Art/SS; 211 (UP), Stuart Armstrong; 212 (LO), Richard Peterson/SS; 212 (1), Leonid Tit/SS; 212 (4), Lars Christensen/SS; 212 (2), Frans Lanting/NGC; 212 (3), Daniel Loretto/SS; 213 (UP RT), Richard Griffin/SS; 213 (UP CTR), GrigoryL/SS; 213 (UP LE), Lori Epstein/NG Staff; 213 (LO LE), Lori Epstein/NG Staff; 213 (LO RT), Lori Epstein/NG Staff; 214 (14), NASA; 215 (UP LE), Pablo Blazquez Dominguez/GI; 215 (LO LE), Francisco Leong/GI; 215 (UP RT), Liu Zhongjun/China News Service/GI; 215 (LO LE), AP/REX/SS; 218 (UP), Lars Christensen/SS; 218 (CTR), Rafael Ben-ari/DRMS; 218 (LO), Francisco Leong/GI

History Happens (220-251)
220-221, travelstock44/AL; 222 (1), Krishna.Wu/SS; 222 (2), volkova natalia/SS; 222 (4), Fotokostic/SS; 222 (3), Museum of London/Heritage Images/GI; 222 (5), Sakdinon Kadchiangsaen/SS; 222 (6), XEG/SS; 222 (9), Nejron Photo/SS; 223 (10), Elena Sherengovskaya/SS; 223 (11), Lebrecht Music and Arts Photo Library/AL; 223 (12), Denis Pepin/DRMS; 223 (13), Josef F. Stuefer/GI; 223 (14), lacostique/SS; 223 (15), Unuchko Veronika/SS; 223 (16), De Agostini Picture Library/GI; 223 (17), Grigorita Ko/SS; 223 (19), Otthon/SS; 224-225, Alessandro Colle/SS; 225 (UP), S.R.Lee Photo Traveller/SS; 225 (LO), warmcolors/IS; 226-227, Jose Fuste Raga/Corbis/GI; 227, 145/Marcaux/Ocean/Corbis/GI; 228 (UP LE), DEA/G. Carfagna/GI; 228 (UP RT), Somyote Tiraphon/SS; 228 (LO), Robert Cravens/GI; 229 (UP), DaleBHalbur/GI; 229 (LO LE), DEA/G.Dagli Orti/GI; 229 (LO RT), alex83/SS; 230 (LE), O. Louis Mazzatenta/NGC; 230 (LO RT), Photo by REX (279524a) Hope Diamond Jewel/Newscom; 230 (CTR RT), STR/EPA/Newscom; 230 (UP RT), Kenneth Garrett/NGC; 231, Kelly Cheng Travel Photography/GI; 232 (UP), Art By Mondolithic; 232 (CTR), Art By Mondolithic; 232 (LO), Art By Mondolithic; 233, Jason Hawkes/Corbis/GI; 234-235 (LE), AP Images/Adam Butler; 235 (RT), Underwood Archives/GI; 236 (UP), Scott Rothstein/SS; 237 (UP), AleksandarNakic/IS; 237 (LO), Gary Blakely/SS; 237 (LO I F), SS; 238 (UP), Marc Dozier/GI; 238 (CTR), Wolfgang Kaehler/GI; 238 (LO), Education Images/UIG/GI; 239 (B), WHHA; 239 (C), WHHA; 239 (D), WHHA; 239 (E), WHHA; 239 (G), WHHA; 239 (H), WHHA; 239 (I), WHHA; 239 (A), WHHA; 239 (LO LE), Larry West/FLPA/MP; 240 (A), WHHA; 240 (B), WHHA; 240 (C), WHHA; 240 (D), WHHA; 240 (E), WHHA; 240 (F), WHHA; 240 (G), WHHA; 240 (H), WHHA; 240 (J), WHHA; 241 (A), WHHA; 241 (B), WHHA; 241 (C), WHHA; 241 (D), WHHA; 241 (E), WHHA; 241 (F), WHHA; 241 (G), WHHA; 241 (H), WHHA; 241 (I), WHHA; 241 (LO RT), Daniel Hurst Photography/GI; 242 (J), WHHA; 242 (A), WHHA; 242 (B), WHHA; 242 (C), WHHA; 242 (D), WHHA; 242 (E), WHHA; 242 (F), WHHA; 242 (G), WHHA; 242 (H), WHHA; 243 (A), WHHA; 243 (C), WHHA; 243 (D), WHHA; 243 (F), WHHA; 243 (G), WHHA; 243 (J), WHHA; 243 (K), WHHA; 243 (I), WHHA; 243 (LO RT), Clint Spaulding/WWD/REX/SS; 244-245, CTON; 246 (LO), Bettmann/Corbis/GI; 246 (UP), Bettmann/Corbis/GI; 247 (background), Reuters/Mannie Garcia/AL; 247 (CTR), Division of Political History, National Museum of American History, Smithsonian Institution; 247 (LO CTR), Charles Kogod/NGC; 248 (UP LE), Archive Photos/GI; 248 (UP RT), Bettmann/Corbis/GI; 248 (LO LE), Michael Ochs Archives/GI; 248 (inset), Underwood & Underwood/Corbis/GI; 248 (LO RT), Patrick Fancy; 248 (UP CTR LE), Stuart, Gilbert (1755-1828)/Art Resource, NY; 249 (UP RT), Jason Reed/Reuters/Corbis/GI; 249 (LO RT), 2011 Silver Screen Collection/GI; 249 (LO LE), Library of Congress Prints and Photographs Division; 249 (UP LE), Jesse Grant/WireImage/

GI; 250 (UP), warmcolors/IS; 250 (CTR), volkova natalia/SS; 250 (LO), O. Louis Mazzatenta/NGC; 251 (UP RT), Janette Pellegrini/Stringer/GI

Geography Rocks (252-337)
252-253, Carsten Peter/SPELEORESEARCH & FILMS/NGC; 259, NASA; 259 (UP), Lori Epstein/NG Staff; 260 (CTR CTR), Maria Stenzel/NGC; 260 (LO CTR), Bill Hatcher/NGC; 260 (UP), Carsten Peter/NGC; 260 (RT CTR), Gordon Wiltsie/NGC; 260 (LO LE), James P. Blair/NGC; 260 (CTR LE), Thomas J. Abercrombie/NGC; 260 (LO RT), Bill Curtsinger/NGC; 261, Dirk Ercken/SS; 262, Ondrej Chvatal/SS; 263 (LO RT), Glowimages/GI; 263 (UP LE), Dennis Walton/GI; 263 (LO LE), Letiziag84/DRMS; 263 (UP RT), Hillary Leo; 263 (UP CTR RT), Martin Harvey/AL; 263 (LO CTR), Kumar Sriskandan/AL; 266, Keith Szafranski/GI; 267 (LO RT), Achim Baque/SS; 267 (UP LE), Izzet Keribar/GI; 267 (LO CTR RT), Dean Lewins/epa/Corbis/GI; 267 (UP RT), Antarctic Search for Meteorites Project; 267 (UP CTR RT), Rick Lee; 267 (LO LE), Stephen J. Krasemann/Science Source; 270, T.Dallas/SS; 271 (UP LE), narvikk/GI; 271 (LO CTR RT), Universal Images Group/GI; 271 (LO CTR), ullstein bild/GI; 271 (UP RT), Kazuyo Sejima and Associates, 271 (UP CTR LE), SeanPavonePhoto/GI; 271 (CTR LE), Gudkov Andrey/SS; 274, Louise Murray/Robert Harding/GI; 275 (UP LE), Jon Arnold/AL; 275 (LO CTR RT), Allan Seiden/Robert Harding World Imagery; 275 (UP RT), Jason Knott/AL; 275 (UP CTR RT), Zig Urbanski/AL; 275 (CTR LE), Philip Game/AL; 278, ale_flamy/GI; 279 (UP LE), Johner Images/AL; 279 (CTR LE), G. Bowater/GI; 279 (LO CTR RT), Sergey Novikov/AL; 279 (LO RT), Grafissimo/GI; 282, PnPy/SS; 283 (UP LE), Pablo Corral V/Corbis/VCG/GI; 283 (UP RT), Suzi Eszterhas/MP; 283 (UP CTR RT), © Universal/Courtesy Everett Collection; 283 (LO CTR RT), Hero Images/GI; 283 (LO RT), Rodrigo Arangua/GI; 283 (CTR LE), Darren Baker/SS; 286, Pete Oxford/MP; 287 (LORT), SOBERKA Richard/hemis.fr/GI; 287 (LO CTR RT), Cristina Mittermeier/NGC; 287 (UP LF), hadynyah/GI; 287 (UP RT), ZSSD/MP; 287 (UP CTR RT), Lee Foster/AL; 287 (CTR LE), Mark Bowler/NPL/MP; 293, Steffen Foerster/SS; 294, Simon Dannhauer/SS; 298, Mint Images - Frans Lanting/GI; 301, Annie Griffiths/NGC; 302, Scorpp/SS; 306, Katarina S/SS; 309, aldarinho/SS; 314, krivinis/SS; 326 (UP RT), Panoramic Images/GI; 326 (UP CTR LE), SS; 326 (UP CTR RT), SS; 326 (LO RT), PhotoDisc; 327 (UP), Alexey Kamenskiy/SS; 327 (UP CTR), Mark Baldwin/SS; 327 (LO LE), Bennie Thornton/AL; 327 (LO), Ron Niebrugge/AL; 328 (1), Pigprox/SS; 328 (LO LE), Robert Preston Photography/AL; 328 (UP RT), Henry Westheim Photography/AL; 328 (LO RT), katjen/SS; 328 (CTR RT), Edwin Verin/SS; 329 (UP RT), Aaron Geddes Photography/AL; 329 (UP CTR RT), Auscape/UIG/GI; 329 (UP CTR LE), Alan John Lander Phillips/GI; 329 (LO LE), Pascaloug5/DRMS; 329 (UP LE), tatraholiday/IS/GI; 329 (LO CTR RT), Sean Pavone/SS; 329 (UP LE), Allen Nolan; 330 (UP LE), Courtesy of Yunak Evleri Cave Hotel; 330 (UP LE), Courtesy of Yunak Evleri Cave Hotel; 331 (UP LE), Matt Cardy/GI; 331 (UP RT), Uwe Zucch/AL; 331 (LO), REUTERS/Lucy Nicholson; 332 (LO), S.Borisov/SS; 332-333, Justin Sullivan/GI; 332 (CTR), Justin Sullivan/GI; 332 (UP), Andy Freeberg; 333 (LO), Nick Ut/AP Photo; 334-335, Chris Hill/NGC; 334 (UP), Mark Campbell/REX/SS; 335 (LO), John Harper/Photolibrary/GI; 336 (UP), Edwin Verin/SS; 336 (CTR), John Harper/Photolibrary/GI; 336 (LO), Dirk Ercken/SS

Since 1888, the National Geographic Society has funded more than
12,000 research, exploration, and preservation projects around the world.
The Society receives funds from National Geographic Partners, LLC,
funded in part by your purchase. A portion of the proceeds from this
book supports this vital work. To learn more, visit natgeo.com/info.

NATIONAL GEOGRAPHIC and Yellow Border Design are trademarks of the
National Geographic Society, used under license.

For more information, visit nationalgeographic.com,
call 1-800-647-5463, or write to the following address:

National Geographic Partners
1145 17th Street N.W.
Washington, D.C. 20036-4688 U.S.A.

Visit us online at nationalgeographic.com/books

For librarians and teachers: ngchildrensbooks.org

More for kids from National Geographic: natgeokids.com

For information about special discounts for bulk purchases,
please contact National Geographic Books Special Sales:
specialsales@natgeo.com

For rights or permissions inquiries, please contact National Geographic
Books Subsidiary Rights: bookrights@natgeo.com

Designed by Ruthie Thompson

National Geographic supports K–12 educators with ELA Common Core
Resources. Visit natgeoed.org/commoncore for more information.

Trade paperback ISBN: 978-1-4263-3013-1
Hardcover ISBN: 978-1-4263-3014-8

Printed in the United States of America
18/WOR/1

The publisher would like to thank everyone who worked to make
this book come together: Angela Modany, associate editor;
Mary Jones, project editor; Sarah Wassner Flynn, writer;
Michelle Harris, researcher; Kathryn Robbins, art director; Lori Epstein,
photo director; Hillary Leo, photo editor; Mike McNey, map production;
Stuart Armstrong, illustrator; Sean Philpotts, production director;
Anne LeongSon and Gus Tello, design production assistants;
Sally Abbey, managing editor; Joan Gossett, editorial production
manager; and Alix Inchausti, production editor.